Human Relations

Human Relations: Principles and Practices

Fourth Edition

Barry L. Reece
Virginia Polytechnic Institute and State University

Rhonda Brandt
Springfield College

Houghton Mifflin Company   Boston   New York

Sponsoring Editor: *Kathleen L. Hunter*
Senior Associate Editor: *Susan M. Kahn*
Senior Project Editor: *Fred H. Burns*
Senior Production/Design Coordinator: *Jill Haber*
Senior Manufacturing Coordinator: *Sally A. Culler*
Marketing Manager: *Melissa Russell*

Cover designer: Rebecca Fagan
Cover illustration by: Minko Dimov, MinkoImages

Printed in the U.S.A.

Library of Congress Catalog Card Number: 99-71919

ISBN: 0-395-96246-3

4 5 6 7 8 9—DC—03   02   01

To Vera, Lynne, Mark, Monique, Michelle, and Colleen

BARRY L. REECE

To Matthew and Patrick

RHONDA BRANDT

About the Authors

The enduring strength of *Human Relations: Principles and Practices* reflects the diverse backgrounds of its authors, who bring together a wealth of experience to ensure the currency, accuracy, and effectiveness of this text.

BARRY L. REECE *Virginia Polytechnic Institute and State University*

Dr. Barry L. Reece is professor at Virginia Polytechnic Institute and State University. He received his Ed.D. from the University of Nebraska. Dr. Reece has been actively involved in teaching, research, consulting, and designing training programs throughout the past three decades. He has conducted more than 600 workshops and seminars devoted to leadership, human relations, communications, sales, customer service, and small business operations. Prior to joining the faculty at Virginia Tech he taught at Ellsworth Community College and the University of Northern Iowa. He has received the Excellence in Teaching Award for classroom teaching at Virginia Tech and the Trainer of the Year Award presented by the Valleys of Virginia Chapter of the American Society for Training and Development.

Dr. Reece has contributed to numerous journals and is author or co-author of twenty books, including *Business, Effective Human Relations in Organizations, Supervision and Leadership in Action,* and *Selling Today—Building Quality Partnerships.* He has served as a consultant to Lowe's Companies, Inc., First Union, WLR Foods, Kinney Shoe Corporation, and numerous other profit and not-for-profit organizations.

RHONDA BRANDT *Springfield College*

Rhonda Brandt received her M.Ed. from University of Missouri-Columbia. She is currently chair of the Administrative Support Department of Springfield College in Springfield, Missouri. Prior to joining Springfield College, she served for ten years as the human relations instructor at the Hawkeye Institute of Technology in Waterloo, Iowa. Ms. Brandt has been active in the training and consulting industry for over twenty years, specializing in human relations and self-esteem programs for small businesses, large corporations, and educational institutions. She was a member of the National Council on Vocational Education's working committee for the Presidential White Paper *Building Positive Self-Esteem and a Strong Work Ethic.* Ms. Brandt is also co-author of *Effective Human Relations in Organizations.*

Brief Contents

Contents

2   Improving Interpersonal Communications   27

5 Attitudes Can Shape Your Life 111

6   Developing a Professional Presence   136

7 Valuing Work Force Diversity   159

Strategies for Resolving Conflict and Achieving Emotional Control

9 A Life Plan for Effective Human Relations

Preface

To be well prepared for employment in the twenty-first century will require a greater understanding of human relations principles and practices. We have seen the evolution of a work environment that is characterized by greater cultural diversity, more work performed by teams, and greater awareness that quality relationships are just as important as quality products in our global economy. The ability to cope effectively with today's work/life issues and problems also requires extensive knowledge of human relations. The fourth edition of *Human Relations: Principles and Practices* has been updated to reflect these important trends and developments. As in earlier editions, the fourth edition includes a number of important components that have been praised by instructors and students.

- The "total person" approach to human relations has been expanded and enriched in this edition. We continue to believe that human behavior at work and in our private lives is influenced by many interdependent traits such as emotional balance, self-awareness, integrity, self-esteem, physical fitness and healthy spirituality. This approach focuses on those human relations skills needed to be well-rounded and thoroughly prepared to handle a wide range of human relations problems and issues.
- This edition, like all previous editions, provides the reader with an overview of the seven major themes of effective human relations: Communication, Self-Awareness, Self-Acceptance, Motivation, Trust, Self-Disclosure, and Conflict Resolution. These broad themes serve as the foundation for contemporary human relations courses and training programs.
- Self-development opportunities are provided throughout the entire text. One of the few certainties in today's rapidly changing work place is the realization that we must assume greater responsibility for developing and upgrading our skills and competencies. In many cases, self-development begins with self-awareness. The text provides multiple opportunities to complete self-assessment activities and then reflect on the results. Each chapter includes thinking/learning starters, application exercises, and a case problem. Every effort has been made to encourage self-assessment, reflection, planning, and self-improvement through goal setting.
- A hallmark of this edition, and all previous editions, is the use of many real world examples of human relations issues and practices at respected organizations. These examples build the reader's interest and promote understanding of major topics and concepts.

IMPROVEMENTS IN THE FOURTH EDITION

The fourth edition of *Human Relations: Principles and Practices* reflects suggestions from the current adopters and reviewers, interviews with human resource development professionals, and a thorough review of the current literature. Up-to-date coverage of key topics is based on a careful review of over 3000 recent books, articles, and reports. It is a practical text that offers timely advice on how to effectively deal with the common human relations problems one will encounter in today's work place. The most significant changes include:

- A major effort was made to create a more concise, tightly focused textbook. Every sentence and every paragraph was carefully examined to be sure it is essential to coverage of the topic or concept. The finished product is very "reader friendly" because the text is focused on important information.
- Greater emphasis has been placed on "how to" information. In numerous areas of the text, the reader is given specific guidelines to follow. For example, Chapter 3 now includes specific instructions on how to build an effective mentor relationship. Chapter 8 includes a new five-step approach to conflict resolution.
- The new edition includes expanded coverage of strategies that can be used to resolve work/life tensions. Throughout the past few years, we have seen an explosion of books, articles, and reports on how to achieve work/life balance. We provide coverage of this important area of human relations.
- The fourth edition keeps the reader in touch with what is happening in the real world with Internet application exercises. These exercises provide students with an opportunity to acquire additional information on important topics in each chapter. Also, the reader will develop a greater appreciation of the Internet as a source of additional information on human relations.
- This edition provides a three-dimensional approach to the study of ethical decision making. One dimension is a major segment of Chapter 4 that explains how to make the right ethical choices when faced with ethical and moral dilemmas. The second dimension is an exciting new instructional game entitled *Ethical Decision Making*. Participation in this game stimulates in-depth thinking about real-life ethical dilemmas. The third dimension is a new video entitled *Ethics* that includes five scenarios depicting typical ethical dilemmas in a work setting. These materials can be used to enhance a teaching unit on character building and integrity.
- Many of the teaching/learning aids featured throughout the text have been updated. Most of the chapter opening vignettes are new to this edition. These real-world examples introduce chapter topics and build reader interest in the material. Over half of the case problems have been replaced or rewritten. Many of these focus on an employee issue or problem within the context of a specific organization. Several of the Thinking/Learning Starters

within each chapter have been rewritten or replaced, and many new Total Person Insights appear throughout the text.

- Four of the chapters in the new edition are presented in a different sequence. We feel the new format provides a more logical presentation of material.

NEW LEARNING TOOLS THAT ENHANCE INSTRUCTION

The fourth edition of *Human Relations: Principles and Practices* includes several new learning tools that will aid both teaching and learning.

- **New video program.** The video package now includes five new segments that illustrate important concepts from the text. The videos focus on ethics, motivation, diversity, leadership, and organizational culture. These videos provide real-world examples from leading organizations and bring chapter content to life. The Video Guide in the Instructor's Resource Manual provides a description of each video, suggested uses, and issues for discussion.
- **New instructional games.** Two new instructional games entitled *Ethical Decision Making* and *Coping with Organizational Politics* have been developed for use with the text. The ethics game stimulates in-depth thinking about the ethical consequences of certain decisions and actions. Politics surface in every organization, and the new instructional game prepares the student to cope effectively with common political situations. Each game simulates a realistic business environment where employees must make difficult decisions. Students play these games to learn without having to play for keeps.
- **New and revised application exercises.** Several new application exercises have been added to the text and the Instructor's Resource Manual. In addition, many of the existing exercises have been rewritten. The instructor can now choose from over 60 application exercises.
- **New transparency package.** A set of two-color transparencies are available for use by adopters of the fourth edition of *Human Relations: Principles and Practices*. The transparency program includes figures, graphs, and key concepts featured in the text, as well as pieces that are exclusive to the program.
- **New PowerPoint® slides.** These slides provide a complete lecture for every chapter. Instructors with PowerPoint can edit the slides, and all instructors with a PC can use the slides with the PowerPoint viewer to present electronic classroom presentations or print out the slides for use as handouts. The slides can be downloaded from our web site by selecting business at http://www.hmco.com/college.

INSTRUCTOR'S RESOURCE MANUAL WITH TEST BANK

The Instructor's Resource Manual is a complete teaching guide for the fourth edition of *Human Relations: Principles and Practices.* The opening material provides a review of the most important teaching and learning principles that facilitate human relations training, a review of several teaching methods, and a description of suggested term projects.

Part I provides a chapter preview, chapter purpose and perspective, a presentation outline, suggested responses to the Thinking/Learning Starters, review questions, and case problem questions for every chapter in the text. Answers, when applicable, are provided for the application exercises. Additional application exercises are included as well. Part II contains the test items and answers. True/False, multiple-choice, fill-in-the-blank, and short-answer questions are provided. Part III includes the instructional games entitled *Ethical Decision Making* and *Coping with Organizational Politics.* This section of the IRM includes complete instructions on how to administer these learning activities in the classroom. Part IV provides the Video Guide as well as a list of videos that can be used in conjunction with the textbook and corresponding video vendors.

THE SEARCH FOR WISDOM

The search for what is true, right, or lasting has become more difficult because we live in the midst of an information explosion. The Internet is an excellent source of mass information, but it is seldom the source of wisdom. Television usually reduces complicated ideas to a sound bite. Books continue to be one of the best sources of knowledge. Many new books, and several classics, were used as references for the fourth edition of *Human Relations.* A sample of the books we used to prepare this edition follow.

Anger, Rage, and Resentment by Kimes Gustin
Complete Business Etiquette Handbook by Barbara Pachter and Majorie Brody
Creative Visualization by Shakti Gawain
Data Smog—Surviving the Information Glut by David Shenk
Do What You Love . . . The Money Will Follow by Marsha Sinetar
Emotional Intelligence by Daniel Goleman
Empires of the Mind by Denis Waitley
Getting to Yes by Roger Fisher and William Ury
How to Win Friends and Influence People by Dale Carnegie
The Human Side of Enterprise by Douglas McGregor
I'm OK—You're OK by Thomas Harris
Minding the Body, Mending the Mind by Joan Borysenko

Multiculture Manners—New Rules of Etiquette For a Changing Society by Norine Dresser

The 100 Best Companies to Work for in America by Robert Levering and Milton Moskowitz

1001 Ways to Reward Employees by Bob Nelson

The Power of 5 by Harold H. Bloomfield and Robert K. Cooper

Psycho-Cybernetics by Maxwell Maltz

Re-Engineering the Corporation by Michael Hammer and James Champy

Reviving Ophelia by Mary Pipher

The Seven Habits of Highly Effective People by Stephen Covey

The Situational Leader by Paul Hersey

The Six Pillars of Self-Esteem by Nathaniel Branden

Spectacular Teamwork by Robert R. Blake, Jane Srygley Mouton, and Robert L. Allen

Stress for Success by James Loehr

The 10 Natural Laws of Successful Time and Life Management by Hyrum W. Smith

When Talking Makes Things Worse by David Stiebel

Working with Emotional Intelligence by Daniel Goleman

You Just Don't Understand: Women and Men in Conversation by Deborah Tannen

ACKNOWLEDGMENTS

Many people have made contributions to *Human Relations: Principles and Practices*. Throughout the years the text has been strengthened as a result of numerous helpful comments and recommendations. We extend special appreciation to the following reviewers and advisors who have provided valuable input for this and prior editions:

James Aldrich, *North Dakota State School of Science*
Garland Ashbacker, *Kirkwood Community College*
Sue Avila, *South Hills Business School*
Shirley Banks, *Marshall University*
Rhonda Barry, *American Institute of Commerce*
C. Winston Borgen, *Sacramento Community College*
Professor Charles Capps, *Sam Houston State University*
Lawrence Carter, *Jamestown Community College*
Cathy Chew, *Cedar Valley College*
John P. Cicero, *Shasta College*
Michael Dzik, *North Dakota State School of Science*
Leann Eilander, *Idaho State University*
John Elias, *Consultant*

Mike Fernsted, *Bryant & Stratton Business Institute*
Dave Fewins, *Neosho County Community College*
Dean Flowers, *Waukesha County Technical College*
Jill P. Gann, *Anne Arundel Community College*
M. Camille Garrett, *Tarrant County Junior College*
Roberta Greene, *Central Piedmont Community College*
Ralph Hall, *Community College of Southern Nevada*
Sally Hanna-Jones, *Hocking Technical College*
Daryl Hansen, *Metropolitan Community College*
Carolyn K. Hayes, *Polk Community College*
John J. Heinsius, *Modesto Junior College*
Stephen Hiatt, *Catawba College*
Larry Hill, *San Jacinto College - Central*
Jolene Holt, *Flint Hills Technical College*
Bill Hurd, *Lowe's Companies, Inc.*
Ronald M. Jimmerson, *Washington State University*
Dorothy Jeanis, *Fresno City College*
Marlene Katz, *Canada College*
Robert Kegel, Jr., *Cypress College*
Vance A. Kennedy, *College of Mateo*
Deborah Lineweaver, *New River Community College*
Thomas W. Lloyd, *Westmoreland County Community College*
Jerry Loomis, *Fox Valley Technical College*
Roger Lynch, *Inver Hills Community College*
Russ Moorhead, *Des Moines Area Community College*
Marilyn Mueller, *Simpson College*
Erv J. Napier, *Kent State University*
Barbara Ollhoff, *Waukesha County Technical College*
Beverly A. Olson, *Dakota County Technical College*
Leonard L. Palumbo, *Northern Virginia Community College*
James Patton, *Mississippi State University*
C. Richard Paulson, *Mankato State University*
Naomi W. Peralta, *The Institute of Financial Education*
William Price, *Virginia Polytechnic Institute and State University*
Shirley Pritchett, *Northeast Texas Community College*
Linda Pulliam, *Pulliam Associates, Chapel Hill, N.C.*
Lynne Reece, *Four Oaks*
Jack C. Reed, *University of Northern Iowa*
Robert Schaden, *Schoolcraft College*
Mary R. Shannon, *Wenatchie Valley College*
J. Douglas Shatto, *Muskingum Area Technical College*
Marilee Smith, *Kirkwood Community College*
Cindy Stewart, *Des Moines Area Community College*
Rahmat O. Tavallali, *Wooster Business College*
V. S. Thakur, *Community College of Rhode Island*

Linda Truesdale, *Midlands Technical College*
Wendy Bletz Turner, *New River Community College*
Chuck Wall, *Bakersfield College*
Marc Wayner, *Hocking Technical College*
Tom West, *Des Moines Area Community College*
Steven Whipple, *St. Cloud Technical College*
Burl Worley, *Allan Hancock College*

We would also like to thank Dr. Denis Waitley and Mr. Charles Haefner for helping us develop a fuller understanding of human relations.

Over 100 business organizations, government agencies, and nonprofit institutions provided us with the real-world examples that appear throughout the text. We are grateful to organizations that allowed us to conduct interviews, observe workplace environments, and use special photographs and materials.

The partnership with Houghton Mifflin, which has spanned two decades, has been very rewarding. Several members of the Houghton Mifflin College Division staff have made important contributions to this project. Sincere appreciation is extended to Susan Kahn who has worked conscientiously on the text from the planning stage to completion of the book. We also offer a hearty thank you to other key contributors: Kathy Hunter, Fred Burns, Jill Haber, and Melissa Russell.

BARRY L. REECE
RHONDA BRANDT

Chapter 1

Introduction to

Human Relations

Chapter Preview

After studying this chapter, you will be able to

1. Understand how the study of human relations will help you succeed in your chosen career.
2. Explain the nature, purpose, and importance of human relations.
3. Identify major trends in the workplace that have given new importance to human relations.
4. Identify major forces influencing human behavior at work.
5. Review the historical development of the human relations movement.
6. Identify seven basic themes that serve as the foundation for effective human relations.

H OWARD SCHULTZ, CEO of Starbucks Coffee Company, grew up in a lower-middle-class family in federally subsidized housing in Brooklyn. His father was a blue-collar worker who held a variety of jobs. Schultz says, "He was not valued as a worker; the system he was part of beat him down and he became a bitter person who lost his self-esteem."[1] Motivated by memories of his father, Schultz is now working hard to make sure every employee feels valued and respected. At Starbucks the employee, not the customer, comes first. This policy is based on the belief that enthusiastic, happy employees will keep customers coming back. Starbucks offers workers an employee ownership plan, excellent training programs, full medical and dental benefits (available even to part-time employees), and career advancement opportunities.

During orientation new employees are introduced to guidelines for on-the-job interpersonal relations. The first guideline is to maintain and enhance self-esteem. Starbucks has discovered that when employees feel respected, they are less likely to leave the company. The annual employee turnover rate is less than 50 percent. The norm in this industry is more like 300 to 400 percent a year. Low employee turnover is important because the company is growing and needs experienced employees. From 11 Seattle stores and fewer than 100 employees, the company has grown to nearly 1,200 stores and several thousand employees.[2] ■

Starbucks's emphasis on relationships is not an isolated case. A growing number of U.S. organizations, from hospitals to hotels, are discovering and rediscovering the benefits of work environments that emphasize employee growth and development opportunities and the human side of enterprise. Most organizations that survive and prosper over a long period of time maintain a balance between concern for productivity and concern for people.

THE NATURE, PURPOSE, AND IMPORTANCE OF HUMAN RELATIONS

Many of America's best-managed organizations are not simply being "nice to people"; they are genuinely helping employees come alive through their work. We have learned that the goals of worker and workplace need not be in conflict. This chapter focuses on the nature of human relations, its development, and its importance to the achievement of individual and organizational goals.

Human Relations Defined

The term **human relations** in its broadest sense covers all types of interactions among people—their conflicts, cooperative efforts, and group relationships. It is the study of *why* our beliefs, attitudes, and behaviors sometimes cause relationship problems in our personal lives and in work-related situations. The study of human relations emphasizes the analysis of human behavior, prevention strategies, and resolution of behavioral problems.

Knowledge of human relations does not, of course, begin in the classroom. Although this may be your first formal course in the subject, your "education" in human relations actually began with your family, friends, and early employment experiences. You learned what was acceptable and what was not. You tested your behavior against that of others, formed close relationships, experienced conflict, developed perceptions of yourself, and discovered how to get most of your needs met. By the time you completed high school, you had probably formed a fairly complex network of relationships and had a pretty good idea of who you were.

The Importance of Human Relations

One of the most significant developments in recent years has been the increased importance of interpersonal skills in almost every type of work setting. In the minds of many employers, interpersonal skills represent an important category of "basic" or "transferable" skills a worker is expected to bring to the job. Technical ability is often not enough to achieve career success. Studies indicate that many of the people who have difficulty in obtaining or holding a job, or advancing to positions of greater responsibility, possess the needed technical competence but lack interpersonal competence.

Several important trends in the workplace have given new importance to human relations. Each of the following trends provides support for the development of competence in human relations:

• *The labor market has become a place of churning dislocation caused by the heavy volume of mergers, buyouts, and business closings.* These activities have been accompanied by nearly 3 million layoffs and the elimination of hundreds of product lines during the past decade. Even industries noted for job security have recently engaged in massive layoffs. A million U.S. defense workers have lost their jobs since the end of the Cold War. At International Business Machines Corp. (IBM), where a job once meant good pay and job security, 170,000 jobs have been cut worldwide in recent years. Even when the economy is strong, many companies continue to eliminate jobs.[3]

Downsizing has produced many negative consequences. The bond of employer-employee loyalty has all but been erased.[4] Large numbers of major U.S. companies are attempting to deal with serious problems of low morale and mistrust of management caused by years of upheaval and restructuring.[5]

• *Temporary work continues to grow.* Massive downsizing has created another phenomenon in the workplace—the large-scale use of temporary workers. Some companies that still have memories of painful layoffs are turning to temporary workers as a hedge against future layoffs. Strong demand for temps has

The Wall Street Journal.
Permission, Cartoon Fea-
tures Syndicate.

surfaced in such diverse fields as telecommunications, banking, heavy manufacturing, and computers. Manpower Inc., now the largest temp employer in the United States, is one of over 2,000 firms providing temporary workers. Today Manpower can provide temporary lawyers, accountants, engineers, and many other types of professional and technical workers.[6] Temporary work is growing in popularity among people who want more flexibility in their lifestyle. Others select this employment route because it can open the door to full-time employment.[7]

• *Organizations are increasingly oriented toward service to clients, patients, and customers.* We live in a service economy where relationships are often more important than products. Restaurants, hospitals, banks, public utilities, colleges, airlines, and retail stores all must now gain and retain the patronage of their clients and customers. In any service-type firm, there are thousands of "moments of truth," those critical incidents in which customers come into contact with the organization and form their impressions of its quality and service. Employees must not only be able to get along with customers; they must also project a favorable image of the organization they represent. Constant contact with the public requires a high degree of patience, versatility, and sensitivity to the needs of a diverse population. Critics of companies that engage in massive downsizing note that anxious survivors are more likely to focus inward on their own careers instead of outward on customer needs.[8]

• *A growing number of organizations are recognizing improved quality as the key to survival.* The notion of quality as a competitive tool has been around for many years, but today it is receiving much more attention. In a period of fierce global competition, a consumer does not have to tolerate poor-quality products or services. Stephen Shepard, editor-in-chief of *Business Week,* states that quality "may be the biggest competitive issue of the late 20th and early 21st centuries."[9] People are at the heart of every quality-improvement program. Committed, well-trained workers who are given authority and responsibility can do the most to improve quality.[10]

• *Many companies are organizing their workers into teams in which each employee plays a part.* Organizations eager to improve quality, raise job satisfaction, increase worker participation in decision making and problem solving, and boost customer service are turning to teams. Typical of the team approach is Motorola, Inc., which now has more than 5,000 specialized "customer satisfaction" teams that work on highly specific ways of improving efficiency or providing new and innovative services.[11] Along with increased use of teams at Motorola has come training to help employees improve their people skills.

Although some organizations have successfully harnessed the power of teams, others have encountered problems. One barrier to productivity is the employee who lacks the skills needed to be a team member. In making the transition to a team environment, team members need skills in group decision making, leadership, conflict resolution, and communications.[12] Another barrier is the poorly prepared team leader. Supervisory-management personnel who provide team leadership must assume the roles of teacher, mentor, and resource person. Leaders who can shift from manager-as-order-giver to manager-as-facilitator are more likely to bring out the best in the people they supervise.

• *Diversity has become a prominent characteristic of today's work force.* A number of trends have contributed to greater work force diversity. Throughout the past two decades, participation in the labor force by Asians, African Americans, and Hispanics has increased; labor force participation by adult women has risen to a record 60 percent—defying the widespread view that it had leveled off; the employment door for people with physical or mental impairments has opened wider; and larger numbers of young workers are working with members of the 50-plus age group. Within this heterogeneous work force we will find a multitude of values, expectations, and work habits. Today, the new buzzwords are "valuing differences" and "managing diversity." There is a need to develop increased tolerance for persons who differ in age, gender, race, physical traits, and sexual orientation. The major aspects of work force diversity are discussed in Chapter 7.

It is safe to say that no line of work, organization, or industry will enjoy immunity from these trends. Today's employee must be adaptable and flexible to achieve success within a climate of change and uncertainty. It is important for everyone to develop those interpersonal skills that are valued by all employers.

The Challenge of Human Relations

To develop and apply the wide range of interpersonal skills needed in today's workplace can be extremely challenging. You will be working with clients, customers, patients, and other workers who vary greatly in age, work background, communications style, values, cultural background, gender, and work ethic. When you make contact with these persons, you present yourself as a multifaceted being with a complex array of values, experiences, and perceptions. The authors of *Workforce America!* point out that "human beings are complex systems and [that] each dimension of diversity adds another element of complexity to the overall functioning of the system."[13] Because every person you come in contact with is unique, each encounter offers a new challenge.

Human relations is further complicated by the fact that we must manage three types of relationships. The first relationship is the one with ourselves. Many people carry around a set of ideas and feelings about themselves that are quite negative and in most cases quite inaccurate. In fact, many people reserve the very harshest criticism for themselves. People who have negative feelings about their abilities and accomplishments, and who engage in constant self-criticism, must struggle to maintain a good relationship with themselves. The importance of high self-esteem is addressed in Chapter 3.

The second type of relationship we must learn to manage is the one-to-one relationships we face in our personal and work lives. People in the health-care field, sales, food service, and a host of other occupations face this challenge many times each day. A nurse, for example, must build one-to-one relationships with patients. In some cases, racial, age, or gender bias serves as a barrier to good human relations.

The third challenge we face is the management of relationships with members of a group. As already noted, many workers are assigned to a team on either a full-time or a part-time basis. At General Motors Corp.'s Saturn plant in Spring Hill, Tennessee, cars move along the line on wooden pallets, and teams of workers travel with them.[14] Lack of cooperation among team members can result in quality problems or a slowdown in production.

The Influence of the Behavioral Sciences

The field of human relations draws on the behavioral sciences—psychology, sociology, and anthropology. Basically, these sciences focus on the *why* of human behavior. Psychology attempts to find out why *individuals* act as they do, and sociology and anthropology concentrate primarily on *group* dynamics and social interaction. Human relations differs from the behavioral sciences in one important respect. Although also interested in the why of human behavior, human relations goes further and looks at what can be done to anticipate problems, resolve them, or even prevent them from happening. In other words, this field emphasizes knowledge that can be *applied* in practical ways to problems of interpersonal relations at work or in our personal life.

Human Relations and the "Total Person"

The material in this book focuses on human relations as the study of *how people satisfy both personal growth needs and organizational goals in their careers.* We believe, as do most authors in the field of human relations, that such human traits as physical fitness, emotional control, self-awareness, self-esteem, and values orientation are interdependent. Although some organizations may occasionally wish they could employ only a person's physical strength or creative powers, all that can be employed is the **total person.** A person's separate characteristics are part of a single system making up that whole person. Work life is not totally separate from home life, and emotional conditions are not separate from physical conditions. The quality of a person's work, for example, is often related to physical fitness and nutrition.

Many organizations are beginning to recognize that when the whole person is improved, significant benefits accrue to the firm. These organizations are establishing employee development programs that address the total person, not just the employee skills needed to perform the job. These programs include such topics as stress management, assertiveness training, physical fitness, balancing work and family life, and values clarification. A few examples follow:

Item: Employees at H. A. Montgomery—a chemical manufacturing firm in Detroit, Michigan—have the option of starting each workday with 20 minutes of Transcendental Meditation.[15]

Total Person Insight

"To me, there's no essential difference between the way we spend time in work and the way we spend the rest of our lives. Time is time; our working life adds up—in a few short decades—to be our life itself."

MARSHA SINETAR

Author, *Do What You Love . . . The Money Will Follow*

Item: Liz Claiborne, Inc. holds seminars on domestic violence issues for its employees.[16]

Item: Texas Instruments offers seminars for dads who need help juggling work and home.[17]

Item: Quaker Oats Company grants bonuses for employees who exercise and shun smoking.[18]

Some of the results of these programs may be difficult to assess in terms of profit and loss. For example, does a person in good physical health contribute more? If an employee is under considerable stress, does this mean he or she will have more accidents on the job? Specific answers vary, but most human resource management experts agree that total person development includes physical, mental, social, emotional, and spiritual development.

The Need for a Supportive Environment

John W. Humphrey, chief executive officer of the Forum Corporation, says, "These days, the only sustainable competitive advantage in any business is people, not product."[19] Unfortunately, not every CEO or manager attributes the same importance to people or people problems. Some managers do not believe that total person training, job enrichment, motivation techniques, or career development helps increase productivity or strengthen worker commitment to the job. It is true that when such practices are tried without full commitment or without full management support, there is a good chance they will fail. Such failures often have a demoralizing effect on employees and management alike. "Human relations" may take the blame, and management will be reluctant to try other human relations methods or approaches in the future.

A basic assumption of this book is that human relations, when applied in a positive and supportive environment, can help individuals achieve greater personal satisfaction from their careers and help increase an organization's productivity and efficiency.

Thinking / Learning Starters

1. How important will human relationship skills be in your future career(s)?

2. Do you believe the trends in the workplace described in this chapter will continue throughout the next decade? What new trends might develop?

THE FORCES INFLUENCING BEHAVIOR AT WORK

A major purpose of this text is to increase your knowledge of factors that influence human behavior in a variety of work settings. An understanding of human behavior at work begins with a review of the six major forces that affect every employee, regardless of the size of the organization. As Figure 1.1 indicates, these are organizational culture, supervisory-management influence, work group influence, job influence, personal characteristics of the worker, and family influence.

FIGURE 1.1

Major Forces Influencing Worker Behavior

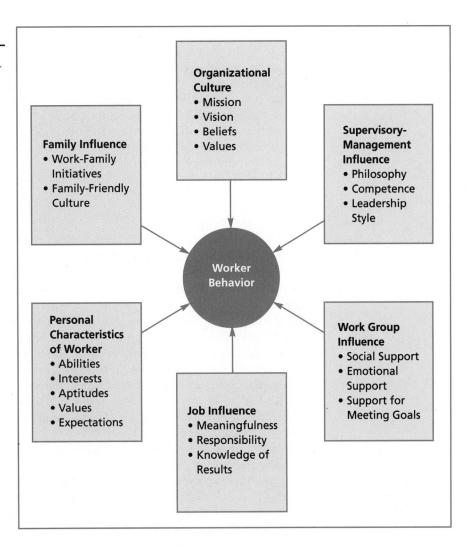

Organizational Culture

Every organization, whether a manufacturing plant, retail store, hospital, or government agency, is unique. Each has its own culture. **Organizational culture** is the collection of shared (stated or implied) beliefs, values, rituals, stories, myths, and specialized language that create a common identity and foster a feeling of community among organization members.[20] The culture at Land's End, the Dodgeville, Wisconsin, mail order company, has been shaped by *Eight Principles of Doing Business* developed by its founder. One of those principles, "We believe that what is best for our customers is best for all of us," no doubt influenced the legendary friendliness of Land's End telephone service representatives and the high quality of the products offered by the company.[21] By contrast, the U.S. Postal Service's authoritarian culture has resulted in poor labor-management relations, thousands of unresolved grievances, and customer service that is often mediocre.[22] The Postal Service hopes to achieve long-term culture change by emphasizing greater employee involvement and empowerment.

A growing number of organizations are creating vision statements that direct the energies of the company and inspire employees to achieve greater heights. Ortho Biotech, based in Raritan, New Jersey, begins its vision statement with a bold prediction: "We will be the best in our business by providing customers with innovative solutions to significant medical problems through biotechnology and related science."[23] Once a vision statement is created, leaders must help every employee see the connection between the employee's job and the organization's vision.

Supervisory-Management Influence

Supervisory-management personnel are in a key position to influence employee behavior. It is no exaggeration to say that supervisors and managers are the spokespersons for the organization. Their philosophy, competence, and leadership style establish the organization's image in the eyes of employees. Each employee develops certain perceptions about the organization's concern for his or her welfare. These perceptions, in turn, influence such important factors as productivity, customer relations, safety consciousness, and loyalty to the firm. Effective leaders are aware of the organization's basic purposes, why it exists, and its general direction. They are able to communicate this information to workers in a clear and positive manner.

Supervisory-management personnel hold the key to both outlook and performance. They are in a unique position to unlock the internal forces of motivation and help employees channel their energies toward achieving the goals of the organization. Effective leadership is shaped by common sense, respect for each worker, good listening skills, and helping people to learn to work together rather than just for themselves.[24]

Total Person Insight

"Jobs do a lot more than merely provide income. They provide the opportunity to learn and enhance skills, to have some control over one's fate and, perhaps most important, to gain a sense of self-worth, a sense of carrying one's own weight."

WILLIAM RASPBERRY

Syndicated Columnist

Work Group Influence

In recent years, behavioral scientists have devoted considerable research to determining the influence of group affiliation on the individual worker. They are particularly interested in group influence within the formal structure of the organization. This research has identified three functions of group membership.[25] First, it can satisfy *social needs*. Many people find the hours spent at work enjoyable because coworkers provide needed social support. Second, the work group can provide the *emotional support* needed to deal with pressures and problems on or off the job. Finally, the group provides *assistance in solving problems and meeting goals*. A cohesive work group lends support and provides the resources we need to be productive workers. The potential value of work group influence helps explain why so many organizations are using various types of teams to improve productivity.

Job Influence

Work in modern societies does more than fulfill economic needs. A job can provide a sense of meaning, a sense of community, and self-esteem.[26] As one organizational consultant noted, work has taken central stage in the lives of many people: "We spend most of our working hours doing our jobs, thinking about work, and getting to and from our workplaces. When we feel good about our work, we tend to feel good about our lives. When we find our work unsatisfying and unrewarding, we don't feel good."[27] Unfortunately, many people hold jobs that do not make them feel good. Many workers perceive their jobs to be meaningless and boring because there is little variety to the work. Some workers experience frustration because they are powerless to influence their working conditions.

Job satisfaction tends to increase when there is compatibility between the wants and needs of the employee and the characteristics of the job. To be completely satisfying, a job must provide three experiences for a worker: meaningfulness, responsibility, and knowledge of results.[28] To enhance both meaningfulness and responsibility, some organizations are redesigning jobs so they provide the employee with more challenge, variety, and personal growth.

Personal Characteristics of the Worker

Every worker brings to the job a combination of abilities, interests, aptitudes, values, and expectations. Worker behavior on the job is most frequently a reflection of how well the work environment accommodates the unique characteristics of each worker. For more than half a century, work researchers and theorists have attempted to define the ideal working conditions that would maximize worker productivity. These efforts have met with some success, but unanswered questions remain.

Identifying the ideal work environment is difficult because today's work force is characterized by such great diversity. A single parent may greatly value

Patience and a caring attitude are two important personal characteristics needed by people who work in our expanding service economy. This elderly nursing home patient appreciates the warm, friendly approach used by this young staff member. (Therese Frare/The Picture Cube, Inc.)

a flexible work schedule and child care. The recipient of a new business administration degree may value challenging work and career advancement opportunities above other benefits. Other workers may desire more leisure time.

Coming into the workplace today is a new generation of workers with value systems and expectations about work that differ from those of the previous generation. Today's better-educated and better-informed workers value identity and achievement. They also have a heightened sense of their rights.

Family Influence

There is general agreement that people need to establish a balance between work life and family life. Balance implies an interconnection among many areas of work and the family.[29] We are just beginning to understand some of these strong linkages. For example, a study of blue-collar fathers in dual-earner households found a powerful tie between conditions at work and treatment of children. Fathers who experienced autonomy at work and worked for supportive bosses tended to have higher self-esteem and to treat their children with greater acceptance and warmth.[30] Researchers have also found fewer behavioral problems in children whose mothers have control over how, where, and when their work gets done.[31] These research studies indicate that children may be the unseen stakeholders in the workplace.

Many organizations have found that family problems are linked to employee problems such as tardiness, absenteeism, and turnover. The discovery has led many companies to develop work-family programs and policies that help employees juggle the demands of children, spouses, and elderly parents.[32] Marriott International, Inc., initiated a number of work-family initiatives after learning that family and personal problems were fueling turnover as high as 300 percent at some of its hotels.[33] Johnson & Johnson, the New Jersey–based maker of health-care products, is considered to have one of the most family-friendly cultures in America. The company maintains four on-site child-care facilities, offers up to $3,000 help to workers who are adopting children, and supports a one-year parental leave program. The company credo includes this sentence: "We must be mindful of ways to help our employees fulfill their family responsibilities."[34]

THE DEVELOPMENT OF THE HUMAN RELATIONS MOVEMENT

The early attempts to improve productivity in manufacturing focused mainly on trying to improve such things as plant layout and mechanical processes. But over time, there was more interest in redefining the nature of work and perceiving workers as complex human beings. This change reflected a shift in values from a concern with *things* to a greater concern for *people*. In this section we examine a few major developments that influenced the human relations movement.

The Impact of the Industrial Revolution

The Industrial Revolution marked a shift from home-based, handcrafted processes to large-scale factory production. Prior to the Industrial Revolution, most work was performed by individual craftworkers or members of craft guilds. Generally, each worker saw a project through from start to finish. Skills such as tailoring, carpentry, and shoemaking took a long time to perfect and were often a source of pride to an individual or a community. Under this system, however, output was limited.

The Industrial Revolution had a profound effect on the nature of work and the role of the worker. Previously, an individual tailor could make only a few items of clothing in a week's time; factories could now make hundreds. Employers began to think of labor as another item in the manufacturing equation, along with raw materials and capital. Employers at that time did not realize how workers' needs affected production. As a result, few owners or managers gave any thought to working conditions, health and safety precautions, or worker attitudes and motivation. Hours were long, and pay was low.

Mayo's Hawthorne Studies

Elton Mayo and his colleagues accidentally discovered part of the answer to variations in worker performance while conducting research in the mid-1920s

---

Total Person Insight

"You can only get so much more productivity out of reorganization and automation. Where you really get productivity leaps is in the minds and hearts of people."

JAMES BAUGHMAN

Director of Management Development, General Electric Co.

at the Hawthorne Western Electric plant, located near Chicago. Their original goal was to study the effect of illumination, ventilation, and fatigue on production workers in the plant. Their research, known as the **Hawthorne studies,** became a sweeping investigation into the role of human relations in group and individual productivity.

For one part of their research, Mayo and his colleagues selected two groups of employees doing similar work under similar conditions and kept output records for each group. After a time, the researchers began to vary the intensity of light for one group while keeping it constant for the other. Each time they increased the light, productivity rose. To determine if the better illumination was responsible for the higher outputs, they began to dim the light. *Productivity continued to rise.* In fact, one of the highest levels of output was recorded when the light was scarcely brighter than the full moon! The researchers realized some other influence was at work.

Mayo made several important discoveries. One of them was that all the attention focused on the test group made these individuals feel important and appreciated. For the first time, they were getting feedback on their job performance. In addition, test conditions allowed them greater freedom from supervisory control. Under these circumstances, morale and motivation increased and productivity rose.[35]

Although some observers have criticized the Hawthorne studies for flawed research methodology,[36] this research can be credited with helping change the way management viewed workers.

From the Great Depression to the 1990s

During the Great Depression, interest in human relations research waned as other ways of humanizing the workplace gained momentum. During that period, unions increased their militant campaigns to organize workers and force employers to pay attention to such issues as working conditions, higher pay, shorter hours, and protection for child laborers. With the passage of the Wagner Act in 1935, businesses were required by law to negotiate contracts with union representatives. Other labor laws passed in the 1930s outlawed child labor, reduced the hours women worked, and instituted a minimum wage for many industries.

During World War II and the years of postwar economic expansion, interest in the human relations field was revived. Countless papers and research studies on worker efficiency, group dynamics, organization, and motivational methods were published. Douglas McGregor, in his classic book *The Human Side of Enterprise,* argued that how well an organization performs is directly proportional to its ability to tap human potential.[37] He introduced his Theory X, a rather pessimistic, authoritarian view of human behavior, and Theory Y, a more positive, optimistic view. Abraham Maslow, a noted psychologist, devised a "hierarchy of needs," stating that people satisfied their needs in a particular order.

Completing a marathon in a wheelchair requires a great deal of motivation. The work of various psychologists and social scientists has added greatly to our understanding of what motivates people and how motivation works. (Gail Hilsenrath/The Picture Cube, Inc.)

Since the 1950s, theories and concepts regarding human behavior have focused more and more on an understanding of human interaction. Eric Berne in the 1960s revolutionized the way people think about interpersonal communication when he introduced transactional analysis, with its "Parent-Adult-Child" model. At about the same time, Carl Rogers published his work on personality development, interpersonal communication, and group dynamics.

There is no doubt that management consultants Tom Peters and Robert Waterman also influenced management thinking regarding the importance of people in organizations. Their best-selling book *In Search of Excellence*, published in 1982, describes eight attributes of excellence found in America's best-run companies.[38] One of these attributes, "productivity through people," emphasizes that excellent companies treat the worker as the root source of quality and productivity.

In 1989 Stephen Covey authored a powerful book on leadership and human relations entitled *The Seven Habits of Highly Effective People*. He describes the principles of fairness, integrity, honesty, patience, and humility as essential ingredients in what he describes as the *character ethic*. Covey believes that character is the foundation for true success and happiness in life.

The most popular buzzword in the 1990s was *re-engineering*, a term coined by Michael Hammer and James Champy in their 1993 bestseller, *Re-engineer-*

ing the Corporation. Re-engineering is a radical approach to improving the performance of a company. Hammer and Champy suggest the starting point for re-engineering is a clean sheet of paper and answers to the question: If you could start the business today, how would you go about it now as opposed to how you have been doing it? Companies that took this challenge seriously often discovered that re-engineered work required fewer workers and far fewer managers.[39] Many workers who live through the re-engineering process say they feel overburdened by work and fear their own job loss.

Thinking / Learning Starters

1. What do you personally find to be the basic rewards of work?

2. The book *In Search of Excellence* cites "productivity through people" as an attribute of excellent companies. Do you agree or disagree with this view?

3. What degree of worker involvement have you experienced in places where you have worked or volunteered?

MAJOR THEMES IN HUMAN RELATIONS

Several broad themes emerge from the study of human relations. They are communication, self-awareness, self-acceptance, motivation, trust, self-disclosure, and conflict resolution. These themes reflect the current concern in human relations with the twin goals of personal growth development and the satisfaction of organizational objectives. To some degree, these themes are interrelated (see Figure 1.2), and most are discussed in more than one chapter of this book.

Communication

It is not an exaggeration to describe communication as the "heart and soul" of human relations. **Communication** is the means by which we come to an understanding of ourselves and others. To grow and develop as persons, we must develop the awareness and the skills necessary to communicate effectively. John Diekman, author of *Human Connections,* says that "if we are going to do anything constructive and helping with one another, it must be through our communication."[40] Communication is the *human* connection.

FIGURE 1.2

Major Themes in
Human Relations

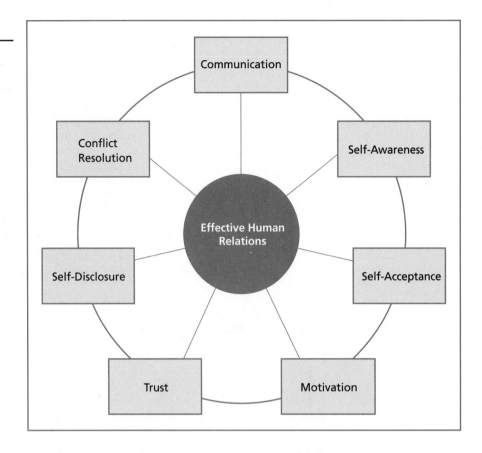

That is why the subject is covered in more than one section of this book. In Chapter 2 we explore the fundamentals of both personal and organizational communication. It is these fundamentals that provide the foundation for all efforts to improve communication. Suggestions on how to improve communication will appear in other chapters.

Self-Awareness

One of the most important ways to develop improved relationships with others is to develop a better understanding of ourselves. With increased **self-awareness** comes a greater understanding of how our behavior influences others. Stephen Covey says that self-awareness enables us to stand apart and examine the way we "see" ourselves. He states that self-awareness "affects not only our attitudes and behaviors, but also how we see other people."[41]

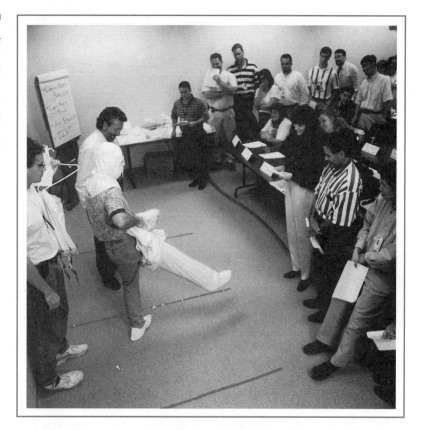

Communication plays a critical role in training programs that teach Samsung employees the correct way to put on a chip-plant bunny suit and mask. (Wyatt McSpadden)

The importance of self-awareness is being recognized by an increasing number of authors, trainers, and educators. Daniel Goleman, author of the best-selling book *Emotional Intelligence,* has given us new insights into the importance of self-awareness. Goleman says IQ accounts for only about 20 percent of a person's success in life. The rest, he says, you can credit to "emotional intelligence." Of all the elements that make up emotional intelligence, Goleman asserts, self-awareness is the most important. He notes that a deficit in self-awareness can be damaging to one's personal relationships and career.[42]

Self-Acceptance

The degree to which you like and accept yourself is the degree to which you can genuinely like and accept other people. **Self-acceptance** is the foundation of successful interaction with others. In a work setting, people with positive self-concepts tend to cope better with change, accept responsibility more readily, tolerate differences, and generally work well as team members. A negative self-concept, however, can create barriers to good interpersonal relations. Self-acceptance is crucial not only for building relationships with others but also for setting and achieving goals. The more you believe you can do, the more you are likely to accomplish. Chapter 3 explains why high self-esteem (complete self-acceptance) is essential for effective human relations. That chapter also helps you identify ways to achieve greater self-acceptance.

Motivation

Most people who engage in the study of **motivation** seek answers to two questions: "How do I motivate myself?" and "How do I motivate others?" If you are really committed to achieving peak performance, you must motivate yourself from within.[43] Inner drives for excellence can be very powerful. Chapter 4 will help you identify the priorities and values that motivate you.

Trust

H. Jackson Brown, Jr., author of *Live and Learn to Pass It On,* says that **trust** is the single most important factor in both personal and professional relationships.[44] Unfortunately, trust is often absent in organizations that are engaged in downsizing and implementing high-speed change. When a lack of trust exists in an organization, a decline in the flow of information almost always results. Employees communicate less information to their supervisors, express opinions reluctantly, and avoid discussions. Cooperation, so necessary in a modern work setting, deteriorates. When a climate of trust is present, frank discussion of problems and a free exchange of ideas and information are encouraged.

Self-Disclosure

Self-disclosure and trust are two halves of a whole. The more open you are with people, the more trust you build up. The more trust there is in a relationship, the safer you feel to disclose who you are. Self-disclosure is also part of good communication and helps eliminate unnecessary guessing games. Managers who let their subordinates know what is expected of them help those employees fulfill their responsibilities. Chapter 2 emphasizes the need of individuals to verbalize the thoughts and feelings they carry within them and provides many practical suggestions on how to use constructive self-disclosure.

Conflict Resolution

Conflict in one form or another surfaces almost daily in the lives of many workers. You may experience conflict during a commute to work when a careless driver cuts you off at a freeway exit ramp. If your job includes supervisory-management responsibilities, you will spend a great deal of time in **conflict resolution** attempting to resolve conflicts among members of your staff. As a team member, you may assume the role of mediator when other team members clash. Resolving conflict with coworkers can require a great deal of energy. Conflict also surfaces when working parents attempt to balance the demands of both work and family. Stressful conditions at home often interfere with work performance, and on-the-job pressures create or magnify problems at home.[45] Chapter 8 provides many valuable suggestions on how conflict can be resolved effectively.

Thinking / Learning Starter

Now that you have had an opportunity to read about the seven themes of human relations, what do you consider your strongest areas? In which areas do you feel you need improvement? Why?

HUMAN RELATIONS: BENEFITS TO YOU

As previously noted, the work force is currently characterized by downsizing, mergers, buyouts, and business closings. We are seeing more emphasis on quality products and quality services. In addition, diversity has become a more prominent characteristic of today's work force. These conditions will very likely continue into the twenty-first century. One of the best ways to cope with these changes is to develop and apply the interpersonal skills needed for success in today's working world.

A basic course in human relations cannot give you a foolproof set of techniques for solving every people-related problem that might arise. It can, however, give you a better understanding of human behavior in groups, help you become more sensitive to yourself and others, and enable you to act more wisely when problems occur. You may even be able to anticipate conflicts or prevent small problems from escalating into major ones.

Many leaders feel that courses in human relations are important because very few workers are responsible to themselves alone. These leaders point out that most jobs today are interdependent. If people in these jobs cannot work effectively as a team, the efficiency of the organization will suffer.

Summary

The study of human relations helps us understand how people fulfill both personal growth needs and organizational goals in their careers. Many organizations are beginning to realize that an employee's life outside the job can have a significant impact on work performance, and some are developing training and education programs in human relations that address the total person. Increasingly, organizations are discovering that many forces influence the behavior of people at work.

Human relations is not a set of foolproof techniques for solving people-related problems. Rather, it gives people an understanding of basic behavior concepts that may enable them to make wiser choices when problems arise, to anticipate or prevent conflicts, and to keep minor problems from escalating into major ones.

The development of the human relations movement involved a redefinition of the nature of work and the gradual perception of managers and workers as complex human beings. A landmark in the study of motivation and worker needs is Elton Mayo's Hawthorne studies. Many industry leaders predict an increased emphasis on human relations research and application. The reasons for this trend include greater awareness that human relations problems serve as a major barrier to the efficient operation of an organization, the employment of workers who expect more from their jobs, and worker organizations and government agencies pressing for attention to employee concerns.

Seven major themes emerge from a study of human relations: communication, self-awareness, self-acceptance, motivation, trust, self-disclosure, and conflict resolution. These themes reflect the current concern in human relations with personal growth and satisfaction of organizational objectives.

Career Corner

Q. The daily newspapers and television news shows are constantly reporting on mergers, business closings, and downsizing efforts. With so much uncertainty in the job market, how can I best prepare for a career?

A. You are already doing one thing that is very important—keeping an eye on labor market trends. During a period of rapid change and little job security, you must continually study workplace trends and assess your career preparation. Louis S. Richman, in a *Fortune* magazine article entitled "How to Get Ahead in America," said, "Climbing in your career calls for being clear about your personal goals, learning how to add value, and developing skills you can take anywhere." After you clarify the type of work that would be rewarding for you, be sure you have the skills necessary to be competitive in that employment area. Keep in mind that today's employers demand more, so be prepared to add value to the company from day one. Search for your employer's toughest problems and make yourself part of the solutions.

The skills you can take anywhere are those transferable skills required by a wide range of employers. These are important because there are no jobs for life. Be prepared to work for several organizations.

Key Terms

human relations
total person
organizational culture
Hawthorne studies
communication
self-awareness

self-acceptance
motivation
trust
self-disclosure
conflict resolution

Review Questions

1. Given the information provided in this chapter, define *human relations.*
2. List and briefly describe the major trends that have given new importance to human relations.
3. Describe the total person approach to human relations. Why is this approach becoming more popular?
4. List and describe the six major forces influencing human behavior at work.
5. In what ways can training in human relations benefit an organization?
6. Briefly describe the three types of relationships people must manage.
7. Mayo's research indicated that workers could influence the rate of production in an organization. What discoveries did Mayo make that led to this conclusion?
8. Liz Claiborne provides seminars on domestic violence issues, and Quaker Oats Company grants bonuses for employees who exercise and shun smoking. Do these two programs represent a good use of company funds? Explain your answer.
9. What seven themes emerge from a study of human relations? Describe each one briefly.
10. Reread the Total Person Insight that quotes Marsha Sinetar and then indicate what you feel is the meaning of this quotation.

Application Exercises

1. Throughout this book you will be given many opportunities to engage in self-assessment activities. Self-assessment involves taking a careful look at those human relations skills you need to be well rounded and thoroughly prepared for success in your work life and fulfillment in your personal life. To assess your human relations skills, complete the self-assessment exercise at the ends of Chapters 2 through 9. These assessment exercises will provide you with increased awareness of your strengths and a better understanding of those abilities you may want to improve.

2. The seven broad themes that emerge from the study of human relations were discussed in this chapter. Although these themes are interrelated, there is value in examining each one separately before reading the rest of the book. Review the description of each theme and then answer these questions:

   a. When you take into consideration the human relations problems that you have observed or experienced at work, school, and home, which themes represent the most important areas of study? Explain your answer.

   b. In which of these areas do you feel the greatest need for improvement? Why?

Internet Exercise

One of the most popular books among job seekers is *The 100 Best Companies to Work for in America* by Robert Levering and Milton Moskowitz. The goal of the authors is to identify and describe the best workplaces. Companies featured in this book are characterized by openness, fairness, camaraderie among employees, job security, opportunities for advancement, and sensitivity to work/family issues. These companies are concerned about the total person, not just the skills that help the company earn a profit. Here are some of the companies that have made the "best companies" list:

Company	Location	Type of Business
Southwest Airlines	Dallas, TX	Airline
SAS Institute	Carey, NC	Computer software
MBNA	Wilmington, DE	Issuer of credit cards
Corning	Corning, NY	Manufacturing
Weyerhaeuser	Federal Way, WA	Forest products

Develop a profile of two of these companies by visiting their Web sites and reviewing the available information. Also, visit Hoover's Online, a resource that provides access to profiles of about 2,800 companies. Additional information on each of these companies may be found in *Business Week, Forbes, Fortune, Working Mother,* and other business publications. For example, *Fortune* publishes an annual list of America's most admired companies, and *Working Mother* publishes a list of the 100 best companies for working mothers.

Case Problem   In Search of Family-Friendly Firms

A growing number of workers are searching for an employer that will help them manage the conflicting demands of home and work. Some are even willing to accept a somewhat smaller paycheck in return for such work-family benefits as child care, elder care, parental leave, and flexible scheduling.

Demographic trends indicate that conflict between family and work will likely increase in the years ahead. Sixty percent of all mothers are employed, and that figure is expected to increase steadily. By the year 2000, dual-earner couples will rise to a majority of all families—a dramatic departure from an earlier era when the husband provided most of the family income. And, as nearly half of marriages end in divorce, single parenting is increasing. Single parents sometimes face special problems balancing work and family responsibilities.

Each year *Working Mother* magazine publishes a list of the 100 best companies for working moms. Companies on the most recent list ranged from small Patagonia, Inc. (577 employees), to giant Eastman Kodak Company (47,014 employees). On-site child-care facilities and flexible work schedules helped Lucasfilm Ltd. (maker of the *Star Wars* trilogy) win a place on the list. The authors of *The 100 Best Companies to Work for in America* recognize many companies that have displayed sensitivity to work-family issues.

The success of family-friendly programs often depends on the attitudes of supervisory-management personnel. Even when employers offer leave for new parents and flexible scheduling, some managers exert subtle pressure to discourage employees from using them. And some companies with the best family-oriented benefits have the worst records for promoting women. Research conducted by Work/Family Directions, a Boston consulting group, found that many women feel that use of family-friendly programs will seriously hamper their career advancement. Deborah Donovan, a lawyer and new mother who works for E. I. du Pont de Nemours & Co., expressed the frustration felt by many other working mothers: "The pressures of middle management are such that flextime means you don't have to work Saturday afternoon. My pet peeve was the occasional Sunday morning meeting."

Questions

1. If you were searching for a new job, would you try to find work with a company that offers family-oriented benefits? Explain your answer.
2. Family-oriented programs such as flexible scheduling and parental leave are not used by some employees because they fear their manager will disapprove of their behavior. What can companies do to resolve this problem?
3. In some cases family-friendly policies breed resentment among employees who must step in when someone leaves work early to pick up a child at day care or takes leave time to care for an elderly parent. How would you respond to such a complaint?

Chapter 2

Improving
Interpersonal Communications

Chapter Preview

After studying this chapter, you will be able to

1. Differentiate impersonal from interpersonal communication.
2. Understand the communication process and the filters that affect communication.
3. Identify ways to improve personal communication, including developing listening skills.
4. Understand how advanced technology is changing the way we communicate.
5. Explain how our global economy has created new communication challenges.

I NTERNATIONAL HARVESTER CO. sold its failing Springfield, Missouri, plant to Jack Stack, the factory manager, and twelve other employees, who formed a new company, Springfield ReManufacturing Corp. (SRC). SRC buys worn-out engines and parts, fixes them to work like new, and sells them to companies such as DaimlerChrysler A.G. and General Motors Corp. Although SRC lost $60,000 in its first year, within a decade it showed profits of $1.3 million on sales of $65 million and employed over 650 people.

One reason for SRC's dramatic success is its open communication climate, which includes opening its financial records to employees. Strategic planning director Dave LaHay explains, "We don't keep any secrets. We get each person to understand the financial statement so they understand why we make the decisions we do."[1] *Inc.* magazine has documented how this "Open Book Revolution" is proving to be successful throughout the world as organizations teach employees how to read financial statements, share the statements with them, set goals to increase profits, and reward achievements toward those goals.[2]

All employees at SRC learn the meaning of such terms as *income statements, balance sheets, cash flow, equity,* and *retained earnings.* Then, on Wednesday afternoons, forty to fifty representatives from different parts of the company meet to play "The Great Game of Business." An exciting exchange of information takes place as some individuals shout out figures while everyone else busily writes them down. After the meeting, the representatives report the companywide results to coworkers in their department.

SRC employees explain their response to this open communication style: "They show us the sales and profits, what they ship; they go through every item. If you are not working up to standard, it's going to show up on that paper. With my prior company, . . . they would come down and say, 'You lost $200,000 this quarter.' [But we wouldn't] know where it was lost. Here you have a total view of everything that is going on." When SRC employees see where money is being lost, they take action to save it because they know that when the company reaches its profit targets at the end of the year, they will be rewarded with a cash bonus of up to 13 percent of their salary.[3] ■

Good communication, which is essential for the smooth functioning of any organization and for the personal development of each worker, depends on the orderly exchange of information. Managers need clear lines of communication to transmit orders and policies, build cooperation, and unify group behavior. Employees must be able to convey their complaints or suggestions and to feel that management has heard what they have to say. Clear communication among coworkers is vital to high productivity, teamwork, problem solving, and conflict management. In short, effective human relations is founded on good communication.

When people in organizations want to send messages, conduct meetings, or communicate person to person, they have many options. Some of these options are creating barriers to effective communication. The growing use of voice mail, electronic mail, fax machines, and pagers has created, for many workers, an information overload. A Gallup poll discovered that the average person working in a large organization sends and receives approximately 178 messages each day.[4] As the number of messages sent and received increases, workers often find themselves distracted and unable to concentrate because of the constant interruptions. This often leads to a breakdown in communications.

Although some communication breakdowns are inevitable, many can be avoided. Leaders like Jack Stack who are candid when sharing information avoid the communication problems so common in organizations. Employees who are treated with respect, are empowered to think for themselves, and feel a sense of responsibility are more likely to communicate openly with other workers and leaders throughout the organization.

THE COMMUNICATION PROCESS

Most people take communication for granted. When they speak or listen to others, they assume that the message given or received is being understood. In reality, most messages are distorted, incomplete, or lost on their way from one person to another. It is estimated that 80 percent of a message gets distorted or lost as it travels through an organization.[5] Therefore, it is important to understand something about the process of communication.

Impersonal Versus Interpersonal Communication

In a typical organization the types of communication used to exchange information can be placed on a continuum ranging from "impersonal" on one end to "interpersonal" on the other.[6] When we use such words as *transmit* or *transfer,* we are talking about a one-way information-giving process. This impersonal, one-way communication process can be used to give basic information such as company policies, instructions, or facts. Generally, organizations use memos, letters, electronic mail, computer printouts, voice mail, manuals, and/or bulletin boards as quick, easy ways to "get the word out." The major limitation of these forms of **impersonal communication** is that people receiving the information usually have no opportunity to ask the sender to clarify vague or confusing wording. Despite this limitation, some organizations are discovering creative ways to keep employees informed using impersonal communication methods. Cray Research, a company that makes supercomputers, uses a variety of communication methods. These include a print newsletter, a video magazine, a confidential question-and-answer program accessible on electronic mail, and frequent communication on business issues by means of E-mail.[7]

In many cases, the national and international geographical location of employees makes two-way communication almost impossible; then organizations often depend heavily on the one-way, impersonal methods such as fax machines, electronic mail, and the Internet. When Texaco Inc. was facing unfavorable publicity concerning a race-discrimination lawsuit, the CEO wasted little time in launching a campaign of damage control. Peter Bijur used the company's satellite broadcast network to address 27,000 employees. He carefully outlined steps that would be taken to redeem the company's reputation.[8]

Interpersonal communication is the verbal exchange of thoughts or information between two or more people. Such words as *share, discuss, argue,* and *interact* refer to this form of two-way communication. Interpersonal communication can take place in meetings, over the phone, in face-to-face interviews, or during classroom discussions between instructors and students. If interpersonal communication is to be effective, some type of **feedback,** or response, from the person receiving the information is necessary. When this verbal exchange happens, the person sending the information can determine whether or not the message has been understood in the way he or she intended. This form of communication is one of the most effective ways to build strong, trusting relationships among people throughout an organization.

Tom Chappell, owner of Tom's of Maine, which makes and sells natural toothpaste, shampoos, and deodorants, relies on face-to-face communication to cope with rumors, downturns in morale, and other communication problems. Several times each year Chappell gets together with his employees and talks about company performance and future plans. He says the best way to communicate with employees is to be honest, be informational, and tell it like it is.[9]

But interpersonal communication takes time, and because it does, many companies use the faster, impersonal means of conveying information. Indeed, the speed of information giving has increased dramatically through the use of

---

Total Person Insight

"'Communication breakdown' has just about taken the place of original sin as an explanation for the ills of the world—and perhaps with good cause. As our world becomes more complex and we spend more time in organized activities, the need for interpersonal understanding has never been greater. And just as important, the cost of failure has never been higher."

PAUL R. TIMM

Educator; author, *The Way We Word*

computers and other technology. Yet many workers say they are out of touch. A young narrator in a television commercial for Volkswagen expressed the feelings of many people:

> I've got gigabytes. I've got megabytes. I'm voice-mailed. I'm e-mailed. I surf the net. I'm on the Web. I am Cyber-Man. So how come I feel so out of touch?[10]

Computers and other forms of technology can be invaluable when it comes to impersonal information giving, but they cannot replace the two-way, interpersonal communication process when feedback and discussion are necessary.

Sender—Message—Receiver

Effective communication, in its most basic form, is composed of three elements: a sender, a receiver, and an understood message.[11] To illustrate, suppose your friend phones from your neighborhood convenience store and asks for directions to your home. You give your friend the appropriate street names, intersections, and compass directions so that he can drive to your door without getting lost. When your friend repeats his understanding of your directions, you clarify any misunderstandings, and he drives directly to your home. A simplified diagram of this communication process would look like Figure 2.1.

Now suppose you are late for an appointment, and the plumber you had requested three days ago calls you from her cellular phone and asks directions to your house. She explains that she has gotten lost in this neighborhood before, and it is obvious that English is her second language. The communication process becomes much more complicated, as shown in Figure 2.2. As your

FIGURE 2.1

Diagram of Simple Communication Process

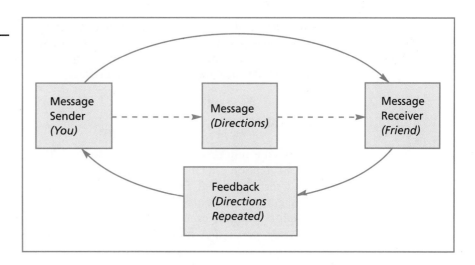

FIGURE 2.2

Diagram of
More Complex
Communication
Process

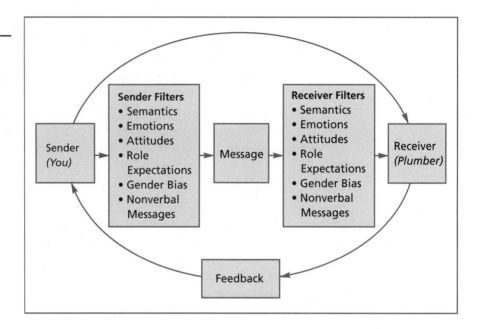

FIGURE 2.2

Diagram of
More Complex
Communication
Process

message travels from you to your plumber, it must pass through several "filters," each of which can alter the way your message is understood. Most communication processes are of the complex type shown in Figure 2.2. Because these filters are so important, let's examine them in greater detail.

COMMUNICATION FILTERS

Messages are filtered through semantics, emotions, attitudes, role expectations, gender bias, and nonverbal messages. When the sender is influenced by any of these filters, the message relayed may be distorted. At the same time, the receiver's filters may further distort the message.

Semantics

We often assume that the words we use mean the same things to others, but this assumption can create problems. Words are not things; they are labels that stand for something. **Semantics** is the study of the relationship between a word and its meaning(s). We have agreed that particular words have associated meanings and usages. We can easily understand what words like *typewriter, computer,* or *envelope* mean. But more abstract terms, such as *job satisfaction,*

From May 1977 *Training* magazine. Used by permission.

"... *PROMISE TO GET THE SHIPMENTS OUT ON TIME AND I'LL PROMISE YOU I WON'T TRY TO EXPLAIN THIS....*"

downsizing, internal customers, or *word processing,* have less precise meanings and will be interpreted by different people in different ways. The more abstract the term, the less likely it is that people will agree on its meaning. Some professionals have been strongly criticized for using abstract words:

Item: Lawyers have been accused of using abstract words and "legalese" to confuse persons who turn to them for help. David Mellinkoff, a law school professor, says that lawyers' writing resembles a foreign language.[12]

Item: Corporate employees often use important-sounding jargon that is almost incomprehensible. Better Communications, a firm that teaches writing skills to employers, clipped this statement from a memo circulated at a Fortune 500 company: "Added value is the keystone to exponentially accelerating profit curves."[13]

People's attitudes, background, experiences, and culture also affect how they interpret the words and phrases they hear. For example, one Midwestern executive sent the following message to his manager, who was born and raised in Peru: "Send me factory and office headcount broken down by sex." The Peruvian manager replied, "249 in factory, 30 in office, 3 on sick leave, none broken down by sex—our problem is with alcohol."[14]

Emotions

Emotions can be a powerful communication filter. Strong emotions can either prevent people from hearing what a speaker has to say or make them too susceptible to the speaker's point of view. If they become angry or allow themselves to be carried away by the speaker's eloquence, they may "think" with their emotions and make decisions or take action they regret later. They have shifted their attention from the content of the message to their feelings about it.

You may have had the experience of your spouse or parent angrily demanding to know why you forgot to run an errand. If you allow someone else's anger to trigger your own, the conversation quickly deteriorates into an argument. The real issue—what happened and what is to be done about it—is lost in the shouting match. Detaching yourself from another's feelings and responding to the content of the message is often difficult. Yet many jobs require that employees remain calm and courteous regardless of a customer's emotional state. Emotional control is discussed in Chapter 8.

Attitudes

Attitudes are beliefs backed up by emotions. They can be a barrier to communication in much the same way emotions can—by altering the way people hear a message. The listener may not like the speaker's voice, accent, gestures, mannerisms, dress, or delivery. Perhaps the listener has preconceived ideas about the speaker's topic. For instance, a person who is strongly opposed to abortion will most likely find it difficult to listen with objectivity to a pro-choice speaker. Negative attitudes create resistance to the message and can lead to a breakdown in communication. Overly positive attitudes can also be a barrier to communication because the listener may hear only what he or she wants to hear. Biased in favor of the message, the listener may fail to evaluate it effectively. More is said about forming attitudes in Chapter 5.

Role Expectations

Role expectations influence how people expect themselves, and others, to act on the basis of the roles they play, such as boss, customer, or subordinate. These expectations can distort communication in two ways. First, if people identify others too closely with their roles, they may discount what the other person has to say: "It's just the boss again, saying the same old thing." A variation of this distortion occurs when we do not allow others to change their roles and take on new ones. This often happens to employees who are promoted from within the ranks of an organization to management positions. Others may still see the new manager as a secretary instead of a supervisor, as "old Chuck" from accounting rather than as the new department head. Coworkers may not take promoted employees seriously in their new roles or listen to what they have to say.

Second, role expectations can affect good communication when people use their roles to alter the way they relate to others. This is often referred to as "position power." For example, managers may expect employees to accept what they say simply because of the authority invested in the position. Employees are not allowed to question the manager's decisions or make suggestions of their own, and communication becomes one-way information giving.

Gender Bias

Men and women tend to color the messages they receive from people of the opposite gender strictly because of the other person's gender. This tendency is a form of **gender bias.**

Men no longer dominate the workplace because women are entering the workplace in greater numbers than ever before and are making major strides in achieving management positions within organizations. One consequence of these changing demographics has been a realization that men and women tend to speak in distinctly different "genderlects," just as people from various cultures speak different dialects.[15] Men are more likely to talk about money, sports, and business; women prefer talking about people, feelings, and relationships. Even when discussing the same topic, men and women may be on different wavelengths because their gender-specific focus is different. For example, if a man and woman are discussing a pending layoff in their organization, the man might approach it from a cost-cutting point of view, and the woman may focus on the feelings of the people involved. Neither view is wrong, but the resulting conversation can frustrate both parties. In her book *Genderflex: Men and Women Speaking Each Other's Language at Work,* Judith Tingle states:

> Men and women assume that the other gender is trying to accomplish the same goal as their own gender, but assume the other gender is going about it the wrong way. . . . Both men and women often become critical and angry at the other gender for not using the "correct" means to the desired end.[16]

This anger and frustration can create a major filter that interferes with effective communication between the genders.

Nonverbal Messages

When we attempt to communicate with another person, we use both verbal and nonverbal communication. **Nonverbal messages** are "messages without words" or "silent messages." These are the messages (other than spoken or written words) we communicate through facial expressions, voice tone, gestures, appearance, posture, and other nonverbal means. Research indicates that our nonverbal messages have much more impact than verbal messages. Albert Mehrabian, author of *Silent Messages*, indicates that only 7 percent of the meaning attached to our messages is conveyed through our choice of words, whereas 55 percent is conveyed by what is seen—facial expressions, posture, eye contact, and gestures. About 38 percent of the message meaning is conveyed by what others hear—tone of voice, vocal clarity, and verbal expressiveness.[17] This chapter limits its discussion to the form of nonverbal communication commonly referred to as "body language."

Many of us could communicate more clearly, more accurately, and more credibly if we became more conscious of our body language. We can learn to strengthen our communications by making sure our words and our body language are consistent. When our verbal and nonverbal messages match, we give the impression that we can be trusted and that what we are saying reflects what we truly believe. But when our body language contradicts our words, we are often unknowingly changing the message we are sending. If a manager says to an employee, "I am very interested in your problem," but then begins to look at his watch and fidget with objects on his desk, the employee will most likely believe the nonverbal rather than the verbal message.

Individuals can improve their communications by monitoring the nonverbal messages they send through the use of eye contact, facial expressions, gestures, and personal space.

Eye Contact Eyes transmit more information than any other part of the body. Because eye contact is so revealing, people generally observe some unwritten rules about looking at others. People who hold direct eye contact for only a few seconds, or avoid eye contact altogether, risk communicating indifference. However, a direct, prolonged stare between strangers is usually considered impolite, even potentially aggressive or hostile. Generally speaking, when you are introduced to someone, maintain eye contact for 10 to 14 seconds.

Workers involved in customer service find that a certain amount of eye contact is necessary to build trust with a prospective customer. Research indicates that tips increase when food service personnel squat down beside the table. Apparently this informal posture promotes eye contact by placing the server on the same level as the customer. When customers perceive the server as friendly and attentive, they tend to give more generous tips.[18]

It is not always fair to base judgments about other people on their ability to make eye contact, however. One interviewer complained that a young man with excellent qualifications would not look him in the eye during the interview. A colleague discovered that the young man was Puerto Rican and explained that Puerto Rican youth are taught to look down as a mark of respect when speaking with adults.

As a general rule, when you are communicating in a business setting, your eyes should meet the other person's about 60 to 70 percent of the time. This timing is an effective alternative to continuous eye contact.

Facial Expressions If you want to identify the inner feelings of another person, watch facial expressions closely. A frown or a smile will communicate a great deal. We have all encountered a "look of surprise" or a "look that could kill." Most of our observations are very accurate. If we are able to assess the inner emotions of the other person, we can be sure that person is doing the same to us, drawing conclusions based on our facial expressions.

Gestures Did you know that you send a nonverbal message every time you place your hand over your mouth, clench your hands together, cross your legs, or grip your arms? These gestures send messages to people about how you are reacting to them and to the situation in which you find yourself.

The next time you are in a business meeting, watch the gestures of your colleagues. Some people will walk into the room with their shoulders slumped forward and head down. They will slouch into their chair, lean their chin on the palm of their hand, play with a pencil or paperclip on the table, or clutch their arms across their chest. Others will walk into the room with chin held high and shoulders back, sit straight in their chairs and lean slightly forward, and take notes with both arms "open" to whoever is speaking during the meeting. Experts agree that the words you say during a meeting with others, no matter how powerful, are often forgotten or disregarded unless your gestures command respect.[19]

In light of our expanding global marketplace, be aware that some gestures that may be common in the American culture may have dramatically different meanings to people from outside the United States (see Figure 2.3). Although nodding your head up and down means "yes" in most countries, it means "no" in Greece and Bulgaria.[20] To use your fingers to call someone forward in a crowd is insulting to most Middle and Far Easterners.[21] And that common American gesture of folding your arms in front of you shows disrespect in Fiji.[22]

Personal Space   Research conducted by Edward Hall provides evidence that people use the space around them to define relationships. It is possible to make others uncomfortable by standing too close to, or too far away from, them. A customer may feel uncomfortable if a salesperson stands too close. A job applicant may feel uncomfortable if the interviewer maintains a distance of several feet. Hall identified four "zones" of comfortable distances that help us understand this nonverbal effect on others:[23]

1. *Intimate distance* includes touching to approximately 18 inches from another person. Most people will respond with defensiveness when strangers intrude into this territory.
2. *Personal distance* ranges from 18 inches to 4 feet. This distance is usually reserved for close friends.
3. *Social distance* is 4 to 12 feet and is used for business meetings and impersonal social gatherings. Business can be conducted with a minimum of emotional involvement.
4. *Public distance,* which usually involves one-way communication from a speaker to an audience, is 12 to 15 feet.

It is important to keep in mind that these distances vary from one culture to another. For example, Asians are accustomed to close contact, but Americans want more space around them.

Thinking / Learning Starters

1. Are you aware of the messages you send through body language? Recall your nonverbal behavior in various situations, including a difficult meeting with a supervisor or a dinner party with friends. Was your behavior consistent with your words? Explain.

2. Acute sensitivity to nonverbal messages is an important skill for people to develop. In general, do you feel that nonverbal messages are more trustworthy than verbal ones? Describe specific nonverbal messages that you have learned to trust in your friends or coworkers.

FIGURE 2.3

The hand-ring finger gesture (hand displayed with the thumb and forefinger tips joined) is a sign of approval in North America. In Belgium, France, and Tunisia this gesture symbolizes the precise opposite—a "big zero." The thumb-up gesture means "OK" or "something good" in almost every part of the world. In Australia, however, it is considered an obscene gesture.

Sources: Hand-ring gesture taken from Desmond Morris, *Bodytalk: The Meaning of Human Gestures* (New York: Crown Trade Paperbacks, 1994), pp. 118–119 and pp. 129–130. Thumb-up gesture: Desmond Morris, *Bodytalk: The Meaning of Human Gestures,* and Rochelle Sharpe, "Work Week," *Wall Street Journal,* October 31, 1995, p. A-1.

Who Is Responsible for Effective Communication?

The sender and the receiver share equal responsibility for effective communication. The communication loop, as shown in Figure 2.2, is complete when the receiver understands, feels, or behaves according to the message of the sender. If this does not occur, the communication process has broken down.

Individuals can improve their human relations by basing all their communications on a simple premise: The message received *is* the message. If the message the receiver hears differs from the one the sender intended, the communication loop has not been completed. The message the receiver hears is, in effect, the only message that exists. If a serious discrepancy exists between what the sender intended to say and what the receiver heard, disagreements or even fights can occur. When emotions calm down, it does not help for the sender to say, "But that's not what I meant. You misunderstood!" By then, human relations between the sender and receiver have already been damaged.

When the sender accepts 100 percent of the responsibility for sending a clear, concise message, the communication process begins. But the receiver must also accept 100 percent of the responsibility for receiving the message as the sender intended. Receivers must provide senders with enough feedback to ensure that an accurate message has passed through all the filters that might alter it.

HOW TO IMPROVE PERSONAL COMMUNICATION

Now that you have been introduced to the communication process and the various filters messages must pass through, you can begin to take the necessary steps to improve your own personal communication skills. As you study the following skills, think about the various settings in which you will apply them. Throughout your working life your success will depend greatly on your ability to be an effective team member. And to become a valued team member, you will need excellent communication skills. You will also apply these skills in your role as leader. In traditional organizations there were leaders and followers, and the followers were not expected to apply leadership skills. Today, progressive organizations are adopting the "employees as leaders" approach, for example, by organizing employees into teams. Communication skills are also critical when you are managing the relationship with your boss.

Send Clear Messages

Become a responsible sender by always sending clear, concise messages with as little influence from filters as possible. As you formulate your messages, keep in mind how filters distort all messages from both the sender's and the receiver's vantage points. A general rule of thumb is to give clear instructions and ask clear questions so you won't be misunderstood. A new employee stood before the paper shredder in her new office. An administrative assistant noticed her confused look and asked if she needed some help. "Yes, thank you. How does this thing work?" "It's simple," said the assistant and took the thick report from the new employee and fed it through the shredder. "I see," she said, "but how many copies will it make?" This kind of miscommunication could easily have been avoided if both parties had followed a few simple rules.[24]

Use Words Carefully As noted previously, abstract words, whether spoken or written, often become barriers to effective communication. Use words that are simple, clear, and concise. Avoid buzzwords or complex, official language. Tailoring the message to the receiver by using words the listener understands will help ensure that your message is understood.

Some companies are now sponsoring business writing courses for their employees. They focus on keeping messages short and simple. The opening and closing paragraphs should be limited to approximately three sentences. Condense the remaining information into three to four bulleted items. The skill of creating memos and letters that convey information clearly and concisely requires practice.[25]

Use Repetition When possible, use parallel channels of communication. For example, by sending a memo and making a phone call, you not only gain the receiver's attention through dialogue but also make sure there is a written record in case specific details need to be recalled. Many studies show that repetition, or redundancy, is an important element in ensuring communication accuracy.

Use Appropriate Timing Keep in mind that most employees, particularly at the managerial level, are flooded with messages every day. An important memo or letter may get no attention simply because it is competing with more pressing problems facing the receiver. Some organizations solve the problem by establishing standard times for particular messages to be sent and received. Important financial information, for example, may be sent on the second Thursday of every month. Timing the delivery of your message will help ensure that it is accepted and acted on.

Develop Listening Skills

In addition to sending clearer messages, we need to practice listening. Most of us are born with the ability to hear, but we have to learn how to listen. Tom Peters, in his book *Thriving on Chaos: Handbook for a Management Revolution,* entitles an entire chapter "Become Obsessed with Listening." Psychologist Carl Rogers has said, "Listening is such an incredible and magical thing." Peters, Rogers, and others agree: We need to accept listening as a skill that can be learned.

Many of the misunderstandings in life are due to poor listening. Most people never learn to listen. This helps explain why people listen at a 25 percent efficiency rate in typical situations. They miss about 75 percent of the messages spoken by other people.[26] All too frequently, most of us hear the message but do not take the time to really listen and blend the messages we hear with critical thinking and human understanding.

Active Listening **Active listening** means concentrating on what you are hearing, listening with your whole body, and feeding back to the speaker what you think the speaker meant.[27] By actively listening, you demonstrate sincere interest in what the other person is saying. This sets into motion a supportive chain in which the speaker feels more accepted and can be more open. When you truly want to create effective communications and enhance your relationships, there are several steps you can follow:

1. *Develop a listening attitude.* Regard the person as worthy of respect and attention. Empathize, or "feel with," the speaker, and really try to understand the

Total Person Insight

"Listening, really listening, is tough and grinding work, often humbling, sometimes distasteful. It's a fairly sure bet that you won't like the lion's share of what you hear."

GERRY MITCHELL

Chairman, Dana Corporation

other person's experience. Drop your expectations of what you are going to hear or what you would like to hear. Don't rush the speaker. Be patient, and refrain from formulating your response until the speaker has finished talking.

2. *Focus your full attention.* This is not easy because the delivery of the messages we hear is often much slower than our capacity to listen. So we have plenty of time to let our minds roam, to think ahead, and to plan what we are going to say next. Our senses are constantly feeding us new information while someone is trying to tell us something. Staying focused is often difficult and involves maintaining eye contact with the speaker and not letting distractions interfere.

3. *Take notes.* One way to focus your attention on what the speaker is saying and away from distractions is by taking notes. Although note taking is not absolutely essential in every verbal exchange, it will greatly improve communications in many situations. If your supervisor is giving you detailed instructions, taking notes will ensure greater accuracy and will build the supervisor's confidence in your ability to remember important details.

4. *Ask questions.* This step ensures your own understanding of the speaker's thoughts and feelings and helps you secure additional relevant information. If you want the speaker to expand broadly on a particular point, ask open-ended questions, such as "How do you feel about that?" or "Can you tell us some ways to improve?"[28]

Empathic Listening   Many workers today face serious personal problems and feel the need to talk about them with someone. They do not expect specific advice or guidance; they just want to spend some time with an empathic listener. Stephen Covey, the noted author and consultant, described **empathic listening** as listening with the intent to understand. This approach gives you an understanding of the other person's frame of reference and lets you understand how the person feels. Empathic listening, according to Covey, requires listening with your ears, your eyes, and your heart.[29] If you want to practice empathic listening, adopt the following practices:

1. *Avoid being judgmental.* Objectivity is the heart and soul of empathic listening. The person is communicating for emotional release and does not seek a specific response.

2. *Accept what is said.* You do not have to agree with what is being said, but you should let the person know you are able to understand his or her viewpoint.

3. *Be patient.* If you are unable or unwilling to take the time to hear what the person has to say, say so immediately. Signs of impatience send a negative message to the person needing to talk.[30]

As a coworker or supervisor, you will likely have many opportunities to engage in empathic listening. Effective empathic listening is one of the highest forms of interpersonal communications.

Thinking / Learning Starters

1. Think of some people you know who are active listeners. How can you tell? Describe an instance when their active listening improved their relations with you or another person.

2. Have you recently been approached by someone who wanted to talk to an empathic listener? Were you able to respond in the manner recommended?

Use Constructive Self-Disclosure

Self-disclosure is the process of letting another person know what you think, feel, or want. It is one of the important ways you let yourself be known by others. The primary goal of self-disclosure is to build strong and healthy interpersonal relationships.

It is important to note the difference between self-disclosure and self-description. **Self-description** involves disclosure of nonthreatening information, such as your age, your favorite food, or where you went to school. This is information that others could acquire in some way other than by your telling them. Self-disclosure, by contrast, usually involves some risk. When you practice self-disclosure, you reveal private, personal information that cannot be acquired from another source. Examples include your feelings about being a member of a minority group or your thoughts on new policies and procedures.

The importance of self-disclosure, in contrast to self-description, is shown by the following situation. You work at a distribution center and are extremely conscious of safety. You take every precaution to avoid work-related accidents. But another employee has a much more casual attitude toward safety rules and often "forgets" to observe the proper procedures, endangering you and other workers. You can choose to disclose your feelings to this person or hide your concerns. If you choose to stay silent, the problem will likely persist.

Benefits of Self-Disclosure   There are a number of benefits you gain from openly sharing what you think, feel, or want. As a general rule, relationships grow stronger when people are willing to reveal more about themselves. When two people engage in an open, authentic dialogue, they often develop a high regard for each other's views. Often they discover they share common interests and concerns, and these serve as a foundation for a deeper relationship.

Self-disclosure often results in increased accuracy in communication. It takes the guesswork out of the communication process. No one is a mind reader; if people conceal how they really feel, it is very difficult for others to know how to respond to them appropriately. People who are frustrated by a heavy work-load but mask their true feelings may never see the problem resolved.

In many cases, constructive self-disclosure can reduce stress. Sidney Jourard, a noted psychologist who has written extensively about self-disclosure, states that too much emphasis on privacy and concealment of feelings creates stress within an individual.[31] To the extent that persons can share with others their inner thoughts and feelings, they experience less stress. Constructive self-disclosure can be a very important dimension of a stress management program. Too many people keep their feelings bottled up inside, which can result in considerable inner tension.

Guidelines for Appropriate Self-Disclosure In the search for criteria to determine appropriate self-disclosure, many factors must be considered. How much information should be disclosed? How intimate should the information be? Under what conditions should the disclosures be made? The following guidelines will help you develop your self-disclosure skills.

1. *Use self-disclosure to repair damaged relationships.* Many relationships are unnecessarily strained. The strain often exists because people refuse to talk about real or imagined problems. Self-disclosure can be an excellent method of repairing a damaged relationship.

   If your actions have caused hurt feelings, anger, or deep-seated ill will, an apology may be in order. A sincere apology can have a tremendous amount of healing power. In addition, it may set the stage for improved communications in the future.

2. *Discuss disturbing situations as they happen.* Your reactions to a work-related problem or issue should be shared as soon after the incident as possible. It is often difficult to recapture a feeling once it has passed, and you may distort the incident if you let too much time go by. Your mem-

---

Total Person Insight

"A genuine apology offered and accepted is one of the most profound interactions of civilized people. It has the power to restore damaged relationships, be they on a small scale, between two people, such as intimates, or on a grand scale, between groups of people, even nations. If done correctly, an apology can heal humiliation and generate forgiveness."

Aaron Lazare, M.D.

ory is not infallible. The person who caused the hurt feelings is also likely to forget details about the situation.

3. *Select the right time and place.* Remarks that otherwise might be offered and accepted in a positive way can be rendered ineffective, not because of what we say but because of when and where we say it.[32] When possible, select a time when you feel the other person is not preoccupied and will be able to give you his or her full attention. Also, select a setting free of distractions.

4. *Avoid overwhelming others with your self-disclosure.* Although you should be open, do not go too far too fast. Many strong relationships are built slowly. The abrupt disclosure of highly emotional or intimate information may actually distance you from the other person. Your behavior may be considered threatening.

Thinking / Learning Starter

Mentally review your previous work or volunteer experience. Identify at least one occasion when you felt great frustration over some incident but avoided disclosing your feelings to the person who could have solved the problem. What factors motivated you not to self-disclose? In retrospect, do you now perceive any benefits you might have gained by choosing to self-disclose?

Improving Team Communications

In an effort to improve productivity and increase employees' involvement in decision making, many companies have formed specific types of teams. Some of these teams have a special purpose, such as devising new work procedures or developing a new product; others are established to solve a specific problem. In making the transition to a team environment, employees often face special challenges in the area of communications. The following ground rules contribute to effective team-member communications.

• At the outset, team members must agree on a clear purpose and establish procedures for getting the work done. Team members must share a common vision. Each team member should have an assigned role and know what he or she is empowered to do.

• All team members should have the information they need to make informed decisions. Open communication builds trust, which is often lacking during the early stages of team development.

- Every team meeting must be meaningful. A specific agenda should be developed for each meeting. Keep meetings short (60–90 minutes), and record minutes for each meeting.
- The importance of working together as a team should not replace the importance of individual contributions. Individual members should feel a sense of responsibility for helping the team achieve its goals.

Developing highly effective teams is a long, complex process. In the case of self-directed teams, the evolution usually takes two to three years. It takes time for people to learn new duties and new ways of interacting.

HIGH-TECH COMMUNICATION

The idea that we need to communicate more so that individuals and their organizations can be more successful is widely accepted. But technological advancements have so dramatically advanced the communications process beyond the traditional memo/letter/telephone that people are often overwhelmed with too much information. Supervisory-management personnel, in particular, are bombarded daily with useless data that they must wade through to find the information they are seeking. High-tech communications alternatives need to be carefully examined to determine their ability to provide useful information, not just masses of data.[33]

Modems, electronic mail, voice mail, faxes, cellular phones, laptop computers, hand-held pen-based electronic notepads, CD-ROM information storage, and the Internet are making it possible for people scattered all over the world to communicate without ever being in the same room. Many organizations now operate from **virtual offices,** which are companies that function like traditional businesses but are actually a network of workers connected with the latest technology.[34] Often a laptop computer, complete with an internal fax/modem, combines with a cellular phone to function effectively as "an office in a briefcase." **Telecommuting,** an arrangement that allows employees to work from their homes, enables people scattered all over the country to work as one office.

The telecommuting trend is increasing dramatically. The greatest boost to this trend has been the expansion of electronic mail, often referred to as E-mail. **E-mail** is a message you send or receive through a computer and its modem (the computer's connection to a telephone line). During recent years, most companies have added E-mail capabilities to their computer networks. In such companies, a salesperson calling on a customer can receive up-to-date information on the status of the customer's order by means of a quick E-mail message to the shipping department. An executive could convene an emergency meeting of all department managers by transmitting an E-mail message directly to their computer monitors. With the inception of the Internet, the service that links computers and databases of libraries, universities, and government agencies throughout the world, E-mail can now travel on a massive global communications "superhighway."

The advantages of using E-mail, both within an organization and globally, are obvious. Time efficiency is unsurpassed, for people can send detailed messages at any time, across all time zones, and the receivers can retrieve their messages as their schedule allows. The cost of an E-mail transmission is usually less than postage and dramatically less than a trans-Atlantic or trans-Pacific phone call. The potential for efficient customer service is enhanced because orders can be placed and changed, and shipping tracked, within seconds.

As E-mail use expands, subtle advantages are beginning to surface. E-mail is now referred to as the "great equalizer." Because the sender's gender and skin color are not immediately obvious, prejudiced attitudes are less likely to alter the message. Before E-mail, lower-level workers had little access to the president or CEO of their organizations. Now they can contact these individuals electronically without anyone in between misinterpreting, sabotaging, or blocking the message. In addition, electronic messages are a wonderful alternative for those individuals who are painfully shy and find it difficult to express themselves when communicating with others face to face.

Despite all these advantages, E-mail has some disadvantages you should be aware of if you are going to be using it. Because E-mail is used to speed up the communications process, many people compose and send hastily written messages, which can be confusing. If you have to send a second message to clarify your first message, E-mail does not save you any time.

Some people believe electronic mail is reviving the lost art of letter writing. If it has been a while since you had to write a letter to anyone, consider these guidelines before you create an E-mail message:

- Think before you write. Take time to compose your thoughts. Don't just "dash out an E-mail."
- Carefully edit your message on the screen before sending it. A typographical error, plural subject and singular verb, or "there" used instead of "their" in a sentence will reflect poorly on your professionalism and competence.
- Summarize your main points, indicate the action or response you are seeking, and be sure you provide all the details the receiver needs to take action.
- Be very careful about the tone of your messages. Remove any potentially offending words and phrasing from your documents. Since correspondents cannot see each other's body language, some mistakenly feel they must use stronger language to get their message across.[35]
- Since E-mail is transmitted instantaneously, be sure you have entered the correct E-mail address! There is no way to retrieve the message once you "send."

Another potential hazard in the use of E-mail is lack of privacy. As communication technology advances, individuals and organizations are devising safeguards that will maintain every individual's right to privacy.

COMMUNICATION IN A GLOBAL ECONOMY

Worldwide telecommunications and international business competition are creating additional communication problems and challenges for modern organizations. U.S. corporations employ more than 60 million overseas workers. More than 100,000 U.S. firms are engaged in global ventures valued at more than $1 trillion.[36] For example, since 1986 American Telephone & Telegraph Co. (AT&T) has grown from 50 people in 10 foreign countries to 52,000 overseas employees in 105 countries.[37] New York–based Colgate-Palmolive Co. currently operates in more than 170 countries and receives about 70 percent of its $7 billion revenues from overseas markets.[38] When we hear the word *transnational* (conducting business with several foreign countries at one time), we may think only of giant corporations like AT&T and Colgate-Palmolive. However, there has been a major increase in middle-size and even small businesses operating transnationally rather than restricting their activities to one or two countries.[39]

As more and more companies send their employees abroad on temporary or permanent assignments, effective communication becomes more critical. Recent studies indicate that more than 25 percent of U.S. corporate overseas assignments fail, at a cost of more than $2 billion a year.[40] Inadequate communication seems to be at the root of many of these failed assignments. For example, learning the language of the new country may be an obvious training need, but more organizations are beginning to realize they must prepare their expatriates—their foreign-based employees—in the language and culture of their host countries.[41] Each country has its own unique view of various aspects of doing business, such as how to spend time, share information, or handle relationships. American employees will function better if they know what to expect. Women should be prepared to cope with far more male chauvinism than they would encounter in the United States. Men and women alike must learn that aggressiveness may be counterproductive in some countries, and that physical contact beyond a handshake is strictly forbidden in many countries. Consider these subtle communication traps for the unwary:

Arab countries: Don't use your left hand to hold, offer, or receive materials because Arabs use their left hand to touch toilet paper. If you must use your left hand to write, apologize for doing so.

China: Don't refuse tea during a business discussion. Always drink it, even if you're offered a dozen cups a day. Never begin to eat or drink before your host does. Also, printed materials presented to Chinese business leaders should be in black and white, since colors have great significance for the Chinese.

France: Don't schedule a breakfast meeting. The French tend not to meet until after 10 A.M.

Germany: Don't address a business associate by his or her first name, even if you've known each other for years. Always wait for an invitation to do so. Also, breakfast meetings are unheard of here too.

Most progressive organizations understand the critical importance of cross-cultural communication in today's global economy. Marriott makes an effective marketing statement with this ad for Marriott hotels located in twenty-seven countries. (Courtesy of the Marriott Corp.)

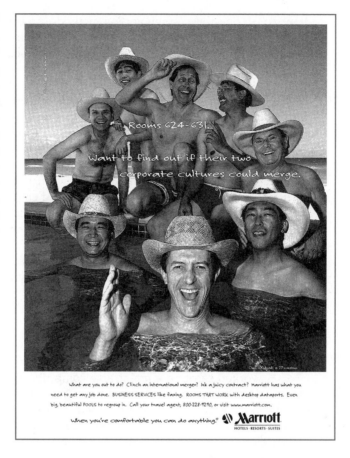

Latin America: People here don't take the clock too seriously. Scheduling more than two appointments in one day can prove disastrous.

Japan: Don't bring up business on the golf course—always wait for your host to take the initiative. Don't cross your legs in Japan. Showing the bottom of the foot is insulting.

Mexico: Don't send a bouquet of red or yellow flowers as a gift. Mexicans associate those colors with evil spirits and death. Instead, send flowers of a different color or a box of premium chocolates.[42]

While many companies are sending employees abroad, others are employing more foreign-born workers than ever before. This trend means that supervisors and managers must have the communication skills to manage a multilingual, multicultural work force here at home. Many of these workers speak English only as a second language and may not be fully fluent in either speaking or receiving English messages.

Summary

Impersonal, one-way communication methods can be effectively used to share basic facts, policies, instructions, and other such information that requires no feedback from the receiver. Interpersonal communication involves a two-way exchange in which the receiver understands the message in the same way the sender intended it.

Communication is often filtered through semantics, emotions, attitudes, role expectations, gender bias, and nonverbal messages. Body language conveys information about a person's thoughts and feelings through eye contact, facial expressions, gestures, and use of personal space.

Individuals can make their messages clearer by choosing words carefully, using repetition, and timing the message so that the receiver can focus on what is being said. They can also learn active and empathic listening skills.

The communications superhighway that connects computers throughout the world has brought with it tremendous opportunities. This technology has also created a major concern about each individual's right to privacy.

The dramatic expansion of the global marketplace means that companies must train their employees to be able to communicate in spite of language and cultural differences.

Career Corner

Q. In our company, all of our individual computer terminals are networked through a mainframe computer. We can access documents and files from any terminal at any time. The human resources department has given us direct access to our individual personnel files and asked us to update our personal data, recording such changes as a new address or an increase or decrease in declared dependents.

Recently, I have received harassing phone calls on my unlisted home telephone. Although I cannot prove it, I believe someone at work has accessed my personnel file and discovered my private phone number. My company has no written policy regarding accessing information electronically. All information, including E-mail messages, can be read by anyone connected to the mainframe. What should I do?

A. Most computer programs that allow information input from multiple sources within a company also have a strong password management device to prevent anyone from accessing sensitive information. Request, in writing, that your organization initiate a password protection system. Different levels of information could be made available to various levels of personnel based on their "need to know" the information.

Currently, employers have the right to monitor employees at work. This includes recording phone conversations, video monitoring, and inspecting employees' personal property on company premises, which can include E-mail. However, because of the increase in the number of lawsuits based on intrusion of privacy and the increase in the use of electronic mail, your organization should establish clear and concise policies as to who can access what information. The policies should include guidelines on such issues as access, business versus personal messages, and offensive messages such as pornography or sexual harassment. If these policies are not firmly established, individual workers tend to lack trust in their coworkers. This atmosphere will eventually interfere with effective human relations throughout the organization.

Key Terms

impersonal communication
interpersonal communication
feedback
semantics
emotions
gender bias
nonverbal messages

active listening
empathic listening
self-disclosure
self-description
virtual office
telecommuting
E-mail

Review Questions

1. Describe the difference between impersonal and interpersonal communication. Explain the communication process in your own words.
2. Why is feedback essential to good communication?
3. What are the responsibilities of both sender and receiver in the communication process?
4. What are communication filters? How can they be stumbling blocks to effective communication?
5. What techniques can be used to send clear messages? How can you know if you have been successful?
6. What happens when a sender's nonverbal cues do not agree with the verbal message being sent?
7. What is the major difference between self-disclosure and self-description?
8. How can self-disclosure contribute to improved teamwork within an organization?
9. List the advantages and disadvantages of using E-mail.
10. What types of communication problems exist in an organization that actively participates in the global economy? What steps should organizations take to help eliminate these problems?

Application Exercises

1. Susan Campbell, author and consultant in the area of interpersonal communication, says the starting point for effective communication is to make sure your intentions are clear. What do you want to accomplish with the next phone call, letter, E-mail message, or visit with a coworker? Some-

times we seek control over the receiver of our message. In some cases, our intention is spiteful or to avoid being blamed for something. If you are honest with yourself about the intention of your communication, you can improve the planning and delivery of your messages. If you are honest with yourself, you are more likely to get what you want. Reflect on your most recent written or spoken communications with another person. What were your intentions? Did you get what you wanted?

2. We can all improve our listening efficiency. First, we need to be aware of our listening habits. By completing this form, you can become more aware of poor listening habits that might reduce your listening efficiency. The results will give you an idea of some listening habits you might want to change.

A—Almost never   *B*—Occasionally   *C*—Frequently   *D*—Most of the time

_____ 1. Do you fail to pay attention? Some listeners allow themselves to be distracted or to think of something else.

_____ 2. Do you give the appearance of listening when you are not? Some people who are thinking about something else deliberately try to look as though they are listening.

_____ 3. Do you tune out the person who says something you don't agree with or don't want to hear? Some people are concentrating on what they are going to say next rather than truly listening to the other person's point of view.

_____ 4. Do you listen only for facts? Some people listen only to facts or details and miss the real meaning of what is being said.

_____ 5. Do you rehearse what you are going to say? Some people listen until they want to say something, at which point they stop listening and begin planning their response.

_____ 6. Do you interrupt the speaker? Some people do not wait until the speaker has completely expressed his or her views.

_____ 7. Do you fail to take notes at a meeting? Some people do not bother to take notes when necessary; consequently, they often forget important details.

Internet Exercise

As noted in this chapter, we spend more time listening than we spend speaking, reading, or writing. However, most of us are not good listeners. To learn more about listening and how to improve your listening skills, visit the Internet and determine what types of resources (such as books, articles, and training programs) are available. Using your search engine, type in "active listening" and "empathic listening," and then examine the information available on these topics. Will this information be useful as you attempt to improve your listening skills? Explain.

Self-Assessment Exercise

The purpose of this application exercise is to help you assess those attitudes and skills that contribute to effective human relations. A similar exercise will appear at the end of each subsequent chapter. Your honest response to each item will help you determine your areas of strength and those areas that need improvement. Completion of this self-assessment will provide you with information needed to develop goals for self-improvement.

Circle the number from 1 to 5 that best represents your response to each statement: (1) strongly disagree (never do this); (2) disagree (rarely do this); (3) moderately agree (sometimes do this); (4) agree (frequently do this); (5) strongly agree (always do this).

a. I am an effective communicator who sends clear, concise verbal messages.   1 2 3 4 5

b. When people talk, I listen attentively and frequently use active listening skills.   1 2 3 4 5

c. I am conscious of how I express nonverbal messages (facial expression, tone of voice, body language, and so on) when communicating with others.   1 2 3 4 5

d. I engage in appropriate self-disclosure in order to achieve improved communication and increased self-awareness and to build stronger relationships.   1 2 3 4 5

e. I am able to share information about myself in appropriate ways, avoiding the extremes of complete concealment and complete openness.   1 2 3 4 5

After recording your response to each item, select an appropriate attitude or skill you would like to improve. Write your goal in the space provided. (The instructions for setting and achieving goals are presented in Chapter 3.)

GOAL: _____

_____

_____

Case Problem   ## Mercedes Learns to Speak 'Bama

The German Chamber of Commerce and Industry conducted a survey of 10,000 businesspeople and discovered that 30 percent of them are considering moving their production outside Germany. The reason: German workers earn wages and benefits that, on the average, are worth $25 an hour (the highest in the world), yet in terms of output per hour they are only two-thirds as productive as their American counterparts. In light of this crushing cost of doing business in Germany, DaimlerChrysler AG, the former Mercedes-Benz AG in Stuttgart, formed a new globalization strategy that included building its new $300 million auto plant nearer to its customers. Mercedes was the top-selling import car in Japan, but the company did not choose that country for its new factory. It could have gone to Mexico and hired low-wage workers, but the company did not make that choice either. Instead, Mercedes chose Vance, Alabama (population 400), for the factory that builds its new sport-utility vehicles.

Not only did the Mercedes management team have to design a new car and a new factory, but they also had to prepare for the cultural upheaval of moving approximately forty German engineers, managers, and their families to Alabama. They conducted seminars at a retreat in the Black Forest to help their employees adjust to the strange habits of their new home and flew some native Alabamians to Stuttgart to help with these "cross-cultural encounter groups."

But Roland Folger, who moved from Germany to Alabama, explained, "We don't want a German enclave in Alabama. We want a real cultural mixing." The Alabamians have learned that Germans are very blunt, perfectionistic, formal, and sometimes humorless, but they love good wine. The German employees have learned that Americans call strangers by their first names, that they leave their office doors open, and that they rarely use public transportation. They have also learned the meaning of such strange expressions as "y'all" and "Howdy."

Despite all the cultural differences, the Vance factory has proven to be a success. Mercedes-Benz has clearly gained valuable experience in how to set up and operate a plant in a distant land and has recently established another new plant in São Paulo, Brazil. The company may well transfer an employee born in Alabama to its plant in Brazil!

Questions

1. Both the Americans and the Germans seem committed to making this multicultural factory operate effectively. What types of training exercises or activities would you use to help these two cultures understand each other better?

2. How might each of the communications filters identified in this chapter affect the messages sent between German-born and American-born workers?

3. What additional communications problems might have been encountered if Mercedes had chosen to build its plant in Japan instead of Alabama? What types of problems might they encounter with an Alabamian working in a German plant in Brazil? Are there any advantages to this situation?

Chapter 3

Building

High

Self-Esteem

Chapter Preview

After studying this chapter, you will be able to

1. Define self-esteem and discuss how it is developed.
2. Explain how self-esteem influences human relations and success at work.
3. Identify the characteristics of people with low and high self-esteem.
4. Explain the roles mentors can play in your professional life.
5. Identify ways to raise your self-esteem.
6. Understand the conditions organizations can create that will help workers raise their self-esteem.

C RYSTAL BURCH, A TEENAGER from a small town in Oregon, learned her early lessons about hard work from her grandmother, who raised four children on a paycheck from Dairy Queen after her husband lost a leg in a construction accident. Crystal's mother, one of 14 children, worked her way up to become supervisor at a packaging plant. Her father picked farm crops and moved irrigation pipe as a child, then rose through the blue-collar ranks to become production manager for a computer-furniture maker. These role models provided a powerful influence on Crystal's ever-changing adolescent view of her place in the world, but her annual visits to Nike Inc.'s Beaverton, Oregon, offices with her grandmother, Lauraine Burch, exposed her to people who wore suits and dresses to work, attended meetings, and solved marketing problems. Crystal noticed that people at Nike didn't have to lift 50-pound loads and were not in constant danger of physical injury. She thought, "I don't have to work like my mom. . . . I'd like to work my way up to be a manager, and maybe run my own business one day."[1]

But her image of her future became dim after entering a large middle school. She was bewildered by the crowds and was scorned by her fellow classmates when she eagerly asked questions in class. Soon she started missing homework deadlines, and her grades plummeted.

Once again a role model, this time Olympic athlete Jackie Joyner-Kersee, helped guide Crystal through her feelings of self-doubt. Grandmother Lauraine had worked with Ms. Joyner-Kersee on a Nike promotion and shared the materials with Crystal. The track star's humble childhood was very similar to Crystal's. She credited her solid hometown roots, close family ties, and the guidance of her role models for helping her achieve many of her goals. Her personal story of overcoming defeat at her first Olympic Games inspired Crystal to think differently.

Joyner-Kersee explained that she was physically ready to compete but lacked the proper mental conditioning: She did not *expect* to win. At the beginning of each event, she fed herself negative thoughts that drained her energy. Through proper mental training, however, Joyner-Kersee took control of her thoughts about her potential success, fed her mind positive self-talk, and came home with two gold medals from the Seoul Olympic Games.[2]

Crystal is once again back on track, and her grade-point average has skyrocketed. Many people, however, go through life never learning these lessons and are guided by negative role models and destructive self-talk that produce dramatically different results. The key seems to be how you feel about yourself and your future. ■

THE POWER OF SELF-ESTEEM

Nathaniel Branden, author of *The Six Pillars of Self-Esteem,* has spent the past three decades studying the psychology of self-esteem. In countless speeches, articles, and books, he has attempted to describe the connection between self-esteem and many of the human problems common to our society today. He notes that high self-esteem enhances our ability to build effective relationships with others:

> The healthier our self-esteem, the more inclined we are to treat others with respect, benevolence, goodwill, and fairness—since we do not tend to perceive them as a threat, and since self-respect is the foundation of respect for others.[3]

The belief that low self-esteem can cause serious problems throughout life prompted the California state assembly to establish the twenty-five-member Task Force to Promote Self-Esteem and Personal and Social Responsibility. This action followed testimony that people with low self-esteem are more likely to exhibit violent behavior, discriminate against others, and abuse drugs. The task force's final report defines **self-esteem** as appreciating your own worth and importance, having the character to be accountable for your own behaviors, and acting responsibly toward others.[4]

The importance of self-esteem as a guiding force in our lives cannot be overstated. Alfred Adler, a noted psychiatrist and author, observed, "Everything begins with self-esteem, your concept of yourself."[5]

Self-Esteem = Self-Efficacy + Self-Respect

Nathaniel Branden states that self-esteem has two interrelated components: self-efficacy and self-respect. **Self-efficacy** is the belief that you can achieve what you set out to do.[6] When your self-efficacy is high, you believe you have the ability to act appropriately. When your self-efficacy is low, you worry that you might not be able to do the task, that it is beyond your abilities. Your perception of your self-efficacy can influence which tasks you take on and which ones you avoid. Albert Bandura, a professor at Stanford University and one of the foremost self-efficacy researchers, views this component of self-esteem as a resilient belief in your own abilities. According to Bandura, a major source of self-efficacy is the experience of mastery, in which success in one area builds your confidence to succeed in other areas.[7] For example, an administrative assistant who masters a sophisticated computerized accounting system is more likely to master future complicated computer programs than is a person who feels computer illiterate and may not even try to figure out the new program, regardless of how well he or she *could* do it.

Self-respect, the second component of self-esteem, is what you think and feel about yourself. Self-respect is the deep-down-inside feeling of your own worth. The conviction of your own value is a primary factor in achieving career success. People who respect themselves tend to act in ways that confirm and reinforce this respect. People who lack self-respect may put up with verbal or physical abuse from others because they feel they are unworthy of praise and deserve the abuse.[8] One key to achieving a sense of self-worth is to set realistic standards. People with low self-esteem are often persons who set unrealistically high standards for themselves and then struggle to achieve them. The result is often a persistent need to prove themselves and an inability to enjoy what they have already accomplished.[9] When you respect yourself, you are less likely to feel a constant need to prove yourself to others. You are proud of your accomplishments and goals and are not dependent on the constant approval of others. One of the great tragedies in life is that people look for respect in every direction except within.

Self-esteem includes your feelings about your adequacy in the roles you play in life, such as that of friend, brother or sister, daughter or son, employee or employer, student or teacher, researcher, leader, and so on. Self-esteem also includes the personality traits you believe you have, such as honesty, creativity, assertiveness, flexibility, and many more. Often your self-esteem derives from your physical characteristics and your skills and abilities. Are you tall, slender, short, or heavy? Do you like what you see in the mirror? Are you good at writing, fixing appliances, researching topics, playing the piano, or engaging in some other skill?

Although high self-esteem is the basis for a healthy personality, it does not mean becoming egotistical—that is, thinking and acting with only your own interests in mind. Genuine self-esteem is not expressed by self-glorification at the expense of others or by the attempt to diminish others so as to elevate yourself. Arrogance, boastfulness, and the overestimation of your abilities reflect inadequate self-esteem rather than, as it might appear, too much self-esteem. Someone with an egotistical orientation to the world sees everything and everyone in terms of their usefulness to her or his own aims and goals. This attitude undermines good human relations.

How Self-Esteem Develops

A Sunday school teacher once asked her class of small children, "Who made you?" Instead of giving the expected reply, an insightful child responded, "I'm not finished yet!" You are not born knowing who and what you are. You acquire your image of yourself over time by realizing your natural abilities and by constantly receiving messages about yourself from the people closest to you and from your environment.

Childhood   Researchers have discovered that a child's potential is determined in the early years. The neurons of the brain—those long wiry cells that carry electrical messages through the nervous system and the brain—literally make their connections during the birth-to-preschool period. If these connections are not made, the child suffers later in life in a variety of ways. For example, emotional stability, which directly affects how individuals feel about themselves, is greatly affected by how the brain develops in the first two years of life.[10]

The childhood experiences of television newsman John Stossel might have had a negative effect on his self-esteem and career had he not taken the necessary action to overcome his stuttering problem. Those suffering from similar experiences might be inspired by this role model's solution to his problem. (Courtesy of the Stuttering Foundation of America)

Beginning at about two months, the distress and contentment that newborns experience start to evolve into more complex feelings such as sadness and joy, envy and empathy, shame and pride. Sadly, children who do not play much or are rarely touched develop brains 20 to 30 percent smaller than normal for their age because of the lack of stimulation.[11] This underscores the importance of effective parenting—that is, finding time to cuddle a baby, talk with a toddler, and provide small children with stimulating experiences. Your potential adult vocabulary is determined by the words filtered through your brain before you were 3, and the foundations for math and logic were set before you were 4.[12] This early, powerful development, or lack thereof,

Total Person Insight

"Is it possible to have too much self-esteem? No, it is not; no more than it is possible to have too much physical health. Sometimes self-esteem is confused with boasting or bragging or arrogance. Such traits reflect, not too much self-esteem, but too little; they reflect a lack of self-esteem."

NATHANIEL BRANDEN

Author, *The Six Pillars of Self-Esteem*

serves as the basis for your success or failure at various endeavors throughout your life.

You may remember that when you started school your childhood friends, siblings, teachers, and various authority figures began sending you messages such as these:

- Bad boy! Bad girl!
- You're so lazy!
- You'll never learn.
- What's wrong with you?
- Why can't you be more like . . . ?
- It's all your fault.

- You're great!
- You can do anything!
- You're a fast learner.
- Next time you'll do better.
- I like you just the way you are.
- I know you did your best.

In most cases, you probably did not stop and analyze these messages; you simply accepted them as true and recorded them in your memory. As a result, you gradually developed a picture of yourself, whether accurate or distorted, that you came to believe as real. The authors of *Staying OK* describe this subconscious level of activity:

> Everyone was once a child. Our experience today is filtered through the events and feelings of childhood, recorded in detail. We cannot have a feeling today that is "disconnected" from similar feelings recorded in the past, the most intense of which occurred to us in the first five years of life. This does not mean that today's feelings are not real, or that we are to discount them by claiming "they're just an old recording." We are today who we once were.[13]

Adolescence   The years from age 12 to age 18 are among the most crucial in developing and consolidating your feelings about yourself. During these years, you are moving away from the close bond between parent and child and are attempting to establish ideals of independence and achievement.[14] You fluctuate between determination to reach your goals and self-doubt about whether or not you are capable. You must also deal with physical changes, relationships with your peers, the loss of a carefree childhood, and the assumption of some adult responsibilities.

Society today, however, unlike previous generations when teens had to help out on the farm or in family business or care for siblings, does not "need" adolescents, and this lack of importance and direction can lead to feelings of insecurity and uncertainty. Teens often feel vulnerable as the media and real life expose them to more violence in the form of drive-by shootings, date rape, sexual harassment, and drug-induced behaviors than ever before. To compensate, they frequently adopt an attitude of not caring.[15] When you do not care about anything or anyone, you do not care about yourself, and the result is low self-esteem. Without some help, this insecurity and lack of direction can last far into adulthood.

A critical factor in self-esteem for large numbers of adolescents is physical appearance. Magazines such as *Glamour, Cosmopolitan,* and *GQ* portray the

© 1992 Lynn Johnson Productions Inc./Distributed by United Feature Syndicate, Inc.

thin body as the height of fashion. The common use of fad diets by young men and women, and eating disorders, can be traced to society's pressure to be thin.[16] It is easy to feel deficient or diminished in comparison to the images projected in movies, on television, or in our favorite magazines. It is also easy to form a negative self-image when making these comparisons.

Mary Pipher, author of the best-selling book *Reviving Ophelia,* says that girls, especially, face difficult challenges during adolescence. This is a time when everything is changing: body shape, hormones, skin, and hair.[17] Recent surveys have discovered that

- 40 to 50 percent of all females have negative body images.[18]
- 60 percent of elementary school girls report being "happy the way I am." But by the time they reach high school, only 29 percent say they are happy with themselves.
- Eighth- and tenth-grade girls were twice as likely as boys to report feeling sad and hopeless.
- 40 percent of the girls in Lancaster County, Nebraska (America's heartland), had considered suicide.[19]

Many people never move beyond the image they had of themselves while in high school. Adolescent problems should not be underestimated, for it is in the resolution of these problems that the self-esteem of the adult is born.

Adulthood When you reach adulthood, your mind has a time-reinforced picture of who you are, molded by people and events from all your past experiences. You have been bombarded over the years with positive and negative messages from your family, friends, teachers, strangers, and the media.

You may compare yourself to others, as was so common in adolescence, or you may focus on your own inner sense of self-worth. Emmett Miller, a noted authority on self-esteem, says that as adults we tend to define ourselves in terms of[20]

1. *The things we possess.* Miller says this is the most primitive source of self-worth. If we define ourselves in terms of what we have, the result may be an effort to accumulate more and more material things to achieve a greater feeling of self-worth. People who define themselves in terms of what they have may have difficulty deciding "what is enough" and may spend their life in search of more material possessions.

2. *What we do for a living.* Miller points out that too often our self-worth and identity depend on something as arbitrary as a job title. Amy Saltzman, author of *Down-Shifting,* a book on ways to reinvent (or redefine) success, says, "We have allowed our professional identities to define us and control us."[21] She points out that we have looked to outside forces such as the corporation, the university, the media, counselors, or our parents to provide us with a script for leading a satisfying, worthwhile life. People pushed into a rigid career track that offers ample financial rewards but no fulfillment of personal needs may dread going to work in the morning even though others admire the job they hold.

3. *Our internal value system and emotional makeup.* Miller says this is the healthiest way for people to identify themselves:

> If you don't give yourself credit for excellence in other areas of life, besides your job and material possessions, you've got nothing to keep your identity afloat in emotionally troubled waters. People who are in touch with their real identity weather the storm better because they have a more varied and richer sense of themselves, owing to the importance they attach to their personal lives and activities.[22]

As an adult, you will be constantly adjusting the level of your self-esteem as you get in touch with your identity. Wally Amos is a prime example of a person who literally lost his identity. He started the gourmet-cookie craze with his Famous Amos Chocolate Chip Cookies, built an extremely successful company, then mismanaged it and lost everything, including two wives and the affections of his children. A court injunction denied him the use of his name and likeness in connection with any food-related venture. He was left without his family, his money, his company, or his name. In typical Wally fashion, however, he realized that there was only *one* name he could not use, and millions more names to choose from, and so the Uncle Noname Cookie Company was born.[23]

Learn to protect your self-esteem against those who try to diminish or limit your potential—by believing in yourself and going around, under, or through obstacles that get in your way. Listen to those who encourage and challenge you. This awareness of how other people are influencing you will help you dis-

> ## *Total Person Insight*
>
> *"If you keep on thinking what you've always thought, you'll keep on getting what you've always got."*
>
> WALLY AMOS
>
> Founder, Uncle Noname Cookie Company

tinguish between what is helpful and what is destructive, what is true and what is false. It will help you expand the range of what you believe you can be and do in the future.

> ## *Thinking / Learning Starters*
>
> 1. Can you recall two or three people from your childhood or adolescence who had a positive effect on your self-esteem? What did these people say or do? Were there any who had a negative effect on you? What did they say or do?
>
> 2. Identify at least two people who exhibit the characteristics of people with high self-esteem. What behaviors helped you identify them?

SELF-ESTEEM INFLUENCES YOUR BEHAVIOR

Your self-esteem has a powerful impact on your behavior at work and in your personal life. In general, people with low self-esteem tend to have more trouble with interpersonal relationships and to be less productive than people with high self-esteem.[24]

Characteristics of People with Low Self-Esteem

1. *They tend to maintain an* **external locus of control.** This means that they believe their behavior is controlled by someone or something in their environment. When you hear a person say, "It's not my fault. He made me do it," you can be assured that the speaker probably has low self-esteem. Rather than taking responsibility for their own choices, such people blame other people or events for controlling them. Even when they succeed, they tend to attribute their success to luck rather than to their own expertise and hard work. This often results in reliance on the approval of others. This seeking of others' approval often pressures us into behaving contrary to our deepest convictions. When we rely too heavily on validation from external sources, we can lose control over our lives.[25]

2. *They tend to participate in self-destructive behaviors.* If you do not like yourself, there is no apparent reason to take care of yourself. Therefore, people with low self-esteem tend to drink too much, smoke too much, and eat too much. Some may develop an eating disorder such as bulimia or anorexia, often with devastating results.

3. *They exhibit poor human relations skills.* Individuals with low self-esteem are more likely to feel hostile, show a lack of respect for others, and attempt to retaliate against others to save face in difficult situations. They tend to blame others for everything that goes wrong. In contrast, people with healthy self-esteem operate from a position of empathy, compassion, and cooperation.[26]

4. *They are poor team members.* Workers with low self-esteem can reduce the efficiency and productivity of a group: They tend to exercise less initiative, hesitate to accept responsibility or make independent decisions, and refuse to ask for help, fearing that others might think them incompetent. Rather than admit an error and handle the consequences, they often lie in an attempt to cover their mistakes.

5. *They may experience the failure syndrome.* As noted previously in this chapter, you form a mental picture of yourself at a very early age. Your subconscious mind was, and continues to be, "programmed" by other people's negative and positive comments. If your subconscious mind has been saturated with thoughts of past failures, these thoughts will continue to undermine your efforts to achieve your goals. If you see yourself as a failure, you will usually find some way to fail. William Glasser, author of *Reality Therapy* and other books on human behavior, calls this the **failure syndrome.** Individuals with a failure syndrome think, "I always fail. . . . Why try?" They have a fear of taking action because they expect to fail . . . again.

Characteristics of People with High Self-Esteem

1. *People with high self-esteem are future oriented and not overly concerned with past mistakes or failures.* They learn from their errors but are not immobilized by them. They believe every experience has something to teach—if they are willing to learn. A mistake can show you what does not work, what not to do. One consultant, when asked whether he had obtained any results in trying to solve a difficult problem, replied, "Results? Why, I've had lots of results. I know a hundred things that won't work!" The same principle applies to your own progress. Falling down does not mean failure. Staying down does.

2. *People with high self-esteem are able to cope with life's problems and disappointments.* Successful people have come to realize that problems need not depress them or make them anxious. It is their attitude toward problems that makes all the difference. In his book *They All Laughed: From Lightbulbs to Lasers,* Ira Flatow examines the lives of successful, innovative people who had to overcome major obstacles to achieve their goals. He discovered that the common thread among these creative people was their ability to overcome disappointing events and press on toward their goals.

3. *People with high self-esteem are able to feel all dimensions of emotion without letting those emotions affect their behavior in a negative way.* This characteristic is one of the major reasons people with high self-esteem are able to establish and maintain effective human relations with the people around them. They realize emotions cannot be handled either by repressing them or by giving them free rein. Although they may not be able to stop feeling the emotions of anger, envy, and jealousy, they can take control of their actions when they are under the influence of these strong emotions by saying to themselves, "I may not be able to control the way I feel right now, but I can control the way I behave."

4. *People with high self-esteem are effective team members.* They are not threatened by helping others to succeed, nor are they afraid to admit weaknesses. Individuals with secure self-esteem realize that in helping other team members succeed, they benefit themselves as well.

5. *People with high self-esteem are able to accept other people as unique, talented individuals.* They learn to accept others for who they are and what they can do. Our multicultural work force makes this attitude especially important. Individuals who cannot tolerate other people who are "different" may find themselves out of a job. People with high self-esteem build mutual trust based on each individual's uniqueness. These trusting relationships do not limit or confine either person because of group attributes such as skin color, religion, gender, lifestyle, or sexual orientation. Accepting others is a good indication that you accept yourself.

6. *People with high self-esteem exhibit a variety of self-confident behaviors.* They accept compliments or gifts by saying, "Thank you," without making self-critical excuses and without feeling obligated to return the favor. They can laugh at their situation without self-ridicule. They let others be right or wrong without attempting to correct or ridicule them. They feel free to express opinions even if they differ from those of their peers or parents. They enjoy being by themselves without feeling lonely or isolated. They are able to talk about themselves to others without excessive bragging. But perhaps most important, they are able to maintain an **internal locus of control**—that is, they make decisions for their own reasons based on their standards of what is right and wrong, and they are not likely to comply with the inappropriate demands of others. This internal control helps raise self-esteem every time it is applied.

HOW TO BUILD SELF-ESTEEM

"The level of our self-esteem is not set once and for all in childhood," says Nathaniel Branden. It can grow throughout our lives or it can deteriorate.[27] Examining your present self-image is the first step in understanding who you are, what you can do, and where you are going.

The person you will be tomorrow has yet to be created. However, most people continue to shape that future person in the image of the past, repeating the old limitations and negative patterns without realizing what they are doing. The development of a new level of self-esteem will not happen overnight, but it can happen. Such a change is the result of a slow evolution that begins with the desire to overcome low self-esteem.

Identify and Accept Your Limitations

The first step toward higher self-esteem is to accept yourself as you are now. Without acceptance, improving your self-esteem is not possible. Accept your limitations, and become realistic about who you are and what you can and cannot do. Demanding perfection of yourself is unrealistic—no one is perfect. The past cannot be changed, so stop dwelling on it. Your future, however, can be effectively shaped by how you think and act from this day forward.

> Accepting ourselves begins with an honest look at who we are. We don't need to like everything we find. We can just say, for example, "Oh, yes, I can recognize that I sometimes feel impatient. This is a human feeling, and I don't need to deny it or dislike myself for feeling it."[28]

Acting as an observer and detaching yourself from negative thoughts and actions can help you break the habit of rating yourself according to some scale of

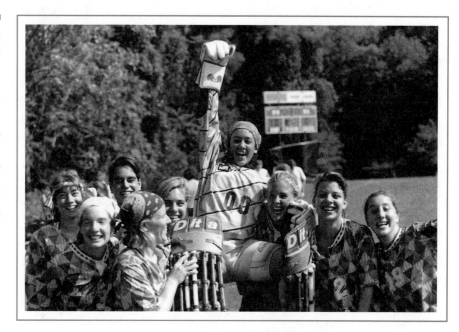

Athletes and successful individuals from all walks of life understand the power of visualizing the successful completion of a difficult task. If you can see your goal, and sincerely believe you are capable, you can achieve it. (Michael McGovern/The Picture Cube, Inc.)

perfection and can enable you to substitute more positive and helpful thoughts. A good first step is learning to hate a behavior you may indulge in, rather than condemning yourself. Hating yourself tends to make the behavior worse. If you condemn yourself for being weak, for example, how can you muster the strength to change? But if you become an "observer" and view the activity as separate from yourself, you leave your self-esteem intact, while you work on changing the behavior.

Take Responsibility for Your Decisions

Psychologists have found that children who were encouraged to make their own decisions early in their lives have higher self-esteem than those who were kept dependent on their parents for a longer period of time. Making decisions helps you develop confidence in your own judgment and enables you to explore options. Take every opportunity you can to make decisions both in setting your goals and in devising ways to achieve them. As you make your decisions, be willing to accept the consequences of your actions, positive or negative.

When Jim Burke became head of a new products division at Johnson & Johnson, one of his first projects was the development of a children's chest rub. The product

Total Person Insight

"To feel competent to live and worthy of happiness, I need to experience a sense of control over my existence. This requires that I be willing to take responsibility for my actions and the attainment of my goals. This means that I take responsibility for my life and well-being."

NATHANIEL BRANDEN

Author, *The Six Pillars of Self-Esteem*

failed miserably, and Burke expected that he would be fired. When he was called in to see the Chairman of the Board, however, he met a surprising reception. "Are you the one who just cost us all that money?" asked Robert Wood Johnson. "Well, I just want to congratulate you. If you are making mistakes, that means you are taking risks, and we won't grow unless you take risks." Some years later, Burke became the chairman of J&J.[29]

The attitude that you must be right all the time is a barrier to personal growth. With this attitude you will avoid doing things that might result in mistakes. Much unhappiness comes from the widespread and regrettable belief that it is important to avoid making mistakes at all costs.[30] Taking risks that reach beyond what you already know how to do can often be fun and extremely rewarding.

Accepting full responsibility for your decisions and actions is an important key to building self-esteem. Most of the factors that generate self-esteem are under your control. Choose to participate in self-improvement activities that will enhance your career and your personal life. Choose to build harmonious relationships with your coworkers, supervisors, customers, and family members. Choose the values by which you want to live your life. Making your own decisions and taking responsibility for the consequences can become a habit that will be a powerful force in your life.

Develop Expertise in Some Area

Developing "expert power" not only builds your self-esteem but also increases the value of your contribution to an organization. Identify and cultivate a skill or talent you have, whether it is a knack for interviewing people, a facility with math, or good verbal skills. Alice Young, a resident partner in the law firm of

Graham & James in New York, developed an expertise in her youth that she did not know would be a major asset in her career. "I speak Japanese, Chinese, French, and English," she says. "I have a knowledge of Asian cultures that I developed before trade with the East opened up." She has been able to capitalize on her expertise to help American and Asian companies do business with each other and to smooth over many cultural differences that would otherwise make negotiations difficult or impossible. She advises others to "use what you know to benefit yourself and your company."[31]

Developing expertise may involve continuing your studies after completing your formal education. Some institutions offer professional courses to enable people to advance in their careers. For example, the Institute of Financial Education conducts courses for persons employed by financial institutions, and the Certified Medical Representatives Institute offers a series of professional development courses for pharmaceutical representatives.

Seek the Support and Guidance of Mentors

Darryl Hartley-Leonard rose from being desk clerk at the Los Angeles Hyatt Hotel to become chief executive officer of the Hyatt Corporation. Ivan Seidenberg began his career at Nynex Corporation as a splicer's assistant earning $89.50 a week and went on to become the CEO. Both credit mentors for their rise from humble beginnings.[32]

Chip Bell, author of *Managers as Mentors: Building Partnerships for Learning,* defines a **mentor** as "someone who helps someone else learn something the learner would otherwise have learned less well, more slowly, or not at all." He also describes a mentor as a sensitive, trusted adviser.[33] Although mentoring is most often a one-on-one partnership, a mentor will sometimes guide a group of protégés through the process of developing their organizational savvy and their careers. In most organizations mentoring is carried out informally, but formal programs are common. Formal programs systematically match mentors and protégés.

Most people who have had a mentoring experience say it was an effective development tool. However, many surveys indicate that only a small percentage of employees say they have had a mentor. In today's fast-paced work environment, where most people have a heavy workload, you must be willing to take the initiative and build a mentor relationship. Here are some tips to keep in mind.

1. *Multiple mentors are recommended.* Some people feel the need for both internal and external mentors. Internal mentors, an experienced associate or supervisor, can provide guidance as you navigate the organizational bumps and potholes. An external mentor, someone who does not work for your company, can provide an objective, independent view of your skills and

talents.[34] Many people benefit from short-term "learning partners" who will coach them on specific skills. A busy person will be less threatened by a request for specific help with a marketing strategy or development of new computer skills.

2. *Search for a mentor who has the qualities of a good coach.* Mentors need to be accomplished in their own right, but success alone does not make someone a good mentor. Look for someone whom you would like to emulate, both in business savvy and in operating style. Be sure it is someone you trust enough to talk about touchy issues.[35] A good mentor is someone who will give you feedback in a straightforward manner.

3. *Market yourself to a prospective mentor.* The best mentor for you may be someone who is very busy. Sell the benefits of a mentoring partnership. For example, point out that you have something to give in return for assistance. You may offer a view from the front lines to a senior manager or some up-to-date technical expertise to an older coworker.[36] Describe specific steps you will take to avoid wasting the time of a busy person. You might suggest that meetings be held during lunch.

Although mentors are not mandatory for success, they certainly help. Indeed, there will always be days when you feel nothing you do is right. Your mentor can help repair damaged self-esteem and encourage you to go on. With the power of another person's positive expectations reinforcing your own native abilities, it is hard to fail.

Set Realistic Goals

Research points to a direct link between self-esteem and the achievement of personal and professional goals. People who consistently set goals are able to maintain high self-esteem. People who fail to set goals wander aimlessly through life with no purpose, and they are more likely to suffer from low self-esteem. The key is making your goals realistic. If they are too far out of sight, you might subconsciously say to yourself, "I can't really see myself doing that." If those are your thoughts, you will probably never succeed at accomplishing that goal. In most cases, you must be able to picture yourself accomplishing the goal.

Visualize Achievement of Your Goals

To **visualize** means to form a mental image of something. The power to visualize is in a very real sense the power to create. If you really want to succeed at something, picture yourself doing it successfully over and over again. Simulate every step in your brain before you ever attempt to make the goal a reality. Visualize yourself overcoming any obstacles that might interfere with your success.[37]

Shakti Gawain, author of *Creative Visualization,* states that when we create something, we always create it first in the form of a thought:

> Imagination is the ability to create an idea or mental picture in your mind. In creative visualization you use your imagination to create a clear image of something you wish to manifest. Then you continue to focus on the idea or picture regularly, giving it positive energy until it becomes objective reality . . . in other words, until you actually achieve what you have been visualizing.[38]

Many famous athletes choreograph their moves in their imagination before going into action. For example, champion skiers imagine themselves negotiating almost every inch of a slope, champion tennis players picture themselves executing successful shots, and gymnasts practice their moves as much in their imagination as in actual rehearsal.[39]

Mary Lou Retton, former Olympic gymnast, spent nine grueling years preparing herself physically and mentally for her performance on one event at the 1984 Olympics and won the gold medal by five one-hundredths of a point. She attributes much of her success to her ability to visualize her perfect performance. "Always prepare yourself for a perfect 10. When I visualized myself going through a beam routine, I didn't imagine myself falling. I visualized myself on the beam—perfect. Always picture it perfect. But also visualize what you can do if something does go wrong."[40]

Denis Waitley, former chair of psychology for the U.S. Olympic teams, believes it is possible to learn a new self-image through the same process—by vividly imagining yourself being the person you want to become.[41] This mental rehearsal can be a powerful step toward improving your self-image. Review the "Characteristics of People with High Self-Esteem" listed earlier in this chapter. If you would like to make them part of your behavior pattern, mentally rehearse these self-confident behaviors. See yourself walking with your chin up and your shoulders straight and speaking with a strong, confident voice. Picture yourself making appropriate eye contact with other people. As you gain confidence, practice these new skills by actually performing them when you are with your friends, family, and coworkers. You will begin to feel more comfortable with these behaviors every day, and soon they will become habits. If it works for the Olympic champions, it can work for you.

Monitor Your Self-Talk

To be sure you achieve the results you have visualized, you need to listen to your self-talk. **Self-talk** takes place silently in the privacy of your mind. It is the series of personal conversations you have with yourself almost continuously throughout the day. Just like statements from other people, your self-talk can dramatically affect your behavior and self-esteem.[42] Unfortunately, many people consistently tell themselves what they have done wrong or how incompetent they are. This negative self-talk often leads to a lack of self-confidence and unhappy relationships. Others talk to themselves with respect and encouragement that lead them toward successful behaviors even when faced with difficult situations. They focus on what they *can* do about the situation, rather than what they *cannot* do. Figure 3.1 indicates how self-talk is part of the cycle of self-esteem, whether that talk is negative or positive.

To constantly improve your self-esteem, you must monitor what you are saying to yourself. When negative thoughts attempt to take over, intentionally create self-talk statements that will replace the negative thoughts and counteract the damage those thoughts have had on your self-esteem in the past. Create self-talk statements for each of your goals by using the following guidelines:

1. Be *specific* about the behavior you want to change. What do you want to do to increase your effectiveness? You should firmly believe that what you want is truly possible.
2. Begin each self-talk statement with a first-person pronoun, such as *I* or *my*. Use a present-tense verb, such as *am, have, feel, create, approve, do,* or *choose*. Don't say "My ability to remember the names of other people *will* improve." Instead, focus on the present: "I *have* an excellent memory for the names of other people."

FIGURE 3.1

Self-Esteem Cycles

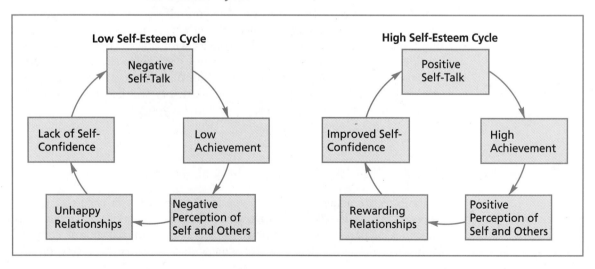

TABLE 3.1

Creating Semantically
Correct Self-Talk

Wrong	Right
I can quit smoking.	I am in control of my habits.
I will lose twenty pounds.	I weigh a trim _____ pounds.
I won't worry anymore.	I am confident and optimistic.
Next time I won't be late.	I am prompt and efficient.
I will avoid negative self-talk.	I talk to myself, with all due respect.
I will not procrastinate.	I do it now.
I'm not going to let people walk all over me anymore.	I care enough to assert myself when necessary.

3. Describe the results you want to achieve. Be sure to phrase the statement as though you have already achieved what you want. Table 3.1 offers several general self-talk statements that might help you improve your self-esteem.[43]

This last step is critical. Because your brain is merely a computer filled with various data from all your past experiences, you need to use literally the correct words. When you think of the words *spider, tornado,* or *blue,* your brain develops an automatic understanding of the word and a response or image based on years of conditioning and training. If you are attempting to quit smoking, don't mention the word *smoke* in your self-talk because your brain will react to the word. "I will not smoke after dinner" conjures an image in your subconscious mind, and your behavior follows accordingly. Say instead, "I am in control of my habits" or "My lungs are clean."

One warning: Every time your self-talk statements use the word *not* you are sending the wrong message to your brain. Consider the following statement: "I will not eat chocolate for dessert." Now remove the word *not* from the statement, and the remaining words represent the message being sent to your brain. Does the remaining statement represent your goal? Be careful to semantically design your self-talk statements so that they take you in the direction you want to go; otherwise, they will take you straight toward what you don't want.

Write positive self-talk statements for different facets of your personal and professional life. Put them on 3-by-5-inch index cards, and attach them to your bathroom mirror, refrigerator, car dashboard, desk blotter, and so on, and review them often. Barbara Grogan, a successful entrepreneur who founded Western Industrial Contractors, has a placard on the dashboard of her car that reads, "I am powerful, beautiful, creative, and I can handle it!"[44] This positive message helps her through the tough times.

Another technique for internalizing your thoughts is to record your affirming statements on a blank cassette tape while quiet, one-beat-per-second music (largo) is playing in the background.[45] Play the tape repeatedly, especially when you are in a relaxed state, such as just before you fall asleep at night. Your brain will accept the information without judgment. When these statements become part of your "memory bank," over time your behavior will follow accordingly. Your brain computer will put out exactly what you put in. If you put positive self-talk in, positive behavior will result.

ORGANIZATIONS CAN HELP

Even though each of us ultimately is responsible for raising or lowering our own self-esteem, we can make that task easier or more difficult for others. We can either support or damage the self-efficacy and self-respect of the people we work with, just as they have that option in their interactions with us. Organizations are beginning to include self-esteem modules in their employee- and management-training programs.

When employees do not feel good about themselves, the result will often be poor job performance. This view is shared by many human resource professionals and managers. Many organizations realize that low self-esteem affects their workers' ability to learn new skills, to be effective team members, and to be productive. Research has identified five factors that can enhance the self-esteem of employees in any organization[46] (see Figure 3.2).

- *Workers need to feel valuable.* A major source of worker satisfaction is the feeling that one is valued as a unique person. Self-esteem grows when an organization makes an effort to accommodate individual differences and to recognize individual accomplishments.
- *Workers need to feel competent.* Earlier in this chapter we noted that self-efficacy grows when people feel confident in their ability to perform job-related tasks. One of the best ways organizations can build employee confidence is to involve employees in well-designed training programs. Effective training programs give employees plenty of opportunities to practice newly acquired job skills.
- *Workers need to feel secure.* Employees are more likely to feel secure when they are well informed and know what is expected of them. Managers need to clarify their expectations and provide employees with frequent feedback regarding their performance.
- *Workers need to feel empowered.* Progressive organizations such as Corning Incorporated and Federal Express Corporation are demonstrating to employees that their opinions and views matter and that their ideas are being implemented in significant ways. These companies make sure that each person has a voice in helping the organization achieve its goals.

FIGURE 3.2

Factors That Enhance
the Self-Esteem of
Employees

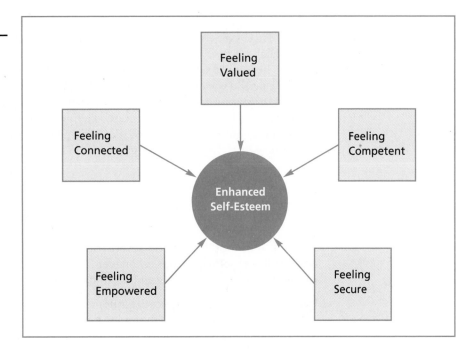

- *Workers need to feel connected.* People are likely to achieve high self-esteem when they feel their coworkers accept, appreciate, and respect them. Many companies are fostering these feelings by placing greater emphasis on teamwork. Team-building efforts help promote acceptance and cooperation.

Summary

Self-esteem is a combination of self-respect and self-efficacy. If you have high self-esteem, you are more likely to feel competent and worthy. If you have low self-esteem, you are more likely to feel incompetent, unworthy, and insecure. Self-esteem reflects your feelings of adequacy about the roles you play, your personality traits, your physical appearance, your skills, and your abilities. High self-esteem is the foundation for a successful personal life and professional life.

A person starts acquiring and building self-esteem from birth. Parents, friends, associates, the media, and professional colleagues all influence the development of that person's self-esteem. As an adult, a person often defines herself or himself in terms of possessions, jobs, and/or internal values. People with high self-esteem tend to be future oriented, cope with problems creatively, handle their emotions well, and exhibit self-confident behaviors. They are effective team members because they willingly help others and appreciate the help others give them. They accept people as talented, unique individuals regardless of their race, gender, age, and so on.

To build high self-esteem, individuals must accept the past and build for the future. They need to accept their limitations and develop expertise in some area. Making decisions and living with the consequences, positive or negative, can also help build self-esteem. Individuals need to set realistic goals by visualizing the person they want to be and monitoring their self-talk.

Many organizations now realize that they need to help build employees' self-esteem and are doing so through offering training sessions, making clear statements about expectations and feedback, giving greater respect to individuals in the workplace, and fostering teamwork.

Career Corner

Q. As a teenager, I was involved in a major car accident in which several bones in my face were broken. I was left with a large scar on my chin. Although I have had several operations to correct the visible damage, I still feel self-conscious whenever I meet new people. It is affecting my career opportunities. What can I do to gain more confidence?

A. In his book *Psycho-Cybernetics,* plastic surgeon Maxwell Maltz demonstrates that what your mind has been conditioned to believe about yourself can override or undermine what you actually see in the mirror. Throughout his twenty-five-year practice, Maltz operated on wounded soldiers, accident victims, and children with birth defects. Many of these individuals saw only their defects and doubted that they could ever be successful. Even after their corrective surgery, these patients' deformities continued to exist in their minds. Their inner self-images had not been changed.

You can learn to use the creative power of your subconscious mind. Even though your external image has been improved, you still need to change the inner self-image you carry within your mind. When you are successful in changing your mental image of yourself, your self-confidence will increase.

Key Terms

self-esteem

self-efficacy

self-respect

external locus of control

failure syndrome

internal locus of control

mentor

visualize

self-talk

Review Questions

1. What is self-esteem? Why is the development of high self-esteem important in a person's life?
2. What influences help shape a person's self-esteem?
3. What characteristics do people with high self-esteem exhibit?
4. Describe the behaviors of people with low self-esteem.
5. List the steps you can take to build high self-esteem. Which two do you feel are the most important? Why?
6. Define *internal* and *external locus of control,* and give an example of each.
7. What influence does self-talk have on a person's self-esteem? How can this influence be controlled?
8. In your own words, explain the two cycles portrayed in Figure 3.1.
9. List the three elements necessary for the construction of positive self-talk statements. Give three examples of such statements.
10. How can organizations help raise the self-esteem of workers?

Application Exercises

1. Describe a situation in which you achieved a goal you had set for yourself. Did any outside positive or negative forces influence your progress toward the goal? If there were negative forces, how did you overcome them? Did you visualize or mentally simulate the completed goal? If so, how did this simulation help?
2. Think about people you know at school, at work, or in your social environment who seem to exhibit low self-esteem. Describe the qualities that give you this impression. Now think about people you know who exhibit high self-esteem. List their qualities. Often these two lists will reflect direct opposites, such as "has a sloppy appearance/keeps a neat appearance," "slumps down the hall/walks tall," or "avoids eye contact during conversations with others/makes eye contact." What steps might the people you identified as having low self-esteem take to enhance their images? How might these steps improve their self-esteem? Could you take any similar steps to improve your own self-esteem? Explain.
3. Identify a quality that you would like to experience more frequently in your life. Examples might be the ability to develop rapport quickly with new acquaintances, the patience to enjoy leisure time, or the perseverance to maintain a daily exercise program. Once you select a specific quality, create in your mind a very detailed mental picture of this behavior. Now develop positive self-talk statements that will guide you toward the desired change in behavior. Use the guidelines on pages 74 and 75 to ensure that you achieve your goal.

Internet Exercise

 As noted in this chapter, self-esteem has two interrelated components: self-respect and self-efficacy. Self-efficacy can be thought of as the confidence you have in your ability to do specific things. Your confidence level can influence which tasks you take on and which ones you avoid. To learn more about self-efficacy and how it can influence your career, visit the Internet and determine what types of resources (such as books, articles, and training programs) are available on this topic. Using your search engine, type in "self-efficacy" and "self-esteem," and then study the available information. Pay special attention to information on how one achieves high self-efficacy. Prepare a written report of your findings.

Self-Assessment Exercise

For each statement, circle the number from 1 to 5 that best represents your response: (1) strongly disagree (never do this); (2) disagree (rarely do this); (3) moderately agree (sometimes do this); (4) agree (frequently do this); (5) strongly agree (almost always do this).

a. I constantly monitor my self-talk in order to maintain high self-esteem.   1   2   3   4   5

b. I tend to be future oriented and not overly concerned with past mistakes or failures.   1   2   3   4   5

c. I have developed and maintained high expectations for myself.   1   2   3   4   5

d. I accept myself as a changing, growing person capable of improvement.   1   2   3   4   5

e. My goals are clearly defined, attainable, and supported by positive self-talk.   1   2   3   4   5

Select an appropriate attitude or skill you would like to improve. Write your goal in the space provided.

GOAL: _____

_____

_____

Case Problem

Altering Your Body Image

A growing number of people seem to be unhappy with how they look. Specifically, they are dissatisfied with the appearance of their body. *Psychology Today* uses the term "body image" to describe the perceptions people have of their physical appearance, attractiveness, and beauty. Body image is our mental representation of ourselves; it is what allows us to contemplate ourselves. The image we see in the mirror influences much of our behavior and self-esteem.

A negative body image can begin to take shape early in life. Teasing during childhood can have a crushing effect on body image. Memories of being teased haunt many people for years. Through adolescence the pressure to achieve an attractive body image is intense, especially among women. Body weight has a major influence on overall satisfaction with appearance. In many cases the ever-present media portray desirable women as thin.

Appearance is more important today than it was in the past, according to Mary Pipher, author of *Reviving Ophelia*. She notes that we have moved from communities of primary relationships in which people know each other to cities where secondary relationships are much more common:

> In a community of primary relationships, appearance is only one of many dimensions that define people. Everyone knows everyone else in different ways over time. In a city of strangers, appearance is the only dimension available for the rapid assessment of others. Thus it becomes incredibly important in defining value.[47]

Preoccupation with body image follows many people throughout adulthood. Large numbers of people wish to conform to the body-size ideals projected in the media. The motivation to be thinner helps support a $50-billion-a-year diet industry. People have learned to judge themselves, in many cases, by the standards of physical attractiveness that appear in fashion magazines and television commercials.

Some people have found ways to remake their self-image and move away from a preoccupation with body image. One approach is to develop criteria for self-esteem that go beyond appearance. To make appearance less significant in your life, you develop other benchmarks for self-evaluation. These might include succeeding at work, forming new friendships, or achieving a greater feeling of self-worth through volunteer work. Another approach is to engage in exercise that makes you feel good about yourself. Exercise for strength, fitness, and health, not just for weight loss. You can also identify and change habitual negative thoughts about your body. When you look in the mirror, try to say nice things about your body.

Questions

1. Professionals in the field of psychology say that people with low self-esteem rely too much on the views of others for a sense of self-worth. Is this a problem you currently face in your life? Explain.
2. Mary Pipher says that in large communities appearance is the only dimension available for rapid assessment of others. Do you find yourself placing a heavy emphasis on appearance when assessing the worth of others?

3. Joan Borysenko, director of the Mind/Body Clinic at Harvard Medical School, says you need to accept yourself as you are. Acceptance, she says, means actually honoring yourself as you are now. Is this good advice? Is it realistic advice? Explain.

4. If you currently have a negative body image, what other criteria could you use to help enhance your self-esteem?

Chapter 4

Personal Values

Influence

Ethical Choices

Chapter Preview

After studying this chapter, you will be able to

1. Explain the advantage of developing a strong sense of character.
2. Understand how personal values are formed.
3. Understand value conflicts.
4. Identify ways to resolve value conflicts.
5. Learn how to make the right ethical decisions based on your personal value system.
6. Understand the danger of corporate crime and the steps being taken to eliminate it.

WHEN MICHAEL MILKEN MEETS with college students and members of the business community to talk about ethical issues, they pay attention. Most people know that in 1990 he pleaded guilty to six felony counts of securities law violations, paid more than $1 billion in fines and restitution, and served nearly two years in prison. He is still barred by the Securities and Exchange Commission from the investment brokerage industry. His employer, Drexel Burnham Lambert, one of the most powerful investment banks on Wall Street, pleaded guilty to a six-count felony indictment and was later forced into bankruptcy.[1] Dennis Levine, a leading merger specialist and partner at Drexel Burnham Lambert, also spent time in prison for illegal trading practices. In his book, *Inside Out,* we learn about the period of "easy morality" that existed on Wall Street. Reflecting on those fast-paced years at Drexel Burnham Lambert, Levine says, "The numbing effect of 60- to 100-hour work weeks helped erode my values and distort my judgment." He admits his ambition was so strong that it went beyond rationality and says, "I gradually lost sight of what constitutes ethical behavior."[2]

On leaving prison, Michael Milken was diagnosed with prostate cancer and immediately began a treatment program that yielded positive results. Today his cancer is in remission, and his image has been greatly enhanced. He started CaPCure, now the largest private provider of research funds for prostate cancer, and he gives large amounts of time and money to many education and medical causes. He is the featured speaker at many national conferences and serves as a consultant to prominent business leaders.[3] ∎

CHARACTER AND INTEGRITY

"The candidate has the kind of work experience we are looking for, but can he pass the 'character' test?" "I always know exactly where she stands . . . she has character." "When I'm in a conflict with someone, I know I can defeat them if they lack character. If they don't stand for something, they'll fall for anything." Statements like these sprinkle daily conversations in every organization because character is such an important element of effective interpersonal relations. **Character** is composed of your personal standards of behavior, including your honesty, integrity, and moral fiber.[4] Your character is based on the judgments you make about what behaviors are right and what behaviors are wrong.

One dimension of character that is getting a great deal of attention today is integrity. Integrity is a basic ingredient of career success. Robert Ringer, author of *Million Dollar Habits,* defined **integrity** as adherence to your moral values, or practicing what you claim to believe in.[5] When your behavior is in tune with your professed standards and values—when you practice what you believe in—you have integrity.

"I'm worried about Junior. He's put a picture of Michael Milken up on his wall."

In a world of uncertainty and rapid change, integrity has become a valuable character trait. People with integrity can be trusted to do what they say they will do. We know what they stand for and what they will fight for. On the other hand, it is difficult to trust people whose behavior contradicts their words. Stephen L. Carter, author of a book entitled *Integrity,* says that anyone who wants to act with integrity must first think hard about what is right and wrong.[6]

How can we achieve integrity? One approach, recommended by author Stephen Covey, is to keep your commitments. "As we make and keep commitments, even small commitments, we begin to establish an inner integrity that gives us the awareness of self-control and courage and strength to accept more of the responsibility for our own lives."[7] Covey says that when we make and keep promises to ourselves and others, we are developing an important habit. We cannot expect to maintain our integrity if we consistently fail to keep our commitments.

Your character and integrity strongly influence your relationships with others. But where can you learn these qualities? College catalogs rarely list a course like "Character Building 101." The Josephson Institute of Ethics acknowledged this lack of character training by forming the Character Counts Coalition. The coalition is an alliance of organizations such as the American Federation of Teachers, the American Association of State Boards of Education, and the American Association of Community Colleges. Their mission is to address the issue of character development through educational institutions and organizations throughout the country. Their efforts focus on a variety of grassroots training activities that encourage the development of the following six "pillars of character":

- **Trustworthiness** Be honest and sincere. Don't deceive or mislead and never betray a trust. Demonstrate your integrity by standing up for your beliefs. Never ask a friend or colleague to do something that is wrong.
- **Respect** Be courteous and polite by being appreciative and accepting of differences. Respect others' rights to make decisions about their own lives. Don't abuse, demean, mistreat, manipulate, exploit, or take advantage of others.
- **Responsibility** Be accountable for your actions. Think about the consequences of your behavior before you act. Don't make excuses or take credit for others' work.
- **Fairness** Treat all people fairly, be open-minded, and listen to opposing points of view. Don't take unfair advantage of others' mistakes.
- **Caring** Show you care about others through kindness, caring, sharing, compassion, and empathy. Be considerate and sensitive to others' feelings.
- **Citizenship** Play by the rules and obey the laws. Respect authority. Stay informed and vote.[8]

If you want to enhance your character, consider building these "pillars" into your lifestyle.

Total Person Insight

"People working together with integrity and authenticity and collective intelligence are profoundly more effective as a business than people living together based on politics, game playing, and narrow self-interest."

PETER SENGE
Author, *The Fifth Discipline*

HOW PERSONAL VALUES ARE FORMED

Hyrum Smith, founder of the Franklin Quest Company, says that certain natural laws govern personal productivity and fulfillment. One of these laws focuses on personal beliefs: Your behavior is a reflection of what you truly believe.[9] **Values** are your deep personal beliefs and preferences that influence your behavior. They are deep-seated in your personality and are more enduring than your attitudes. To discover what really motivates you, carefully examine what it is you value.

Table 4.1 details the values clarification process. These five steps can help you determine whether or not you truly value something. Many times you are not consciously aware of what is really driving your behavior because values exist at different levels of awareness.[10] Unless you clarify your values, life events are likely to unfold in a haphazard manner. Once you are aware of your value priorities and consistently behave accordingly, your character and integrity are enhanced, and life in general is much more satisfying and rewarding. Hyrum Smith says that everything starts with your **core values,** those general statements of principles and beliefs that guide the development of intermediate and long-range goals:

> If you set goals that aren't aligned with your values, you may accomplish a great deal, but you won't ever be satisfied, because you'll be neglecting the things that matter most to you.[11]

Our values may be influenced by our religious beliefs. Here students at Gujarat Vidyapith weave khadi, *a coarse fabric that has become a symbol of self-reliance for the people of India. Gandhi, religious leader and founder of the school, reasoned that if Indians could spin and wear their own cloth, they could get rid of their dependence on the British and their textile mills. (Steven McCurry/National Geographic Image Collection)*

TABLE 4.1

A Five-Part Valuing
Process to Clarify and
Develop Values

Thinking

We live in a confusing world where making choices about how to live our lives can be difficult. Of major importance is developing critical thinking skills that help distinguish fact from opinion and supported from unsupported arguments. Learn to think for yourself. Question what you are told. Engage in higher-level thinking that involves analysis, synthesis, and evaluation.

Feeling

This dimension of the valuing process involves being open to your "gut level" feelings. If it doesn't "feel right," it probably isn't. Examine your distressful feelings such as anger, fear, or emotional hurt. Discover what you prize and cherish in life.

Communicating

Values are clarified through an ongoing process of interaction with others. Be an active listener and hear what others are really saying. Be constantly alert to communication filters such as emotions, body language, and positive and negative attitudes. Learn to send clear messages regarding your own beliefs.

Choosing

Your values must be freely selected with no outside pressure. In some situations, telling right from wrong is difficult. Therefore, you need to be well informed about alternatives and the consequences of various courses of action. Each choice you make reflects some aspect of your values system.

Acting

Act repeatedly and consistently on your beliefs. One way to test whether or not something is of value to you is to ask yourself, "Do I find that this value is persistent throughout all aspects of my life?"

Source: Howard Kirschenbaum, *Advanced Values Clarification* (La Jolla, Calif.: University Associates, 1977).

Core values influence the actions of both individuals and organizations. Anne Mulcahy, an executive at Xerox Corporation and mother of two sons, says she and her husband make decisions at home and work based on their core values: "Our kids are absolutely the center of our lives—and we never mess with that."[12] Volvo, the Swedish automaker, has for years been guided by the core values of safety, quality, and environmental concern. Although some critics say the company makes solid, safe, but profoundly boring cars, its traditional core values will not be abandoned.[13]

As you engage in the values clarification process, it helps to reflect on those things that influence the development of your values. Let's look at some of the important factors that shape our values.

Environmental Influences

Aristotle said, "If you would understand virtue, observe the conduct of virtuous men." But where are these "virtuous men," the role models we should observe? As a nation, we have witnessed many examples of shabby values. When you look to Wall Street, you learn about the transgressions of Dennis Levine and Michael Milken. Turn to religion and you learn about the moral failures and financial excesses of leaders such as Jim Bakker and Jimmy Swaggart. Look at sports and you discover that some of our heroes are motivated by greed and lust. And our political leaders, from the oval office down, often seem to lack the moral courage to do the right thing.

Many events and individuals have influenced the formation of values in the United States in this century. Some of them are shown in Table 4.2. In general, the major environmental influences that shape our values are the family, religious groups, schools, the media, and people we admire.

Influence of the Family Katherine Paterson, author of books for children, says being a parent these days is like riding a bicycle on a bumpy road—learning to keep your balance while zooming full speed ahead, veering around as

TABLE 4.2

People and Events That Have Influenced the Formation of Values in the United States

Matures (born 1928–1945)	Baby Boomers (born 1946–1961)	Generation X (born 1962–1972)
Eisenhower	Television	AIDS
MacArthur	Beatniks	Wellness movement
A-bomb	Sputnik	Iran-Contra affair
Dr. Spock	Civil Rights Act	Operation Desert Storm
John Wayne	The pill	Oklahoma City bombing
Mickey Mantle	Drug culture	TV rating system
Doris Day	Women's movement	World Wide Web
Frank Sinatra	Vietnam War	Health-care reform
The Waltons	Watergate	Work/family balance concerns
Andy and Opie Taylor	JFK and MLK assassinations	Clinton impeachment hearings

many potholes as possible.[14] Parents must assume many roles, none more important than moral teacher. In many families in contemporary society, one parent must assume full responsibility for shaping children's values. Some single parents—those overwhelmed with responsibility for career, family, and rebuilding their own personal lives—may lack the stability necessary for the formation of the six pillars of character. And in two-parent families, both parents may work outside the home and at the end of the day may lack the time or energy to intentionally direct the development of their children's values. The same may be true for families experiencing financial pressures or the strains associated with caring for elderly parents. Author James Michener, who was an orphan and had no family, offered another perspective: "It is thoughtless beyond imagination for older people to say rigidly, 'The child must learn his or her values at home' when there is no home. Some substitution must be found."[15]

Influence of Religious Groups   Many people learn their value priorities through religious training. This may be achieved through the accepted teachings of a church, through religious literature such as the Koran and the Bible, or through individuals in churches or synagogues who are positive role models. William Wilson, founder of Pioneer/Eclipse Corporation of Sparta, North Carolina, when asked to comment on the impact of religious beliefs on his success, responded:

> I guess my religious beliefs did have one important impact on my approach to business—in terms of the ethics and principles I live by. I've always had the attitude that profits don't come first. They can never come first. People have to come first—customers and employees. The funny thing is, if you treat people right, the profits always follow.[16]

Religious groups that want to define, instill, and perpetuate values may find an eager audience. Stephen Covey and other social observers say that many people are determinedly seeking spiritual and moral anchors in their lives and in their work. People who live in uncertain times seem to attach more importance to spirituality.[17] Healthy spirituality is discussed in Chapter 9.

Influence of the Schools   Many parents, concerned that their children are not learning enough about moral values and ethical behavior, want character education added to the curriculum.[18] Some have been influenced by William J. Bennett's *The Book of Virtues*. Bennett sees moral education as a fundamental purpose of education. In support of this practice, Thomas Lickona, professor of education at the State University of New York, says children have very little sense of right and wrong, so schools must help out.[19]

   In the 1970s, many schools included values clarification in their curriculum. As various factions of society objected, fearing that values would be "imposed" on children, schools eliminated these classes, and teachers learned to be "value neutral." Today, however, there is a nationwide resurgence of the movement to teach moral values and ethics in the classrooms. Sanford McDonnell, chairman of the Character Education Partnership, says the schools have the greatest potential for overcoming what he describes as "the national crisis of character." The Character Education Partnership defines "good character" as understanding, caring about, and acting on core ethical values. McDonnell says our nation will not be strong if we graduate young people who are brilliant but dishonest or have great intellectual knowledge but do not care about others.[20] In higher education, we are now seeing the addition of more courses on values and ethics. Over 500 business-ethics courses are currently taught on American campuses.[21] In some cases, entire departments or centers are devoted to this type of education.

Influence of the Media   Some social critics say that if you are searching for signs of civilization gone rotten, you can simply tune into the loud and often amoral voices of mass entertainment on television and radio. They point out that viewers too often see people abusing and degrading other people without any significant consequences. Mainstream television continues to feature a great deal of violence and antisocial behavior, and the programs are seen by a large number of young viewers. It is estimated that the average preschool child watches more than 27 hours of television per week and that the average teenager spends 21 hours watching TV.[22] Is it any wonder that, with this constant bombardment, our children have difficulty determining right from wrong?

Several organizations have taken steps to influence the content and presentation of mass entertainment. Children Now, a national children's advocacy group, has asked television programmers to show viewers the consequences of antisocial behavior. The National Political Congress of Black Women has initiated a campaign to get rid of recordings that contain messages that are demeaning to women. The Time Warner recording label has been a frequent target of this organization.[23] And in Richmond, Virginia, the owners of the Ukrop supermarket chain initiated an advertising boycott aimed at a radio station that began airing Howard Stern's controversial talk program. A letter from the Ukrop family described his program content as "racist, sexist, filth."[24]

Influence of People We Admire   In addition to being influenced by the media, your values are likely to be influenced by **modeling**—shaping your behavior to resemble that of people you admire and embracing the qualities those people demonstrate. The heroes and heroines you discover in childhood and adolescence help you form a "dominant value direction."[25] Opie and Andy Taylor were positive role models for most children growing up in the 1950s and 1960s. Today Bart Simpson's unique family relationships teach children a new way of interacting with authority figures. We would be better served to point children and adolescents in the direction of humanitarian and tennis champion Arthur Ashe, who led an exemplary family and professional life until his untimely death from AIDS contracted after heart bypass surgery, or Oprah Winfrey, whose open and honest style can have a positive effect on girls and women of all ages. If we truly want to develop a more moral society, we need to keep track of the men and women our children are modeling and encourage our children to look for positive qualities such as Ashe's integrity and

Winfrey's honesty. We would all be wise to focus on and emulate the positive qualities of those we admire.

Avoiding Values Drift

Core values represent the starting point for personal and organizational success. As individuals, we need to reflect on our core values when making decisions related to important work-life issues. All great institutions have answered the questions "What do we stand for?" and "Why do we exist?" Successful companies like Hewlett-Packard, Disney, and Boeing have one thing in common. They have successfully adapted over the decades to a changing environment without losing sight of their core values. They have not drifted away from their strong foundations.[26]

Debbie and Randy Fields, cofounders of Mrs. Fields' Cookies, hold strong opinions about what it takes to successfully operate a large chain of retail stores. They are constantly looking for "drift." Drift is the slow erosion of the company's standards and values. When the company was expanding, they opened a new store in Hawaii and staffed it with capable employees. Over a period of five months, the people made tiny, infinitesimal changes in the cookie recipes. When Debbie Fields visited the store, she discovered that her original chewy cookies had become spongy cakes.[27] Tiny changes in personal values can have a similar effect, steering a person slightly off course. That is why it is so important to constantly monitor your commitment to your values and make adjustments when necessary to get your life back on track. In his book *Conversations with God*, Neal Donald Walsch discusses the process of building a strong foundation for everything from your daily decisions to your long-range goals. He suggests: "Do not dismantle the house, but look at each brick, and replace those which appear broken, which no longer support the structure."[28] This careful examination of each of your values will help keep you on track toward your ideal future and help you avoid values drift.

Thinking / Learning Starters

1. Identify the events and individuals that have been influential in forming your value system. Are those of your childhood and adolescence still important to you?

2. Based on the media's influence and the concept of modeling, what do you predict the next generation's values will be? The children of today will be your coworkers in the future. Will their attitudes and values be a potential problem for you?

VALUES CONFLICTS

One of the major causes of conflict between people within an organization is a clash between each individual's personal values. There is no doubt about it, people are different. Everyone has been raised with different family backgrounds, religious experiences, education, role models, and media exposure. These differences can pop out anywhere and anytime people get together. Many observers suggest that organizations look for **values conflicts** when addressing such problems as declining quality, absenteeism, and poor customer service. The trouble may lie not so much in work schedules or production routines as in the mutual distrust and misunderstanding brought about by clashes in workers' and managers' value systems. Here are some examples of values conflicts:

Item: Manny Garcia, a very successful Burger King franchise owner, was upset when the company launched an advertising campaign that included the slogan "Sometimes you gotta break the rules." He felt the slogan sent the wrong message to his teenage customers. To protest the ad campaign, he flipped his Burger King signs upside down.[29]

Item: Workers struck the General Motors plant at Flint, Michigan, to protest excessive required overtime. They complained that workweeks that sometimes

People with shared values often unite against those whose values conflict with their group. Here a group opposed to David Duke confronts those in support of the political candidate and former Ku Klux Klan advocate. (Michael Dwyer/Stock, Boston, Inc.)

stretch to 66 hours disrupt their personal lives. Management says the overtime is necessary because the cost of health insurance and other benefits for new workers is so high the company cannot afford to hire more workers.[30]

Item: Herbert Lanese, former president of McDonnell Douglas Aerospace, was abruptly fired six months after he was hired because of a values clash with Chief Executive Harry Stonecipher. One problem became obvious during a 99-day machinists' strike at the St. Louis plant. Local newspapers quoted Lanese as saying that convenience store clerks with two weeks' training could do the machinists' jobs. Union members were elated when Lanese was removed.[31]

Internal Values Conflict

A person who is forced to choose between two or more strongly held values is experiencing an **internal values conflict.** As a manager, you may be torn between loyalty to your workers and loyalty to upper management. As an employee, you may find yourself in conflict between fulfilling family obligations and devoting the time and energy required to succeed at work. Trudy Desilets spent many years searching for a balance between her personal and professional life. Because travel demands left her exhausted, she gave up a fast-track sales job soon after the birth of her first child. When she asked to share her job with an equally qualified employee, her bosses turned her down. She loved her next job, but by the time her daughter was 3 she was facing burnout. The demands of being a good worker, a good mother, and a good wife were overwhelming.[32]

How you resolve internal values conflicts depends on how much time you are willing to invest in the values clarification process described in Table 4.1. Once you have completed the process and identified your core values, be sure to rank them in order of importance to you. This ranking process will help you make decisions when life gets complicated and you have to make difficult choices.[33] If one of your values is to be an outstanding parent and another is to maintain a healthy body, you should anticipate an internal values conflict when a busy schedule requires a choice between attending your daughter's soccer game and your weekly workout at the fitness center. However, when you rank which value is more important, the decision will be much easier.

Values Conflicts with Others

Some of the most common interpersonal values conflicts arise between workers of different generations, races, cultures, ethnic backgrounds, or religions; between men and women; and between supervisors and workers. Employees from diverse backgrounds may clash over different interpretations of the work ethic and the priorities of job and personal life. Unless such conflicts are handled skillfully, confrontation can make the situation worse, not better.

How will you handle a tense situation where it is obvious your values conflict with those of a colleague? You may discover your supervisor is a racist and you strongly support the civil rights of all people. Perhaps a coworker is a homosexual and your religious background does not accept this alternative lifestyle. These are highly emotional issues that can disrupt friendships, work teams, and the productivity of organizations. There are no easy answers. You *can* attempt, however, to develop respect for the other person, even though you disagree with his or her beliefs. Find a common ground concerning things you and the other person do agree on, and avoid discussions concerning your values conflict. Attempt to really listen to and understand where the other person is coming from, and share your thoughts and opinions in a calm manner. You will never be too old to learn something new and make adjustments to your beliefs based on new insights that may have never presented themselves during your formative years. If these techniques do not work and your values conflict continues to surface, you may need to determine whether or not the relationship is worth saving and make your decisions accordingly.

PERSONAL VALUES AND ETHICAL CHOICES

Ethics are the rules that direct your conduct and moral judgments.[34] They help translate your values into appropriate and effective behaviors in your day-to-day life. Personal ethics determine how you do business and with whom. Kickbacks and payoffs may be acceptable practices in some parts of the world yet may be viewed as unethical practices elsewhere. Where will you draw the line between right and wrong?

As competition in the global marketplace increases, moral and ethical issues can become cloudy. Although most organizations have adopted the point of view that "Good ethics is good business," exceptions do exist. Some organizations encourage, or at least condone, unethical behaviors. Surveys show many workers feel pressure to violate their ethical standards in order to meet business objectives.[35] Thus, you must develop your own personal code of ethics.

Every job you hold will present you with new ethical and moral dilemmas. These challenges can surface almost daily for people who direct and supervise the work of others. It may be tempting to tell employees to "do whatever is necessary" to get a job done on time, or to look the other way when employees engage in unethical or illegal acts. Simply taking credit for the accomplishments of others or displaying favoritism when establishing the work schedule represents a lapse in ethical conduct.

As a laborer, salesperson, or office support worker, you too will be faced with ethical choices. Faced with the demands of overtime, balancing work and family, and layoffs due to downsizing, workers seem to feel more pressure to act unethically.[36] A survey sponsored by the International Association of Administrative Professionals discovered an alarming frequency of unethical behaviors, including breaching confidentiality about hiring, firing, or layoffs; removing or destroying information, and falsifying documents.[37] Other studies indicate that underpaid employees who feel unappreciated are more prone to steal from their employers, with the price tag reaching over $120 billion a year—and climbing rapidly.[38]

How to Make the Right Ethical Choices

In today's turbulent, fast-paced, highly competitive workplace, ethical dilemmas surface frequently, and telling right from wrong has never been more difficult. Here are a few guidelines to help you make the right ethical choices.

Learn to distinguish between right and wrong Although selecting the right path can be difficult, a great deal of help is available today. Many current books and articles offer good advice. The book *The Measure of Our Success* by Marian Wright Edelman presents a collection of "lessons for life" that can offer guidance in making ethical choices. A few examples follow:

- There is no free lunch. Don't feel entitled to anything you don't sweat and struggle for.
- Never work just for money or for power. They won't save your soul or build a decent family or help you sleep at night.
- Be honest. Struggle to live what you say and preach. Act with integrity.
- Sell the shadow for the substance. Don't confuse style with substance; don't confuse political charm or rhetoric with decency or sound policy.[39]

Help in making the correct ethical choices may be as close as your employer's code of ethics, ethical guidelines published by your professional organization, or advice provided by an experienced and trusted colleague.

Make certain your values are in harmony with those of your employer You may find it easier to make the right ethical choices if your values are compatible with those of your employer. Many organizations have adopted a set of beliefs, customs, values, and practices that attract a certain type of employee (see Figure 4.1). Harmony between personal and organizational values usually leads to success for the individual as well as the organization. These **shared values** provide a strong bond among all members of the work force.

Item: When selling their long-distance telephone service, employees of Working Assets assure their customers that 1 percent of every phone bill will be donated to liberal causes such as Greenpeace, the American Civil Liberties Union, gun control, abortion rights, and protection of redwoods. One marketing campaign read, "Be Socially Responsible: Talk on the Phone." Chief Executive Officer Laura Sure says that people are looking for other reasons to make a choice beyond the cost of services rendered.[40]

FIGURE 4.1

Lotus Development Corporation's Operating Principles

OPERATING PRINCIPLES

These Operating Principles are intended to serve as guidelines for interaction between all employees. Their purpose is to foster and preserve the spirit of our enterprise and to promote the well-being of all concerned.

Commit to excellence

Insist on integrity

Treat people fairly; Value diversity

Communicate openly, honestly, and directly

Listen with an open mind; Learn from everything

Take responsibility; Lead by example

Respect, trust, and encourage others

Encourage risk-taking and innovation

Establish purpose before action

Work as a team

Have fun

Source: © Lotus Development Corporation. Used with permission of Lotus Development Corporation.

Total Person Insight

"Nothing is more powerful for employees than seeing their managers behave according to their expressed values and standards; nothing is more devastating to the development of an ethical environment than a manager who violates the organization's ethical standards."

DAN RICE AND CRAIG DREILINGER

Management Consultants; Authors, "Rights and Wrongs of Ethics Training"

Item: In a Duke University survey of 650 M.B.A. graduates of eleven top schools, 70 percent indicated that they would not work for certain industries because of ethical or political concerns. About 82 percent said they would shun tobacco companies, 36 percent would avoid firms with environmental problems, 26 percent would refuse to work for liquor marketers, and 20 percent would not get involved with defense contractors. Dan Nagy, who conducted the survey for Duke's Fuqua School of Business, says, "Today's students have strong values and limit the compromises they're willing to make for money."[41]

Item: Lotus Development Corp. was awarded *Personnel Journal*'s coveted Optimas Award, Quality of Life Category, for its continual re-evaluation of its values relative to its workers. One of Lotus's operating principles, treating people fairly and valuing diversity, led to the creation of an innovative benefits policy that offers medical, dental, vision, and hearing insurance benefits to gay and lesbian partners of employees. Russell Campanello, vice president of human resources for Lotus, stated this about the company's prior plan: "Our benefits program was out of synch with our stated values around not discriminating based on sexual orientation. It has to reflect the needs, interests and values [of the workers] because that's what makes [the relationship] mutual."[42]

Research conducted by the Families and Work Institute indicates that work/family decisions continue to be a battlefield for clashing values. Increasingly, employees want the opportunity to openly discuss family issues such as child care, requests for a flexible schedule, or care for an ailing parent. Johnson & Johnson is one of several companies that is training managers to sensitize them to values priorities that are different from their own.[43]

Don't let your life be driven by the desire for immediate gratification
Progress and prosperity have almost identical meanings to many people. They equate progress with the acquisition of material things. One explanation is that young business leaders entering the corporate world are under a great deal of pressure to show the trappings of success. This is the view expressed by John

Delaney, who is a professor at the University of Iowa and has done extensive research on ethics. He says, "You're expected to have the requisite car and summer house to show you're a contributor to society, and many people do whatever it takes to get them."[44]

To achieve immediate gratification often means taking shortcuts. It involves pushing hard, cutting corners, and emphasizing short-term gains over the achievement of long-term goals. M. Scott Peck, author of the best-selling book *The Road Less Traveled,* discusses the benefits of delaying gratification: "Delaying gratification is a process of scheduling the pain and pleasure of life in such a way as to enhance the pleasure by meeting and experiencing the pain first and getting it over with. It is the only decent way to live."[45]

If delaying gratification is "the only decent way to live," why do so many people seek immediate gratification? The answer to this question is somewhat complex. Some people feel pressure from friends and family members to climb the ladder of success as quickly as possible. They fail to realize that the road to peace of mind and happiness is not paved with Rolex watches, Brooks Brothers suits, and a Lexus. In Chapter 9 we describe a new definition of success and discuss the nonfinancial resources that make the biggest contribution to a happy and fulfilling life.

Thinking / Learning Starter

1. Think about the last time you felt guilty about something you did. Did you hurt someone's feelings? Did you take credit for something someone else accomplished? Which of your basic values did your actions violate?

2. When was the last time you broke off a friendship or relationship with another person in your personal or professional life? Does the reason for the breakup reflect back to a values conflict between the two of you? Explain.

CORPORATE VALUES AND ETHICAL CHOICES

This chapter began with a look at the dark side of Wall Street. In the securities industry, as in other industries, it is easy to focus on the individuals and organizations that have been motivated by greed and have failed to establish strict standards of business conduct. Nevertheless, some of the most successful companies play by the rules. At Legg Mason, one of the nation's top ten securities and investment management companies, employees are guided by strict stan-

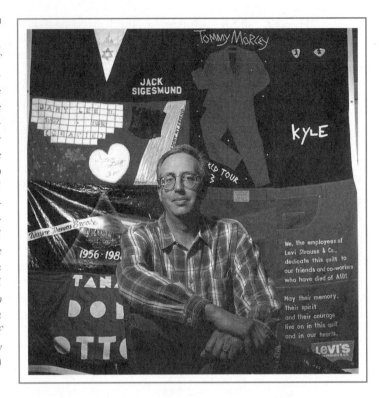

Robert D. Haas, chairman and CEO of Levi Strauss & Company, believes that the corporation should be an ethical creature capable of both making profits and making the world a better place to live. He has established high standards regarding work environment, ethics, and social responsibility. He is pictured here in front of the Levi Strauss contribution to the AIDS quilt, a memorial to victims of the disease. (Andy Freeberg)

dards of business conduct. Chip Mason, chief executive officer at Legg Mason, has told employees that honesty is the *number-one* business principle guiding the company. His leadership has been rewarded with steady revenue growth.[46] Similarly, Ben Edwards, chairman of A. G. Edwards and Sons, Inc., the seventh-largest securities firm in the nation, says that following the golden rule is still the best way to achieve success in business. This attitude has had a positive influence on the company's 7,400 employees. He encourages employees who are faced with an ethical conflict to ask the question "Is it right?"[47]

Corporate Crime

Many organizations have gotten into serious trouble by ignoring ethical principles. In recent years, the media have carried headlines concerning organizations involved in corporate crime.

Item: Eighteen former Honda Motor Co. executives were convicted on federal fraud and racketeering charges. The executives admitted that they had accepted over $15 million in bribes from dealers in exchange for generous supplies of fast-selling Honda cars.[48]

Item: Prudential Insurance Company agreed to pay $410 million to customers who were misled by sales representatives. The agents involved were guilty of using a practice called "churning." Churning occurs when agents pressure customers to use built-up cash value in an old policy to buy a new, more expensive policy.[49]

Item: Stew Leonard, founder of the well-known Stew Leonard's Dairy Store, pleaded guilty to conspiring to defraud the federal government of taxes. He installed a computer software program that reduced sales data on an item-by-item basis and skimmed $17 million in cash.[50]

Those items represent only a small fraction of the corporate crime that goes on today. Many offenders are not caught or brought to trial. But, on the positive side, recent surveys indicate that a large majority of America's major corporations are actively trying to build ethics into their organizations.

Item: Minnesota Mutual Life Insurance Company has been able to steer clear of scandal for more than one hundred years by adopting a values-based management philosophy that rewards integrity and honesty. Success at the management level requires commitment to the company's core values. Managers must demonstrate their ability to infuse ethical values in their subordinates.[51]

Item: At Harley-Davidson the soul of the "Hog" can be traced to values that emphasize strong working relationships. The company's idea of a healthy working relationship is embedded in five formal values that constitute a code of behavior for everyone:[52]

- Tell the truth.
- Be fair.
- Keep your promises.
- Respect the individual.
- Encourage intellectual curiosity.

Many say they have difficulty determining the right course of action in difficult "gray-area" situations. And even when the right ethical course of action is clear, competitive pressures sometimes lead well-intentioned managers astray.[53] Tom Chappell, author of *The Soul of a Business* and founder of Tom's of Maine, explains why organizations often have difficulty doing what is morally right and socially responsible: "It's harder to manage for ethical pursuits than it is to simply manage for profits."[54]

How to Prevent Corporate Crime

Develop Ethics Codes Mark Twain once wrote, "To be good is noble. To tell people how to be good is even nobler, and much less trouble." Many corporate leaders have decided that it is time to put their views on ethics in writing. Most organizations today have written codes of ethics. A written code, highly publicized throughout the company and enforced without exception, can be a powerful force in preventing unethical behavior. A Tulane University study, however, discovered that the drive for a "comfortable life" and "pleasure" controlled the decisions of many managers even though their organizations had codes of ethics in place. Researchers say corporations need to do more to create an overall "ethical climate" that includes a reward system that recognizes acts of moral courage.[55] Also, organizations need to enforce their ethics codes with greater zeal.

Hire with Care   Thomas Melohn, president of North American Tool & Die Inc., located in San Leandro, California, says the key to operating a successful company is to first identify a guiding set of values and then "make sure you find people who have those values and can work together."[56] He says the hiring process should be given a very high priority. Melohn never hires any employee without checking references and conducting a lengthy job interview.

Jerry Pardue, vice president of loss and prevention for Super D Drugs, a southeastern drugstore chain, uses integrity tests (also called honesty tests) to screen out dishonest persons and drug users. He is one of a growing number of businesspeople who use some form of psychological testing. (Reid Psychological Systems developed the first honesty test more than forty years ago.) Company officials say that people who get involved in tangible theft (stealing cash or merchandise) are more likely to commit intangible thefts such as coming to work late or using the telephone for personal calls.[57]

As the popularity of integrity tests grows, so does the debate over their use. Many people are questioning the accuracy of the tests and the fairness of using them to hire or turn away applicants. Some states have made it illegal to deny someone a job on the basis of low test scores. Even the testing companies admit that the tests are not foolproof. But the American Psychological Association has studied the accuracy of integrity tests and has stated that some are in fact reliable.[58]

Provide Ethics Training   Many ethical issues are complex and cannot be considered in black-and-white moral terms. It is for this and other reasons that ethics training has become quite common in the business community. In some cases, the training involves little more than a careful study of the company ethics code and its implications for day-to-day decision making. Employees are notified where the code of ethics is displayed in the building and are asked to sign a document that verifies they have read, understand, and agree to abide by the code of ethics. In other cases, employees participate in in-depth discussions of ethical decisions. At Martin Marietta Corp., ethics training includes the use of a game called Gray Matters, in which a game leader presents mini-cases to teams of players. Each team also receives a list of potential responses to an ethical dilemma presented in the minicase. After discussing the responses, each team selects what it thinks is the best answer. The team leader then discloses the point value of each answer. Learning takes place as team members debate the pros and cons of each possible response.[59] Sears, Roebuck and Company provides its employees with a booklet entitled *Code of Business Conduct*. It outlines the company's position on a wide range of issues such as receiving gifts, employee discounts, care of company assets, and foreign business dealings. It also includes guidelines for making ethical decisions (see Table 4.3).

Is it possible to instill ethical values in employees through the use of training programs? Some critics say ethics training programs prepare employees to make the right decision only when actions are covered by specific rules. They see more merit in providing guidelines that employees can use to resolve many ethical issues. Almost everyone agrees that ethics training must start at the top of the organization. Business leaders must realize that unethical conduct is destructive and usually generates no more than short-term gains. The long-term consequences of ethical misconduct can be very costly.

Develop Support for Whistle-Blowing   When you discover your employer or a colleague is behaving illegally or unethically, you have three choices. You can keep quiet and keep working. You can decide you can't be party to the situation and leave. Or you can report the situation in the hope of putting a stop to it. When you reveal wrongdoing within an organization to the public or to those in positions of authority, you are a **whistle blower.**

Whistle blowers are sounding alarms in industries from tobacco companies to airlines. Jeffrey Wigand, a former chief researcher for Brown & Williamson Tobacco, testified that his company misled the public about the danger of nicotine. Sylvia Robins reported that she knew about a procedural flaw at Unisys, a National Aeronautics and Space Administration subcontractor that

TABLE 4.3

Sears's Guidelines for Ethical Decision Making

> **Guidelines for Making Ethical Decisions:**
>
> **1.** Is it legal?
> **2.** Is it within Sears' shared beliefs and policies?
> **3.** Is it right/fair/appropriate?
> **4.** Would I want everyone to know about this?
> **5.** How will I feel about myself?

Source: *Code of Business Conduct,* Sears, Roebuck and Co., 3333 Beverly Road, Hoffman Estates, IL 60179. Courtesy of Sears, Roebuck and Co.

produces software programs for the space shuttle program, that resulted in invalid test results that endangered space shuttle crews. A Florida Power & Light engineer blew the whistle on safety concerns at a nuclear plant. Each of these individuals chose to come forward with information even though they knew they might be subject to harassment from their employers. And all were successful in their efforts. The tobacco industry is being forced to take legal and financial responsibility for years of tobacco-related health hazards. Engineers at Florida Power & Light and Unisys were severely punished for taking shortcuts that led to hazardous conditions, and both organizations were forced to pay huge penalties for their neglect.[60]

Many people were raised by parents who discouraged "tattling." Those who were raised during the baby-boom/Vietnam War era, however, learned to question authority and are now moving into the upper ranks of corporations and government agencies. Books such as *Blowing the Whistle: Organizational and Legal Implications* are finding an audience eager to learn how to effectively clean up unethical business practices without endangering their personal or professional futures. Cutting-edge management theories such as "total quality management" and "re-engineering" encourage workers to be a proactive part of the organization's team. If organizations focus on quality, then workers from the leadership ranks to the assembly lines must be able to report problems. Whistle-blowing is not an easy path to take. You may be right, win your case, and still lose friends and perhaps your job. However, taking steps to get rid of unethical practices is often your responsibility.

VALUES AND ETHICS IN INTERNATIONAL BUSINESS

If the situation is complex on the domestic scene, values and ethical issues become even more complicated at the international level. The subject is too broad to treat in detail in this chapter, but we can provide an overview of some conflicts that exist in international business. Here are some examples of situations in which a lack of shared values can create difficult situations:

Item: The values of Asian executives often differ from those of their American counterparts. To most Asians, the important values are hard work, respect for learning, and honesty. To most Americans, freedom of expression, personal freedom, and self-reliance are the important values, followed by individual rights, hard work, personal achievement, and thinking for oneself.[61] These contrasts offer special challenges in the global marketplace.

Item: In China, the highly regulated economy gives government officials many opportunities to seek payments for special favors. If you make the first payment, expect continued demands for money.[62] The United States Congress passed the Foreign Corrupt Practices Act, which bars American companies from engaging in the bribery of government officials common in many countries. In some cases, this law puts American businesspeople at a disadvantage because some representatives of other countries participate freely in bribery.

Item: As more Americans complete business transactions with the Japanese, value differences become clearer. **Naniwabushi** is the Japanese expression for establishing close personal terms with someone so that she or he will owe you a favor, a commonly accepted business practice in Japan. In this environment, potentially awkward obligations could arise for Americans if they accept gifts from Japanese business acquaintances.

Item: Value differences can also arise in business matters between French and American business representatives. The French tend to be prompt about considering a decision, but they like to examine all the details. This means that final decisions can be slow in coming. Once made, however, they are expressed candidly—whether the decision is in your favor or not.

Now that trade relations have been resumed with countries such as Vietnam, South Africa, and China, it is important for all parties to recognize value differences and to spend time and effort building mutual respect and understanding.

Summary

A strong sense of character grows out of your personal standards of behavior. When you consistently behave in accordance with your values, you maintain your integrity. Your values are the personal worth or importance you give to an object or idea. People's values serve as the foundation for their attitudes, preferences, opinions, and behaviors. Personal values are largely formed early in life and are influenced by family, religious upbringing, schools, the media, and role models.

Internal values conflicts arise when we must choose between strongly held personal values. Values conflicts with others, often based on age, racial, religious, gender, or ethnic differences, require skilled intervention before they can be resolved.

Once you have clarified your personal values, your ethical decisions will be easier. You must learn to distinguish right from wrong, choose an employer whose values you share, and avoid the pursuit of immediate gratification. Shared values unify employees in an organization by providing guidelines for behavior and decisions.

Corporate values and ethics on both the domestic and the international levels are receiving increasing attention because of the devastating effect and expense of corporate crime. Many organizations are developing ethics codes to help guide employees' behaviors, hiring only those individuals who share their corporate values, and offering ethics training opportunities to all employees. As multinational organizations increase in number, the individuals involved will need to consciously examine their values and ethical standards to deal effectively with differing value structures in each country.

Q. I will soon graduate from college and would like to begin my career with an organization that shares my values. I have carefully examined what is most important to me and believe I know the type of organizational culture in which I can thrive. But how do I discover the "real" values of an organization when my interviews are permeated with buzzwords such as "family-friendly" and "teamwork-oriented." How can I determine whether or not they truly mean what they seem to say?

A. Direct questions about an organization's values often result in well-rehearsed answers from the interviewer. Try using *critical incident* questions such as "How did you handle the recent downsizing of your middle managers?" or "Tell me about the heroes in your organization." And don't depend solely on the interviewer's answers. Ask current and former employees as well as the organization's customers or clients. Listen carefully to the language used during your interviews. Do you hear a lot of talk about "love," "caring," and "intuition," or do you hear statements like "We had to send in the SWAT team," "They beat their brains out," and "We really nailed them!" If possible, sit in on a team meeting with your potential coworkers. A perfect match between your values and your potential employers' is hard to find, so be patient. You may need to compromise.

Key Terms

character
integrity
values
core values
modeling

values conflict
internal values conflict
ethics
shared values
whistle blower
Naniwabushi

Review Questions

1. How do values differ from attitudes, opinions, or behavior?
2. How are our values formed? How have the sources of our values changed in recent years?
3. Differentiate between internal values conflicts and values conflicts with others.
4. Explain the five dimensions of Kirschenbaum's valuing process (see Table 4.1).

5. Describe the advantages and disadvantages of employees sharing the same values as their organization.
6. Explain the negative effects of the pursuit of immediate gratification.
7. How do top management values affect the purpose and direction of an organization?
8. List some of the steps corporations are taking to eliminate crime in their organizations.
9. How might an ethics code help organizations be more productive?
10. How do seemingly accepted unethical business practices in foreign countries affect Americans' ability to compete for business contracts in those countries?

Application Exercises

1. Guilt and loss of self-respect can result when we say or do things that conflict with what we believe. One way to feel better about yourself is to "clean up" your integrity. Make a list of what you are doing that you think is wrong. Once the list is complete, look it over and determine if you can stop these behaviors. Consider making amends for things you have done in the past that you feel guilty about.[63]
2. In groups of four, discuss how you would react if your manager asked you to participate in some sort of corporate crime. For example, the manager could ask you to help launder money from the company, give a customer misleading information, or cover up a budget inaccuracy and keep this information from reaching upper management. You might want to role-play the situation with your group. Follow up with class discussion.
3. One of the great challenges in life is the clarification of our values. The five-part valuing process described in Table 4.1 can be very helpful as you attempt to identify your core values. Select one personal or professional value from the following list, and clarify this value by applying the five-step process.
   a. Respect the rights and privileges of people who may be in the minority due to race, gender, ethnicity, age, physical or mental abilities, or sexual orientation.
   b. Conserve the assets of my employer.
   c. Utilize leisure time in order to add balance to my life.
   d. Maintain a healthy lifestyle.
   e. Balance the demands of my work and personal life.

Internet Exercise

As the Internet grows in popularity, we are seeing some unethical uses of this technology. Ethical issues related to privacy, security, and confidentiality are receiving increasing attention. Many sites on the World Wide Web focus on ethical issues pertaining to computers and technology. To learn about important ethical issues raised by the use of computers and the Internet, use your search engine to identify appropriate resources. Type in "computer ethics," and then examine the information available. Prepare a list of the most important ethical issues related to the use of computers, and place a checkmark next to each issue that currently affects you.

Self-Assessment Exercise

1. For each of the following statements, circle the number from 1 to 5 that best represents your response: (1) strongly disagree (never do this); (2) disagree (rarely do this); (3) moderately agree (sometimes do this); (4) agree (frequently do this); (5) strongly agree (always do this).

   a. I base my personal and professional decisions on clearly defined personal values.   1   2   3   4   5

   b. I accept the fact that others' values may differ from mine, and I respect their right to maintain a value system that differs from my own.   1   2   3   4   5

   c. I have a clear sense of what is right and wrong, and my character reflects the fundamental strengths of honesty, fairness, service, humility, and modesty.   1   2   3   4   5

   d. I maintain my integrity by practicing what I believe in and keeping my commitments.   1   2   3   4   5

   Select an appropriate attitude or skill you would like to improve. Write your goal in the space provided.

   GOAL: _____

   _____

   _____

Case Problem

Disney Versus the Southern Baptist Convention

If you look up *wholesome* in the dictionary, you might expect the Walt Disney Company logo beside it because Disney has become *the* family-entertainment giant known for its theme parks and G-rated movies. The Walt Disney Company has been functioning on the family-oriented values passed on by its revered founder and is now the largest entertainment company in the world since purchasing the American Broadcasting Company. Recently, however, Disney's organizational culture has been changing to reflect new company initiatives and to value the diversity of its work force as well as its customers. Disney has extended health care benefits to all company employees with same-sex partners, allowed gays and lesbians to gather annually at Disney parks, and contracted with film producers that make R-rated movies.

In response, leaders of the 16-million-member Southern Baptist Convention voted to boycott Disney to protest what they see as its drift away from commitment to traditional family and Christian values. The Southern Baptists believe that same-sex relationships do not qualify as "family," that Disney should stop the annual gay/lesbian get-togethers, and that Disney should refuse to participate in the creation or marketing of R-rated movies. Their nonbinding resolution specifically requests members to cancel plans to visit Disney theme parks, refuse to pay to see Disney movies, and cut Disney product purchases by $100 each year. Sixteen million members times $100 can equal a devastating blow to any corporation's bottom line.

A Disney spokesperson called the boycott "misguided" because it targets the most family-friendly media company in the world.

Questions

1. Do you agree or disagree with the decision to launch a boycott? Explain.
2. If you were a Southern Baptist Convention member who did not vote at the convention and who had children who had saved money for their trip to Disney World, would you go on the trip? Explain.
3. If you were a Southern Baptist minister who did not vote at the convention and did not agree with the vote, how would you guide your church's membership?
4. What steps should Disney take to reduce the potentially destructive effect of the boycott? Would these actions violate the values of any other groups?

Chapter 5

Attitudes Can Shape
Your Life

Chapter Preview

After studying this chapter, you will be able to

1. Understand the impact of employee attitudes on the success of individuals as well as organizations.
2. List and explain the ways people acquire attitudes.
3. Describe attitudes that employers value.
4. Learn how to change your attitudes.
5. Learn how to help others change their attitudes.
6. Understand what adjustments organizations are making to develop positive employee attitudes.

PRIOR TO THE OPENING of the Grand Hyatt Wailea Beach resort hotel on the island of Maui, the personnel department screened 6,000 applicants to fill 1,200 jobs. When Nordstrom opened its first department store on the East Coast, the company interviewed 3,000 people to fill 400 front-line jobs.[1] Both of these service-driven companies are searching for employees who display a positive attitude toward customer service.

When General Motors opened its Saturn plant, applicants were screened for "compatibility" from a huge pool of people. Hal Rosenbluth, CEO of Rosenbluth International, the nation's fourth-largest travel agency, interviews his potential executives by playing basketball with them. He explains, "I like to see who's passing the ball, who's hogging it, who's taking shots they shouldn't."[2] GM and Rosenbluth are searching for employees who exhibit attitudes that help them work effectively as team members.[3]

The National Center on the Educational Quality of the Work Force at the University of Pennsylvania asked 3,000 employers what matters most when hiring nonsupervisory workers. The applicant's attitude ranked number one among eleven characteristics.[4] A close look at this survey and at similar studies tells us that the qualities that make up "attitude" vary from one employment setting to another. Lynn Mercer, manager of a Lucent Technologies plant, says she is guided by the principle that you should hire attitude over aptitude. She searches for employees who display initiative, curiosity, and collegiality— characteristics that she views as hallmarks of a self-directed work force. Mercer is searching for self-starters and team players.[5] John Guffey, Coltec Industries Inc. CEO, is continually searching for employees who do not have an attitude of entitlement. In other words, he wants to avoid hiring a person who is continually asking, "What's in it for me?"[6] ■

WHAT IS AN ATTITUDE?

An **attitude** is a relatively strong belief about or feeling toward a person, object, idea, or event. It is an "emotional readiness" to behave in a particular manner.[7] Values serve as a foundation for attitudes, and attitudes serve as a foundation for behavior (see Figure 5.1). Throughout life we form attitudes toward political movements, religions, national leaders, various occupations, government programs, laws, and other aspects of our daily lives. They become deeply ingrained in our personalities as we learn and grow. We tend to be very much in favor of those things toward which we have a positive attitude. And we are very much against those things toward which we have a negative attitude. Some of our attitudes are so strong that we encourage others to adopt

Habitat for Humanity International is a nonprofit ministry dedicated to providing housing for the homeless by making adequate, affordable shelter a matter of conscience and action. Volunteers and the selected homeowners invest hundreds of hours to reduce the monetary cost of the house, increase the personal stake of the family members in their house, and foster attitudes of partnership with other people in the community. (David Young-Wolff/PhotoEdit)

our views and copy our behaviors. When others hold strong contrasting attitudes, based on their values and past experiences, a potential human relations challenge exists.

Some attitudes, such as job satisfaction, are multidimensional. The feelings we have about our work, for example, are made up of attitudes toward the company's compensation plan, opportunities for promotion, coworkers, supervision, the work itself, and other factors.[8] Job satisfaction is usually of major concern to an employer because management knows there is a link between attitudes and behavior. Persons who are dissatisfied with their jobs are more likely to be late or absent from work, become unproductive, or quit. Therefore, improved job satisfaction can reduce tardiness, absenteeism, and employee turnover.[9]

FIGURE 5.1

The Relationship Between Values, Attitudes, and Behaviors

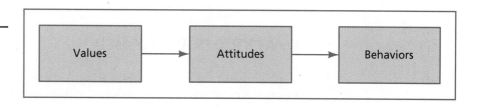

The Powerful Influence of Attitudes

Charles Swindoll is credited with saying, "The longer I live, the more I realize the impact of attitude on life." He is convinced that attitude is more important than appearance, giftedness, or skill.[10] For example, people who go through life with a positive mental attitude see daily obstacles as opportunities rather than roadblocks and are therefore more likely to achieve their personal and professional goals. People who filter their daily experiences through a negative attitude tend to focus on what is going wrong and find it difficult to achieve contentment or satisfaction in any aspect of their lives. It makes no difference how attractive, intelligent, or skilled they are; their attitude holds them back.

Our attitudes can greatly influence our mental and physical health. Bernie Siegel, author of *Peace, Love and Healing* and *Love, Medicine and Miracles,* sees a strong connection between a patient's mental attitude and his or her ability to heal. Siegel, who is a surgeon, says that when a doctor can instill some measure of hope in the patient's mind, the healing process begins. As part of his treatment plan, Siegel attempts to give patients a sense of control over their destinies. He wants his patients to believe in the future and know that they can influence their own healing.[11]

Attitudes represent a powerful force in any organization. An attitude of trust, for example, can pave the way for improved communication and greater cooperation between an employee and a supervisor. A sincere effort by management to improve working conditions, when filtered through attitudes of suspicion and cynicism, may have a negative impact on employee-management relations. These same actions by management, filtered through attitudes of trust and hope, may result in improved worker morale. As another example, a caring attitude displayed by an employee can increase customer loyalty and set the stage for repeat business.

HOW ATTITUDES ARE FORMED

Throughout life you are constantly making decisions and judgments that help formulate your attitudes. These attitude decisions are often based on behaviors your childhood authority figures told you were right or wrong, childhood and adult behaviors for which you were rewarded or punished, role models you selected, and the various environmental and corporate cultures you chose to embrace.

Socialization

The process through which people are integrated into a society by exposure to the actions and opinions of others is called **socialization.**[12] As a child, you interacted with your parents, family, teachers, and friends. Children often feel that statements made by these authority figures are the "proper" things to believe. For example, if a parent declares, "People who live in big, expensive houses are either crooked or born rich," the child may hold this attitude for many years.

Children learn a great deal by watching and listening to family members, teachers, and other authority figures. In some cases, the influence is quite subtle. Children who observe their parents recycling, using public transportation instead of a car to get to work, and turning off the lights to save electricity may develop a strong concern for protection of the environment.

Peer and Reference Groups

As children reach adolescence and begin to break away psychologically from their parents, the **peer group** (persons their own age) can have a powerful influence on attitude formation. In fact, peer-group influence can sometimes be stronger than the influence of parents, teachers, and other adult figures. With the passing of years, reference groups replace peer groups as sources of attitude formation in young adults. A **reference group** consists of several people who share a common interest and tend to influence one another's attitudes and behaviors. The reference group may act as a point of comparison and a source of information for the individual member. For example, a fraternity or sorority may serve as a reference group for a college student. In the business community a chapter of the American Society for Training and Development or of Sales and Marketing Executives International may provide a reference group for its members. As members of a reference group, we often observe other people in the group to establish our own norms. Reference groups often have a positive influence on the professional development of members.

Rewards and Punishment

Attitude formation is often related to rewards and punishment. People in authority generally encourage certain attitudes and discourage others. Naturally, individuals tend to develop attitudes that minimize punishments and maximize rewards. A child who is praised for sharing toys with playmates is likely to develop positive attitudes toward caring about other people's needs. Likewise, a child who receives a weekly allowance in exchange for performing basic house-keeping tasks learns an attitude of responsibility.

As an adult, you will discover that your employers will continue to attempt to shape your attitudes through rewards and punishment at work. Many organizations are rewarding employees who take steps to stay healthy. Dominion Resources, a Virginia-based utility, rewards healthy checkups for both employee and spouse. Some companies offer employees annual health checkups with precise targets for blood pressure, cholesterol levels, and other indicators of good health. Those who achieve the targets get a discount on their health premiums; those who fall short of the goal pay the standard rates.[13]

Role Model Identification

Most young people would like to have more influence, status, and popularity. These goals are often achieved through identification with an authority figure or a role model. A **role model** is that person you most admire or are likely to emulate. Preschoolers are most likely to identify their parents as their role models. At this early stage parents are seen as almost perfect, as real heroes. During early elementary school, children begin to realize that their parents have flaws, and they search for other heroes—perhaps a popular athlete, a rock star, or an actor. During later stages of development, new role models are adopted. As you might expect, role models can exert considerable influence—for better or for worse—on developing attitudes.

The media have a tremendous influence on people's selection of role models. By the time they graduate from high school, most young adults will be spending about four hours a day watching television.[14] Many of the programs they watch are dominated by crime, violence, and stereotyped or deviant characters and life situations. At the other extreme, other programs present positive superheroes with superhuman abilities. With this constant reinforcement from fictional negative and positive role models, young people sometimes have difficulty sorting out which behaviors and attitudes are acceptable in the real world.

Role models at work can have a major influence on employee attitude development. The new salesperson in the menswear department naturally wants help in adjusting to the job. So does the new dental hygienist and the recently hired auto mechanic. These people will pay special attention to the behavior of coworkers and managers. Therefore, if a worker leaves work early and no negative consequences follow, new employees may develop the attitude that staying until quitting time is not as important as they had thought. If a senior employee is rude to customers and suffers no negative consequences, new employees may imitate this attitude and behavior.

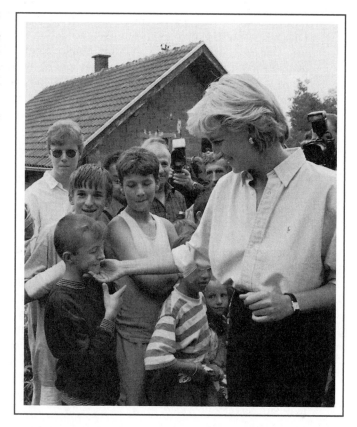

The late Princess Diana successfully used her highly publicized life to share her humanitarian actions and attitudes with people around the world. (AP/Wide World Photos)

In most organizations, supervisory and management personnel have the greatest impact on employee attitudes. The supervisors' attitudes toward safety, cost control, accuracy, dress and grooming, customer relations, and the like become the model for subordinates. Employees pay more attention to what their supervisors *do* than to what they *say*.

Cultural Influences

Our attitudes are influenced by the culture that surrounds us. **Culture** is the sum total of knowledge, beliefs, values, objects, and customs that we use to adapt to our environment. It includes tangible items, such as foods, clothing, and furniture, as well as intangible concepts, such as education and laws.[15]

People strive to define themselves in every culture. The definition varies from culture to culture. If you ask an adult living in Japan, "Who are you?"

that person is likely to respond, "I'm an employee of Sony Corporation." In Japanese culture, people are more likely to define themselves by the organization that provides them with lifetime employment.[16] In the United States, a person's job and employer are somewhat less likely to be the major source of identity. For instance, a young woman who spends hours each week trying to improve the environment may define herself as an environmentalist. That she works as a department supervisor at a local supermarket may be incidental to how she defines herself.

As noted in Chapter 1, many organizations today are striving to define their own culture in order to influence the attitudes of their workers. Generally speaking, organizational culture represents the "social glue" that binds members of an organization together.

Item: Federal Express Corp., America's first nationwide overnight delivery service, recognizes that a successful service company must do everything possible to keep employees satisfied and highly motivated. After all, it is the employees who make the guaranteed overnight deliveries possible. The Federal Express culture incorporates four basic beliefs that many companies would consider revolutionary: (1) Be as concerned about investments in people as about investments in machines. (2) Use technology to support the efforts of men and women on the front line. (3) Make recruitment and training as crucial for salespeople and housekeepers as for managers. (4) Link compensation to performance for employees at the entry level, not just for those at the top.[17] Does all this attention to employees make a difference? The customers say yes. Ninety-five percent of Federal Express customers say they are completely satisfied with services provided.

Item: When Amy Miller started her first ice cream store, her market niche was safe from competition. However, it was not long before national companies such as Baskin-Robbins and Steve's were setting up shop nearby. Miller decided the best way to differentiate her store from the others was to provide some entertainment along with each purchase. When you visit an Amy's Ice Creams store, you may see an employee break-dance on the freezer top or juggle serving spades. Employees might be wearing pajamas (because it's Sleep-Over Night) or masks (because it's Star Wars Night). Employees are likely to do anything to create fun, including contests that involve the customers. Miller communicates her cultural message to prospective employees the day they show up looking for a job. Instead of a formal application form, they are given a white paper bag along with instructions to do anything they want with it and bring it back in a week. Applicants use the bag to create masks, cartoons, and works of art. Today Amy's Ice Creams is a seven-store chain of shops in Austin and Houston, Texas, with annual sales of $2.2 million.[18]

Item: The United States Marines have developed an eleven-week basic training program that has a dramatic impact on those who complete it. Recruits emerge as self-disciplined Marines who are physically fit, courteous to their elders, and drug-free. Many have had to overcome deep differences of class and race and have learned to live and work as a team. They live in an organizational culture where a hint of racism can end a career and the use of illegal drugs is minimized by a "zero tolerance" policy.[19]

Thinking / Learning Starters

1. Identify at least one matter you feel strongly about. Do you know how you acquired this attitude? Is it shared by any particular group of people? Do you spend time with these people?

2. Think of an attitude that a friend or coworker holds but that you strongly disagree with. What factors do you believe contributed to the formation of this person's attitude?

ATTITUDES VALUED BY EMPLOYERS

Chapter 1 noted that the current labor market is characterized by churning dislocation and uncertainty. The large number of mergers, buyouts, business closings, and downsizing efforts has resulted in the loss of many jobs. Layoffs have come in every segment of the work force. Even managers and professionals have experienced job losses. As these victims of job turnover seek new employment opportunities, they are discovering that employers are looking for candidates who display several important attitudes. The following discussion suggests several of these attitudes.

Be Self-Motivated

Dawn Overstreet, a lecturer associated with the Americana Leadership College, once said, "People need to be leaders of themselves." In her presentations she emphasizes the importance of self-sufficiency—the ability to handle life despite difficulties.[20] People who are self-motivated are inclined to set their own goals and monitor their own progress toward those goals. They do not need a supervisor hovering around them making sure they are on task and accomplishing what they are supposed to be doing. Many find ways to administer their own rewards after they achieve their goals. Employers who are participating in

Raised in a welfare family, Michael Bradford was homeless, battled drug and alcohol addiction, and spent time in jail for burglary. Today, Bradford has turned his life around by changing his outlook on life and graduating from a welfare-to-work program sponsored by Marriott Corporation. (David Peterson)

downsizing often retain those employees who are capable of making their own decisions and following through.

Become a Self-Directed Learner

Organizations from hospitals to retail outlets are being forced to train and retrain employees quickly and more frequently. Established industries are discovering the advantages of adopting new technology, and new industries are developing new processes that offer them a competitive edge in the marketplace. Given this enormous demand for the work force to learn new things faster, people with curiosity and a desire to keep up-to-date will be in great demand.

But most organizations depend on each individual becoming a **self-directed learner.** Self-directed learners take responsibility for their own learning; they diagnose what it is they need to learn, develop objectives, discover learning experiences, find resources, and evaluate learning outcomes.[21] They seek out opportunities to enhance their skills and knowledge through on-the-job training as well as seminars and workshops offered outside the workplace. They read professional journals and monitor news media for research and technology advances that might affect their jobs in the future. Ideally, employees should prepare a self-directed learning plan that targets where they would like their professional life to lead them and indicates how they will get there.

Most people are eager to learn new jobs or new ways of doing their old jobs, but many do not know *how* to learn. Do you learn best by reading about a new process, by listening to someone describe it, by watching someone perform the new procedure, or by doing it yourself with an expert's guidance? Although there is no right or wrong learning style, it is important to understand the way you learn. Employees who know how to approach and master any new situation are more cost-effective to their employers because the time and other resources spent on their training can be reduced.[22] Employees who have the desire and ability to learn fast will have the cutting edge when it comes time to get their dream job or retain their position during downsizing.

Be a Team Player

In sports, the person who is a "team player" receives a great deal of praise and recognition. A team player is someone who is willing to step out of the spotlight, give up a little personal glory, and help the team achieve a victory. Team players are no less important in organizations. Employers are increasingly organizing employees into teams (health teams, sales teams, product development teams) that build products, solve problems, and make decisions. Saturn's automobile manufacturing plant is made up of a network of highly effective teams. Each team functions as a small-business unit responsible for its own product, budget, and accounting, and for doing business with the other teams within the organization. Management screens potential employees, but each team has the final say on whether a person will be hired. An employee who is not an effective team member can be thrown off the team.[23]

Be Concerned About Your Health and Wellness

The ever-growing cost of health care is one of the most serious problems facing companies today. Many organizations are promoting wellness programs for all employees as a way to keep costs in line. These programs include tips on healthy eating, physical-fitness exercises, stress management practices, and other forms of assistance that contribute to a healthy lifestyle. Employees who actively participate in these programs frequently take fewer sick days, file fewer medical claims, and bring a higher level of energy to work. Some companies even give cash awards to employees who lose weight, quit smoking, or lower their cholesterol levels. Employees who pay a great deal of attention to their health needs can be a real asset.

Value Coworker Diversity

To value diversity in the work setting means to make full use of the ideas, talents, experiences, and perspectives of all employees at all levels within the organization. People who differ from each other often add richness to the organization. An old adage states: If we both think alike, one of us is not necessary.

Development and utilization of a talented, diverse work force can be the key to success in a period of fierce global competition. Women and people of color make up a large majority of the new multicultural, global work force. Many people, however, carry prejudiced attitudes against those who differ from them. They tend to "prejudge" others' value based on the color of their skin, gender, age, religious preference, lifestyle, political affiliation, or economic status. Although deeply held prejudices that have developed over a long time are difficult to change, employers are demanding these changes. Wisconsin Power and Light is typical of many organizations that have made a strong commitment to valuing diversity. One of the company's expectations concerning diversity says, "Employees at all organizational levels must be intolerant of behaviors in the workplace that are inconsistent with the objectives of equal opportunity and the building of a diverse workforce."[24] Chapter 7 contains specific guidance on how to develop positive attitudes toward joining a diverse work force.

"I'm giving you a 'marginal' on your attitude toward constructive criticism." (Kaser, Phi Delta Kappan. *Reprinted by permission.*)

HOW TO CHANGE ATTITUDES

If you begin to notice that successful people will not associate with you, that you have been overlooked for a promotion you thought you should have had, or that you go home from work depressed and a little angry at the world, you can almost always be sure you need an attitude adjustment. Unfortunately, people do not easily adopt new attitudes or discard old ones. It is difficult to break the attachment to emotionally laden beliefs. Yet attitudes *can* be changed. There may be times when you absolutely hate a job, but you can still develop a positive attitude toward it as a steppingstone to another job you actually do want. There will be times as well when you will need to help colleagues change their attitudes so that you can work with them more effectively. And, of course, when events, such as a layoff, are beyond your control, you must strive to maintain a positive attitude. It is often said that life is 10 percent what happens to you and 90 percent how you react to it. Knowing how to change attitudes in yourself and others can be essential to effective human relations—and your success—in an organization.

Changing Your Own Attitude

You are constantly placed in new situations with people from different backgrounds and cultures. Each time you go to a new school, take a new job, get a promotion, or move to a different neighborhood, you may need to alter your attitudes to cope effectively with the change. In all these situations, the events are out of your control. But you can control your attitude toward these events. If you allow yourself to dwell on the negative aspects of change, you can expect to exhibit negative, self-destructive behaviors. When you make an effort to focus on the positive, you will find your world a much more pleasant place in which to live. If you are happy, other people enjoy working with you.

Being able to control your attitudes is a powerful human relations skill that usually involves certain basic changes:

1. *Become an optimist.* Optimistic thoughts give rise to good moods that tend to serve as a foundation for developing positive attitudes and effective human relationships. When you are an optimist, your coworkers, managers, and—perhaps most important—your customers feel your energy and vitality and tend to mirror your behavior. An optimistic view of life events can make life far less stressful.

In a work setting, it does not take long to identify people with an optimistic outlook. Optimists are more likely to bounce back after a demotion, layoff, or some other disappointment. According to Martin Seligman, professor of psychology at the University of Pennsylvania and author of *Learned Optimism,* optimists are more likely to view problems as merely temporary setbacks on

Total Person Insight

"You'll never entirely get rid of the negative voices inside you—but that doesn't mean you have to listen to them. Get into the habit of challenging negative ideas."

PAMELA R. JOHNSON AND CLAUDIA RAWLINS

Authors, "Daydreams and Dialogues: Key to Motivation"

their road to achieving their goals. They focus on their potential success rather than on their failures.[25]

Pessimists, in contrast, tend to believe bad events will last a long time, will undermine everything they do, and are their own fault. A pessimistic pattern of thinking can have unfortunate consequences. Pessimists give up more easily when faced with a challenge, are less likely to take personal control of their life, and are more likely to take personal blame for their misfortune.[26] Often pessimism leads to **cynicism,** which is a mistrusting attitude regarding the motives of people. When you are cynical, you are constantly on guard against the "misbehavior" of others.[27] If you begin to think that everyone is screwing up, acting inconsiderately, or otherwise behaving inappropriately, cynicism has taken control of your thought process, and it is time to change.

Fortunately, pessimism and optimism are both learned attitudes, so they can be changed. If you feel the need to become a more optimistic person, you can spend more time visualizing yourself succeeding, a process that is discussed in Chapter 3. Monitor your self-talk, and discover whether or not you are focusing on the negative aspects of the problems and disappointments in your life or are looking at them as learning experiences that will eventually lead you toward your personal and professional goals. Try to avoid having too much contact with pessimists, and refuse to be drawn into a group of negative thinkers who see only problems, not solutions. Surround yourself with other optimists because attitudes can be contagious.

2. *Think for yourself.* Determine whether the attitudes that seem to get you in trouble are your own or the result of socialization. If you have been socialized into holding negative attitudes, you need to re-examine them. Authority figures, family ties, and peer pressure are strong influences. But you are an intelligent adult now, and you can control your own thoughts and feelings about people, ideas, and events, rather than being controlled by others' attitudes.

Buckminster Fuller, the respected architect and inventor, stated that learning to think for himself was the turning point in his life. He discovered at age 32 that he needed to become a more independent thinker and stop relying on others to influence every aspect of his life. Once he made the decision to think for himself, he became highly motivated to discover what he described as the "operating principles" of his world.[28]

3. *Keep an open mind.* We often make decisions and then refuse to consider any other point of view that might lead us to question our beliefs. Many times our attitudes persist even in the presence of overwhelming evidence to the contrary. If you have been raised in a family or community that supports racist views, it may seem foreign to you when your colleagues at work openly accept and enjoy healthy relationships with people whose skin color is different from your own. Pay attention. Expose yourself to new information and experiences beyond what you have been socialized to believe. Maybe your coworkers have discovered qualities of these individuals that you have overlooked because you could not see beyond the color of their skin.

We live in a world where generalizations are commonplace: Men are too competitive. Women are too emotional. People on welfare are lazy. You cannot trust government officials. These generalizations need to be assessed with an open mind if you want to advance in your chosen career. James Allen, the famous Harvard psychologist, discovered that you can change many of the outer aspects of your life by changing the inner attitudes of your mind. When you face things you cannot change, take a few moments to reflect on the Serenity Prayer.

FIGURE 5.2

Serenity Prayer

SERENITY PRAYER

Grant me the serenity to
accept the things I cannot change,
the courage to change the things I can,
and the wisdom to know the difference.

Source: "Serenity Prayer" by Dr. Reinhold Niebuhr.

Helping Others Change Their Attitudes

It is true that you are really in control of only your own attitudes. Although you can bend and flex and alter these as often as you find it beneficial, sometimes you need to stand firm and maintain your position. At that point, you may want to help other people change their attitudes. Unfortunately, you cannot hand your colleagues "a ready-made box of attitudes." But often you can help produce an atmosphere in which they will want to change their thinking.

Some people attempt to beg, plead, intimidate, or even threaten others into adopting new attitudes. This process is similar to attempting to push a piece of yarn across the top of a table. When you *push* the yarn in the direction you want it to go, it gets all bent out of shape. When you gently *pull* the yarn with your fingertips, it follows you wherever you want it to go. Two powerful techniques can help you pull people in the direction you want them to go, often without their even realizing that you are attempting to change their attitudes:

1. Change the *conditions* that precede the behavior.
2. Change the *consequences* that follow the behavior.

Change the Conditions   If you want people to change their attitudes, identify the behaviors that represent the poor attitudes and alter the conditions that precede the behavior. Consider the following situation.

A new employee in a retail store is having a problem adjusting to her job. From the first day, she has found the job frustrating. Because the store is understaffed and the manager needed her on the sales floor as soon as possible, he rushed through her job training procedures without taking time to answer her questions. Now she finds there are many customers' questions she cannot answer, and she has trouble operating the computerized cash register. The manager does not seem to care whether she succeeds or fails; he apparently just wanted the job filled. She wants to quit, and her negative attitudes are affecting her job performance and the way she handles her customers.

The manager could easily have prevented this employee's negative attitudes by changing the conditions surrounding her training. He could have been careful to answer all her questions *before* she was placed on the sales floor. Perhaps he could have asked an experienced salesperson to stay with her as she helped her first few customers. Above all, he could have displayed a caring attitude toward her and her success.

Change the Consequences   Another way to help other people change their attitudes is to alter what happens *after* they exhibit the behavior and attitude you are attempting to change. A simple rule applies: When an experience is followed by positive consequences, the person is likely to repeat the behavior. When an experience is followed by negative consequences, the person will soon learn to stop the behavior. For example, if you are a supervisor, and several of your employees are consistently late for work, you might provide some form of negative consequence each time they are tardy, such as a verbal reprimand or reduced pay. Keep in mind, however, that we tend to focus attention on the people who exhibit disruptive attitudes and to ignore the employees exhibiting the attitudes we want to encourage. Saying: "Thank you for being here on time. I really appreciate your commitment" can be an extremely effective reward for those who arrive at work on time. Attitudes rewarded will be repeated.

One note of caution: It is important to view consequences through the eyes of the person you are trying to influence. What you see as a negative consequence—a one-week leave of absence without pay—might be a positive consequence to someone else—an extra week's vacation. Robert Mager, a nationally known authority in the field of training and development, says:

> It doesn't matter what I might seek out or avoid: It is what is positive or aversive to the person whose behavior I am trying to influence that counts. And this, incidentally, is one reason we don't succeed more often than we do in the area of human interaction. We try to influence others by providing consequences that are positive to us but not to them.[29]

Thinking / Learning Starters

1. Are you holding a grudge against someone? Describe the situation. What are the benefits of holding on to this attitude? What are the benefits of letting go of it and moving on to a more productive atmosphere?

2. Think of a situation that is upsetting to you at work or home. How can you alter the situation to help change the other person's opinions? If it is absolutely impossible to change the situation, what will result if you change your attitude? Which direction is the best solution to the problem?

ORGANIZATIONS' EFFORTS TOWARD IMPROVING EMPLOYEES' ATTITUDES

Many companies are realizing that an employee's attitude and performance cannot be separated. When employees have negative attitudes about their work, their job performance and productivity suffer. When they have positive

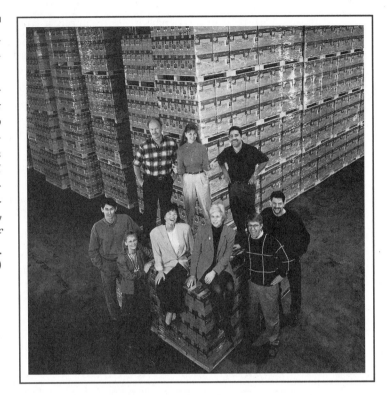

Employers like Hewlett Packard are seeking employees who are willing to be part of self-managed teams that create solutions to problems within the organization. This team of HP workers created a better system of moving boxes while management vigorously refused to tell any of them what to do. (Andy Freeberg)

attitudes, job performance and productivity are likely to improve. For generations, employers and labor unions focused on salaries and fringe benefits as the rewards that would keep workers producing at top efficiency. But gradually, both labor and management discovered that money was not always the primary ingredient of a satisfying job.

People who are asked what they most want from their job typically cite mutual respect among coworkers, interesting work, recognition for work well done, the chance to develop skills, and so forth. If employers want to maintain or improve the positive attitudes of their workers, and thereby maintain or improve productivity, they need to provide the benefits workers consider important. Of course, workers expect the pay to be competitive, but they want so much more. As author and management consultant Peter Drucker says, "To make a living is not enough. Work also has to make a life."[30] Organizations are finding creative ways to influence worker attitudes.

Item: Greyhound Lines Inc., the Chicago-based bus company, developed a training program that put new employees in the role of customers and required them to endure realistic simulations of actual customer service failures. Trainees waited in long lines, were treated rudely and indifferently, and were given rides in dirty, smelly buses. One month after "reality training" began, Greyhound realized a 50 percent decrease in customer complaints. Employees who completed this training exhibited a better attitude toward customers than did employees who had not received the training.[31]

Item: Starbucks Coffee Company has taken the position that the quality of its work force provides the only sustainable competitive advantage. The business is built on making every employee feel respected. Full- and part-time workers receive a generous and comprehensive employee benefits package. Starbucks's company culture has a positive influence on employees' attitudes toward customer service, product quality, and honesty. Orin Smith, chief financial officer at Starbucks, says, "The biggest defense against pilferage is a strong culture."[32]

Item: Intracorp, a Philadelphia-based managed care services firm, has found a way to reduce clients' worker compensation claims and aid workers' recovery after a work-related injury:

1. Explain workers' compensation policies before on-the-job mishaps occur.
2. Demonstrate genuine concern after an injury.
3. Refer the injured worker to doctors who treat quickly and aggressively.

When Intracorp's clients took these steps, workers recovered and returned to work more quickly. They discovered that workers who were satisfied with their treatment were less likely to see a lawyer.[33]

What do these organizations have in common? Each has given thought to the attitudes that are important for a healthy work environment and has taken steps to shape these attitudes. Many organizations are attempting to improve employee attitudes and productivity by enhancing the quality of their employees' work life. This might involve developing training programs that employees want, joint review of monthly profit and loss statements, enhanced fringe benefit programs, and collaborative efforts to improve safety. It might also include building day-care centers, sponsoring drug treatment programs for employees, or paying for employee memberships at local health clubs.

A FINAL WORD

Viktor Frankl, a survivor of the Auschwitz concentration camp and author of *Man's Search for Meaning,* said, "The last of the freedoms is to choose one's attitude in any given set of circumstances." We have noted throughout this chapter that attitudes have a major impact on our day-to-day lives. Given the importance of attitudes, you should regularly re-examine yours and choose the ones that will take you where you want to go in life. Changing an attitude that is detrimental to your personal or professional life can be a challenge, but the process can also be a critical step toward your continued growth and success. The happiest people don't necessarily *have* the best of everything; they just *make* the best of everything. It's all in their attitude.

Summary

An attitude is any strong belief toward people and situations. It is a state of mind supported by feelings. People possess hundreds of attitudes about work, family life, friends, coworkers, and the like.

Attitudes represent a powerful force in every organization. If the persons employed by a service firm display a caring attitude toward customers, the business will likely enjoy a high degree of customer loyalty and repeat business. If the employees of a manufacturing firm display a serious attitude toward safety rules and regulations, fewer accidents will likely occur.

People acquire attitudes through early childhood socialization, peer and reference groups, rewards and punishment, role model identification, and cultural influences.

Employers hire and attempt to retain employees who are self-motivated, self-directed learners; are willing to be team players; are concerned about health and wellness; and value coworker diversity.

You can choose to change your attitude by becoming an optimist; thinking for yourself without undue pressure from your peers, family, and others; and keeping an open mind. You can help others change their attitudes by altering the consequences and conditions that surround the situation. Positive consequences and conditions produce positive attitudes. Organizations are taking steps to improve employee attitudes by enhancing the quality of their work life.

Career Corner

Q. I am a 24-year-old recent college graduate. Six months ago I accepted a job as assistant to the office manager of a small manufacturing plant. She is in her late 50s and has been with the company since she graduated from high school. She has made it perfectly clear that she never had the opportunity to go to college. Her attitudes about how work is to be done in our office seem so old-fashioned. I have so many creative ideas to improve our efficiency, but she seems to believe I am too young to know anything. Every time she says, "That's the way it has always been done; don't change it," my skin crawls and I feel very bitter for the rest of the day. What can I do to change her attitude toward my potential?

A. Begin by changing your attitude toward her traditional way of performing routine tasks in the office. Remember, she has had to adjust to many changes over the years to keep her organization running smoothly. Respect her past successes, and assure her that you are there to help with the changing demands of the future.

Second, begin to alter the conditions in the office so that they are conducive to your creative ideas. Bring your professional journals to work, and invite her to read various articles discussing innovative ideas that have been successfully implemented in other offices. Invite her to attend a seminar with you or to enroll in a class on some new software package that makes tedious office tasks easier. If she accepts a new idea, praise her intelligence and openness. When she receives positive feedback from you and others in the organization, she will likely repeat the behavior and seek out additional ways to improve the efficiency of the office. Changing attitudes is not easy, so be patient.

Key Terms

attitude
socialization
peer group
reference group
role model

culture
self-directed learner
cynicism

Review Questions

1. It has been said that "attitudes represent a powerful force in any organization." What examples can you give to support this statement?
2. List five ways in which we form our attitudes.
3. Describe how rewards and punishment can shape the attitudes of employees in an organization. Give at least one example of each.
4. How can selecting a positive role model within an organization help an individual reach his or her goals?
5. Describe the attitudes employers are looking for in their employees.
6. Explain how consequences can influence the shaping of attitudes in an organization.
7. Robert Mager says that the conditions that surround a subject can play an important role in shaping attitudes. Provide at least one example to support Mager's statement.
8. Identify the difference between a person with an optimistic attitude and one with a pessimistic viewpoint. Which one are you? Explain.
9. What are organizations doing to help improve the attitudes of their workers? Why do they bother to keep their workers happy?

10. Explain in your own words the meaning of Waitley's Total Person Insight on page 114.

Application Exercises

1. Describe your attitudes concerning
   a. a teamwork environment
   b. health and wellness
   c. life and work
   d. learning new skills
   How do these attitudes affect you on a daily basis? Do you feel you have a positive attitude in most situations? Can you think of someone you have frequent contact with who displays negative attitudes toward these items? Do you find ways to avoid spending time with this person?

2. Identify an attitude held by a friend, coworker, or spouse that you would like to see changed. Do any conditions that precede this person's behavior fall under your control? If so, how could you change those conditions so the person might change his or her attitude? What positive consequences might you offer when the person behaves the way you want? What negative consequences might you impose when the person participates in the behavior you are attempting to stop?

3. For a period of one week, keep a diary or log of positive and negative events. Positive events might include the successful completion of a project, a compliment from a coworker, or just finding time for some leisure activities. Negative events might include forgetting an appointment, criticism from your boss, or simply looking in the mirror and seeing something you don't like. An unpleasant news story might also qualify as a negative event. At the end of one week, review your entries and determine what type of pattern exists. Also, reflect on the impact of these events. Did you quickly bounce back from the negative events, or did you dwell on them all week? Did the positive events enhance your optimism? Consider each negative event in relation to the Serenity Prayer (Figure 5.2). What did you discover?

Internet Exercise

The qualities that make up the "right attitude" vary somewhat from one employment setting to another. To learn more about what attitudes employers view as important, visit the Internet and discover what information is available on this important topic. Using your search engine, type in "attitude," and then examine the resources (such as books, articles, and training programs) available on this topic. Pay special attention to information on how attitudes are formed, attitudes valued by employers, and efforts organizations are making to improve attitudes. Prepare a brief written report that summarizes your findings.

Self-Assessment Exercise

For each of the following statements, circle the number from 1 to 5 that best represents your response: (1) strongly disagree (never do this); (2) disagree (rarely do this); (3) moderately agree (sometimes do this); (4) agree (frequently do this); (5) strongly agree (almost always do this).

a. When forming attitudes about important matters, I maintain an open mind, listen to the views of others, but think for myself.   1   2   3   4   5

b. I make every effort to maintain a positive mental attitude toward other people and the events in my life.   1   2   3   4   5

c. I seek feedback and clarification on the influence of my attitudes and behaviors on others.   1   2   3   4   5

d. I am willing to change my attitudes and behaviors in response to constructive feedback from others.   1   2   3   4   5

Select an appropriate attitude or skill you would like to improve. Write your goal in the space provided.

GOAL: _____

_____

_____

Case Problem

Office Politics

Typically, a workplace operates under two sets of rules: a formal system, which includes the publicly acknowledged reporting structure, rules, and regulations; and a political system, which is the dynamic informal network of friends and influence. Most people have an attitude of resentment about having to play office politics in order to get ahead. They want to be judged by their performance, skills, and knowledge as they strive to succeed in their chosen careers. However, when you reach a certain level, everyone is smart, works hard, and is competent. Then the standard may be "who you know, not what you know."

Office politics is part of being an effective team player in most organizations. It is nothing more than getting to know people on an informal basis and learning their strengths and weaknesses. It involves getting to know who can get things done, whose opinion is respected, who gets ignored and why. The better you understand the values and attitudes underlying others' behaviors, the better you will be able to adjust your behavior accordingly. At the same time, the informal network allows you to share your talents and abilities that might not be discovered merely by looking at the work you produce. The goal of the team is not to work within your personal comfort zone but to get things done quickly while taking into account members' emotions and personalities so the team can produce quality decisions. This often requires you to play the political game. There are a few guidelines for playing this game effectively:

1. *Don't try to please everyone.* One aspiring young executive was bemoaning the fact that someone in the organization did not like her. A respected colleague commented, "Who do you think you are that *everyone* is going to like you!"

2. *Build a solid base of trusted allies throughout the organization.* These are people who will tell you what is going on and stand up for you.

3. *Maintain your visibility outside the company.* Speak at community events, volunteer your help to local charities, or write an article for your professional journal or local newspaper. You will be bringing credit to yourself and your company, and fellow workers will notice.

4. *Confront anyone who attempts to stab you in the back.* If you ignore one attempt, you will increase your vulnerability to other attempts. Intercept any false rumors by finding the person responsible for the grapevine messages and explaining your side of the story. If you are left out of important meetings or decisions, explain to those in charge how valuable your input might be to them.

5. *If you are not a "politician," consider working for a small business.* It will be easier for you to get to know individuals and gain their trust when there are only a few players.

Questions

1. What is your attitude toward playing office politics? Is this attitude based on past experience or stories you have heard from others? Explain.

2. What can you do to maintain a positive attitude toward office politics? What would be the consequences of your positive attitude?

3. Is there any way to assess a company's political environment before you go to work for the company? What kinds of mistakes might you avoid if you were aware of this information?

Chapter 6

Developing

a Professional

Presence

Chapter Preview

After studying this chapter, you will be able to

1. Explain the importance of professional presence.
2. Discuss the factors that contribute to a favorable first impression.
3. Distinguish between assumptions and facts.
4. Define *image* and describe the factors that form the image you project to others.
5. List and discuss factors that influence your choice of clothing for work.
6. Understand how manners contribute to improved interpersonal relations in the workplace.

H ERTZ CORPORATION, the U.S. Air Force, Hyatt Hotels Corporation, the City of Dallas, and the Neiman-Marcus Group, Inc., have one thing in common: All have purchased the services of Feedback Plus, an agency that dispatches professional shoppers who pose as consumers. These "mystery" shoppers visit the client's business, purchase products or services, and report back to the client on the quality of service they receive. The City of Dallas hired Feedback Plus to see how car-pound employees treat citizens picking up their cars. The Air Force uses professional shoppers to assess customer service at on-base supply stores. Banks, hospitals, and public utilities are also hiring mystery shoppers. Vickie Henry, chief executive of Feedback Plus, notes that many similar firms compete for clients' business, and service really does differentiate one firm from another.[1] Sears, Roebuck and Company officials say Sears's mystery shopper program has helped the company achieve a new level of service and profitability. The amount that Sears and other companies spend on mystery shopper programs is estimated at $100 million a year.[2] ■

As organizations experience increased competition for clients, patients, and customers, awareness of the importance of public contact increases. They are giving new attention to the old adage "First impressions are lasting impressions." Research indicates that initial impressions do indeed tend to linger. Therefore, a positive first impression can be thought of as the first step in building a long-term relationship.

Of course, it is not just *first* contacts with clients, patients, customers, and others that are important. Positive impressions should be the objective of *every* contact. A major goal of this chapter is to discuss the important factors that help us make positive impressions. Another important goal is to examine the factors that shape the image we project to others.

MAKING A GOOD IMPRESSION

There are many personal and professional benefits to be gained from a study of the concepts in this chapter. You will acquire new insights regarding ways to communicate positive impressions during job interviews, business contacts, and social contacts made away from work. You will also learn how to shape an image that will help you achieve your fullest potential in the career of your choice. Most important, the material in this chapter will very likely increase your self-awareness. As we noted in Chapter 1, self-awareness is an important first step toward building more effective relationships with others.

This is not a chapter about ways to make positive impressions with superficial behavior and quick-fix techniques. We do not discuss the "power look" or the "power lunch." The material in this chapter will not help you become a more entertaining conversationalist or win new customers by pretending to be interested in their hobbies or families. Stephen Covey, author of *The 7 Habits of Highly Effective People,* says that the ability to build effective, long-term relationships is based on character strength, not quick-fix techniques. He notes that outward attitude and behavior changes do very little good in the long run *unless* they are based on solid principles governing human effectiveness. These principles include service (making a contribution), integrity and honesty (which serve as a foundation of trust), human dignity (every person has worth), and fairness.[3]

Few people can fake a sincere greeting or a caring attitude. If you really do not care about the customer's problem, the customer will probably sense your indifference. Your true feelings will be difficult to hide. Ralph Waldo Emerson was right on target when he said, "What you are shouts so loudly in my ears I cannot hear what you say."

Professional Presence

We are indebted to Susan Bixler, president of Professional Image, Inc. and author of *Professional Presence,* for giving us a better understanding of what it means to possess professional presence. **Professional presence** is a dynamic blend of poise, self-confidence, control, and style that empowers us to be able to command respect in any situation.[4] Once acquired, it permits us to be perceived as self-assured and thoroughly competent. We project a confidence that others can quickly perceive the first time they meet us.

Bixler points out that in most cases, the credentials we present during a job interview or when we are being considered for a promotion are not very different from those of other persons being considered. It is our professional presence that permits us to rise above the crowd. Debra Benton, a career consultant, says, "Any boss with a choice of two people with equal qualifications will choose the one with style as well as substance."[5] Learning to create a professional presence is one of the most valuable skills we can acquire.

The Primacy Effect

The development of professional presence begins with a full appreciation of the power of first impressions. The tendency to form impressions quickly at the time of an initial meeting illustrates what social psychologists call a **primacy effect** in the way people perceive one another. The general principle is that first impressions establish the mental framework within which a person is viewed, and information acquired later is often ignored or reinterpreted to coincide with this framework.[6]

During his first term as president, Bill Clinton often appeared in brief jogging shorts and garish print shirts; his suits were loose fitting and in need of tailoring; and his military salute was viewed as halfhearted by many observers.

Toby Fischer-Mirkin, fashion consultant and author of *Dress Code,* said the president did not communicate a very commanding image.[7] Early in his first term, Clinton appeared vulnerable to many people, and this image had a negative influence on his popularity. Later in his first term, he communicated a more "presidential" image and went on to be re-elected to a second term. He discovered, or perhaps rediscovered, the power of the primacy effect.

The First Few Seconds

When two people meet, their potential for building a relationship can be affected by many factors. Within a few moments, one person or the other may feel threatened, offended, or bored. Roger Ailes, communication adviser to three presidents and consultant to numerous Fortune 500 executives, says people begin forming an opinion of us in a matter of seconds. He believes that most people assess the other person very quickly and then settle on a general perception of that individual. Ailes says it is very difficult for us to reverse that first impression.[8] The following examples support his view of first impressions.

Dee Soder, a psychologist who helps unemployed senior executives find work, likes to give clients the fish test. If a person fails to comment on the wahoo, the large blue fish hanging on the wall outside her office, Soder sees a problem. When entering the office of a prospective boss, she says, you should pick out something unusual and comment on it. It creates a good first impression. (Nicole Bengiveno/Matrix)

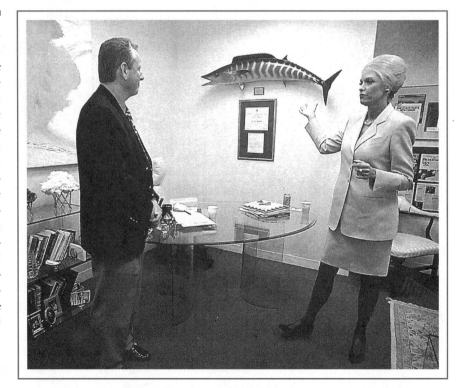

Thinking / Learning Starter

To test the practical application of Roger Ailes's guideline in a real-life setting, examine it in the context of your past experiences. Review the following questions and then answer each with yes or no.

1. Have you ever entered a restaurant, hotel, or office and experienced an immediate feeling of being welcome after your first contact with an employee?

2. Have you ever met someone who immediately communicated to you the impression that he or she could be trusted and was interested in your welfare?

3. Have you ever placed a telephone call and known instinctively within seconds that the person did not welcome your call?

Item: Paula rushed into a restaurant for a quick lunch—she had to get back to her office for a 1:30 P.M. appointment. At the entrance of the main dining area was a sign reading "Please Wait to Be Seated." A few feet away, the hostess was discussing a popular movie with one of the waitresses. The hostess made eye contact with Paula but continued to visit with the waitress.

Item: When Sandy and Mike entered the showroom of a Mercedes-Benz dealer, they were approached by a salesperson wearing sport slacks (khaki color), a blue knit pullover shirt (short sleeve), and casual gum-soled shoes. The salesperson smiled and said, "Are you looking or buying?"

Total Person Insight

"If people aren't quickly attracted to you or don't like what they see and hear in those first two to four minutes, chances are they won't pay attention to all those words you believe are demonstrating your knowledge and authority. They will find your client guilty, seek another doctor, buy another product, vote for your opponent or hire someone else."

JANET G. ELSEA

President, Communication Skills, Inc.

In each of these examples, a negative first impression was created in a matter of seconds. The anxiety level of the restaurant customer increased because she was forced to wait while two employees talked about a personal matter. And the potential customers made judgments about the automobile salesperson based solely on his appearance. Unfortunately, these employees were probably not fully aware of the impression they communicated to customers.

Assumptions Versus Facts The impression you form of another person during the initial contact is made up of both assumptions and facts. Most people tend to rely more heavily on **assumptions** during the initial meeting. If a job applicant sits slumped in the chair, head bowed and shoulders slack, you might assume the person is not interested in the position. If the postal clerk fails to make eye contact during the transaction and does not express appreciation for your purchase, you may assume this person treats everyone with indifference. Needless to say, the impression you form of another person during the initial contact can be misleading. The briefer the encounter with a new acquaintance, the greater the chance that misinformation will enter into your perception of the other person. The authors of a popular book on first impressions state that "Depending on assumptions is a one-way ticket to big surprises and perhaps disappointments."[9]

Cultural Influence

Cultural influences, often formed during the early years of our life, lead us to have impressions of some people even before we meet them. People often develop stereotypes of entire groups. Although differences between cultures are often subtle, they can lead to uncomfortable situations. We need to realize that the Korean shopkeeper is being polite, not hostile, when he puts change on the counter and not in your hand. Many Asian students do not speak up in class out of respect for the teacher, not boredom.[10]

Many American companies are attempting to create a new kind of workplace where cultural and ethnic differences are treated as assets, not annoyances. Yet some employees feel pressure to conform to dress and grooming standards that their employer considers "mainstream." When LaToya Rivers, a black college student, applied for a position at the Boston Harbor Hotel, she asked whether braids were allowed. She was told, "Yes, as long as they are neat and professional in appearance." Once hired, the policy seemed to change. A manager told her to restyle her braided hair or leave.[11]

Norine Dresser, author of *Multiculture Manners—New Rules of Etiquette for a Changing Society,* notes that it is becoming more difficult for organizations to develop policies that do not offend one ethnic group or another. She argues that it is the collective duty of the mainstream to learn the customs and practices of established minority groups as well as the ways of the latest arrivals from other countries.[12]

THE IMAGE YOU PROJECT

Image is a term used to describe how other people feel about you. In every business or social setting, your behaviors communicate a mental picture that others observe and remember. This picture determines how they react to you. Your image depends on more than exterior qualities such as dress and grooming. In the words of James Gray, author of *The Winning Image,* "Image is more than just a veneer."[13] He observes,

> Image is a tool for communicating and for revealing your inherent qualities, your competence, abilities and leadership. It is a reflection of qualities that others associate with you, a reflection that bears long-lasting influence in your bid for success. Image is not a tool for manipulation. Nor is it a false front. It cannot substitute for substance.[14]

In many respects, the image you project at work is very much like a picture puzzle, as illustrated in Figure 6.1. It is formed by a variety of factors, including manners, self-confidence, voice quality, versatility, integrity (see Chapter 4), entrance and carriage, facial expression, surface language, competence,

FIGURE 6.1
_____

**Major Factors That
Form Your Image**

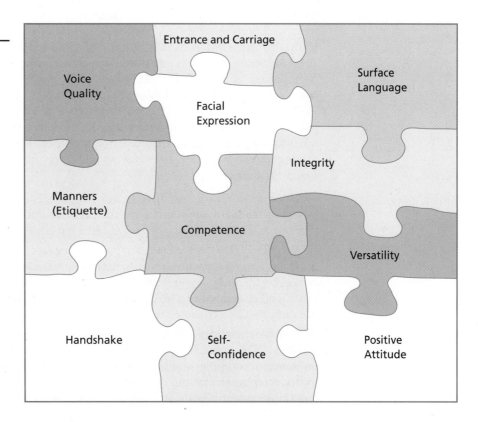

positive attitude, and handshake. Each of these image-shaping components is under your control.

A growing number of organizations have discovered a direct link between profitability and the image projected by employees. Financial institutions, public utilities, airlines, retail stores, restaurants, hospitals, and manufacturers face the problem of not only gaining but also retaining the patronage of clients and customers. When the Oldsmobile division of General Motors Corp. decided to reshape the image projected by dealers, it developed a $25 million training program. Dealers and employees learned how to improve service to customers and to sell the Aurora, a more luxurious car than the models that Olds dealers were used to selling.[15]

Surface Language

As noted earlier, we base opinions about other people on both facts and assumptions. Unfortunately, assumptions often carry a great deal of weight. Many of the assumptions you develop regarding other people are based on **surface language,** a pattern of immediate impressions conveyed by appearance. The clothing you wear, your hairstyle, the fragrances you use, and the jewelry you display all combine to make a statement about you to others.

According to many writers familiar with image formation, clothing is particularly important. John Molloy, author of *Dress for Success* and *The Woman's Dress for Success Book,* was one of the first to acknowledge publicly the link between image and wardrobe. According to his research, what you wear influences your credibility and likability.[16]

Although a more relaxed dress code has evolved in recent years, people judge your appearance long before they judge your talents. It would be a mistake not to take your career wardrobe seriously. Bixler suggests that those making career wardrobe decisions should keep in mind that three things haven't changed:[17]

1. *If you want the job, you have to look the part.* Establish personal dress and grooming standards appropriate for the organization where you wish to work. Before you apply for a job, try to find out what the workers there are wearing. If in doubt, dress conservatively.

2. *If you want the promotion, you have to look promotable.* A good rule to follow is to dress for the job you want, not the job you have. If you are currently an office worker and want to become an office manager, identify the successful office managers and emulate their manner of dress.

3. *If you want respect, you have to dress as well as or better than your industry standards.* One would expect to find conservative dress standards in banking, insurance, accounting, and law, and more casual dress standards in advertising, sports entertainment, and agriculture. Spend time researching the dress and grooming standards in the industry in which you hope to find a job.

Thinking / Learning Starter

Do you recall a teacher, coworker, or supervisor whose surface language impressed you—either positively or negatively? What specific elements (such as dress or hairstyle) were evident in this person's surface language? What type of image do you think he or she was trying to project?

Selecting Your Career Apparel

Over 23 million American workers wear a uniform especially designed for a particular job. The judges on the U.S. Supreme Court and the technicians at the local Midas Muffler and Brake shop have one thing in common—both groups wear a special uniform to work. Today more and more people are donning uniforms to go to work. Companies that have initiated extensive career apparel programs rely on uniforms to project an image of consistent quality, good service, and uniqueness. Uniforms enhance company credibility, which in turn increases customer confidence in the firm.[18] Wearing a uniform can also have a positive effect on employees. Wearing the same uniform seems to create a sort of bond among coworkers. Thus, a uniform can make at least a small contribution to building company spirit at your local McDonald's restaurant or Holiday Inn hotel.

Wells Fargo Bank adopted a custom line of clothing for employees working at banking centers located in Safeway and other supermarkets. The goal was to create a professional look that would define the bank's identity and build customers' confidence in the financial services that Wells Fargo offered. The bank also wanted to make sure that people distinguished its employees from supermarket workers.[19]

The uniforms worn by United Parcel Service employees, United Airlines reservation clerks, and the employees at your local restaurant might be classified as special-design **career apparel.** In addition to special-design uniforms, there is another type of career apparel, somewhat less predictable, worn by large numbers of people in the labor force. Here are some examples:

- A female lawyer representing a prestigious firm would be appropriately dressed in a gray or blue skirted suit. A dress with a suit jacket would also be acceptable. She should avoid clothing in brash colors or casual styles that might reduce her credibility.
- A male bank loan officer would be appropriately dressed in a tailored gray or blue suit, white shirt, and tie. This same person dressed in a colorful blazer, sport shirt, and plaid slacks would be seen as too casual in most bank settings.

- A female receptionist at a prominent accounting firm would be appropriately dressed in a skirt and blouse. This same person would be inappropriately dressed if she showed up for work wearing designer jeans, a sweater, and Birkenstock sandals.
- A technician employed by an auto dealership that sells new cars would be appropriately dressed in matching gray, tan, or blue shirt and pants. The technician would be inappropriately dressed in jeans and a T-shirt.

Many organizations seek advice about career apparel from image consultants. One source of image consultants is the Association of Image Consultants International.

Wardrobe Engineering

The term **wardrobe engineering** was first used by John Molloy to describe how clothing and accessories can be used to create a certain image. This concept was later refined by several other noted image consultants in hundreds of books and articles on dress and grooming. Although these authors are not in complete agreement on every aspect of dress, they do agree on a few basic points regarding wardrobe.

The quality of your wardrobe will influence the image you project A wardrobe should be regarded as an investment, with each item carefully selected to look and fit well. Purchase a few basic items each year and you will soon have everything you need.

The newest dress fad is often inappropriate in a business or professional setting In most cases, the world of work is more conservative than college, the arts, or the world of sports. If you are a fashion setter, you might be viewed as unstable or insincere. To be taken seriously, avoid clothing that is faddish or too flashy.

Women generally have more latitude than men in selecting appropriate attire, but they should still exercise some caution in choosing their wardrobe. In some cases, women are entering positions formerly dominated by men. They need to be taken seriously, and the wardrobe they select can contribute to this end.

Your wardrobe should be appropriate for your field and for you Although you should consider the dress and grooming standards of others in your field, don't give in to blind conformity or duplication. As one image consultant noted, "Effective packaging is an individual matter based on the person's circumstances, age, weight, height, coloring, and objectives."[20] In addition to these personal factors, you need to consider what's appropriate for your career. In general, four factors influence your choice of clothing for work:

1. *Products and services offered.* In some cases the organization's products and services more or less dictate a certain type of dress. For example, a receptionist employed by a well-established law firm would likely wear clothing that is conservative, modest, and in good taste. These same dress standards would apply to a pharmaceutical sales representative who calls on medical doctors.

2. *Type of person served.* Research indicates that first impressions created by dress and grooming are greatly influenced by unconscious expectations. Throughout life we become acquainted with real estate salespeople, nurses, police officers, and others employed in a wide range of occupations. We form mental images of the apparel common to each of these occupations. When we encounter someone whose appearance does not conform to our past experiences, we often feel uncomfortable.

3. *Desired image projected by the organization.* Some companies establish dress codes that help shape the image they project to the public. Walt Disney Company, for example, maintains a strict dress and grooming code for all its theme-park employees. They are considered "cast members" and must adhere to dress and grooming standards that complement the image projected by Disney theme parks.

4. *Geographic region.* Dress in the South and Southwest tends to be more casual than dress in the Northeast. Climate is another factor that influences

the clothing people wear at work. In Texas, for example, the warm climate calls for short sleeves and open collars in some work settings.

Thinking / Learning Starter

Assume you are planning to purchase (1) a life insurance policy, (2) a Rolex wristwatch, and (3) eyeglasses. What types of career apparel would you expect persons selling these products to wear? What grooming standards would you recommend?

The Business Casual Look

The terms *business casual* and *corporate casual* have recently been used to describe the movement toward dress standards that emphasize greater comfort and individuality. **Business casual** is clothing that allows you to feel comfortable at work but looks neat and professional. It usually means slacks, cotton shirts, and sports coats for men, and slacks, casual dresses, or skirts for women.[21] Business casual bridges the gap between the suits, white shirts, and silk blouses traditionally worn in business, and casual dress, such as jeans, shorts, and T-shirts. Some companies have established "casual Fridays" or "dress-down weeks," while others have shifted from a strict dress code to a relaxed dress code. The casual look in corporate America was triggered, in part, by efforts to improve teamwork and empower employees. Bottom-up initiatives often emphasize getting rid of symbols of top-down authority.[22] The casual

Reprinted with special permission of King Features Syndicate.

trend has also been fueled by the influx of Generation Xers who are entering the work force. These new workers are more relaxed and are looking for ways to express their individuality.

Growing acceptance of the casual look has created some problems for both employers and employees. Many companies are struggling to develop casual dress guidelines and offer assistance to employees who find dressing down for casual days a mind-boggling experience. What is business casual? What is "dressy" casual? The answer to these questions varies from one company to another. Some companies have developed written policies that describe what is and is not acceptable casual attire, but others say this approach is too intrusive. Chrysler Financial, a division of Chrysler Corporation, found that some employees did not follow the company's new casual-Fridays dress code. So the company hired a local department store to put on a fashion show involving professional models and Chrysler employees. The show gave employees many examples of casual clothing that is appropriate for work.[23]

Your Facial Expression

After your overall appearance, your face is the most visible part of you. Facial expressions are the cue most people rely on in initial interactions. They are the "TelePrompTer" by which others read your mood and personality.[24]

Studies conducted in nonverbal communication show that facial expressions strongly influence people's reactions to each other. The expression on your face can quickly trigger a positive or negative reaction from those you meet. How you rate in the "good-looks" department is not nearly as important as your ability to communicate positive impressions with a pleasant smile.

If you want to identify the inner feelings of another person, watch the individual's facial expressions closely. A frown may tell you "something is wrong." A smile generally communicates "things are OK." Everyone has encountered a "look of surprise" or a "look that could kill." These facial expressions usually reflect inner emotions more accurately than words.

In many work settings, a cheerful smile is an important key to creating a positive first impression. A deadpan stare (or frown) can communicate a negative first impression to others. If you find it hard to smile, take time to consider the reasons. Are you constantly thinking negative thoughts and simply find nothing to smile about? Are you afraid others may misinterpret your intentions?

Your Entrance and Carriage

The way you enter someone's office or a business meeting can influence the image you project, says Susan Bixler. She notes that "your entrance and the way you carry yourself will set the stage for everything that comes afterward."[25]

A nervous or apologetic entrance may ruin your chances of getting a job, closing a sale, or getting the raise you have earned. If you feel apprehensive, try not to let it show in your body language. Hold your head up, avoid slumping forward, and try to project self-assurance. To get off to the right start and make a favorable impression, follow these words of advice from Bixler: "The person who has confidence in himself or herself indicates this by a strong stride, a friendly smile, good posture, and a genuine sense of energy. This is a very effective way to set the stage for a productive meeting. When you ask for respect visually, you get it."[26] Bixler says the key to making a successful entrance is simply believing—and projecting—that you have a reason to be there and have something important to present or discuss.

Your Voice

Several years ago, a Cleveland-based company, North American Systems, Inc., developed and marketed Mr. Coffee, an appliance that makes coffee quickly and conveniently. Some credited the quick acceptance of this product to an effective advertising campaign featuring baseball Hall of Famer Joe DiMaggio. He came across to the consumer as an honest, sincere person. When Joe DiMaggio said Mr. Coffee worked and made good coffee, people believed him.

The tone of your voice, the rate of speed at which you speak (tempo), and the volume of your speech contribute greatly to the meaning attached to your verbal messages. In the case of telephone calls, voice quality is critical because the other person cannot see your facial expressions, hand gestures, and other body movements. You cannot trade in your current voice for a new one, but with a little practice you can make your voice more pleasing to other people and project a positive tone.

Although there is no ideal voice for all business contacts, your voice should reflect at least these four qualities: confidence, enthusiasm, optimism, and sincerity. Above all, try to avoid a speech pattern that is dull and colorless. Joanne Lamm, founder of Professional Speech Associates, says the worst kind of voice has no projection, no color, and no feeling.[27]

African Americans, Hispanics, Asians, Native Americans, and recent immigrants to America often face special challenges in verbal communication. New arrivals may have a unique accent because the phonetic habits of the speaker's native language are carried over to his or her new language. Many people born and raised in America have a dialect that is unique. Should this uniqueness be viewed as a problem or an opportunity? Kim Radford, vice president of marketing at Wachovia Trust Company, had to answer this question soon after graduating from college. He took a position as a stockbroker in Charleston, West Virginia. Radford, a black, conducted most of his business on the telephone and seldom met clients face to face. Early on, someone said, "Kim, you need to get that black accent out of your voice if you're going to be successful in this business." Radford faced a real dilemma: He wanted to be successful, but he did not want to compromise his personal integrity. He talked to several people, black and white, and the advice he received boiled down to this guideline:

> Stay honest to yourself, but communicate and be understood. There's no need to clean up the fact that you sound black as long as you're articulate and your diction's good and people can understand you.[28]

Your Handshake

When two people first meet, a handshake is usually the only physical contact between them. A handshake is a friendly and professional way to greet someone, or take leave, regardless of gender. The handshake can communicate warmth, genuine concern for the other person, and strength. It can also communicate aloofness, indifference, and weakness. The message you send the other party through your handshake depends on a combination of the following factors:

1. *Degree of firmness.* Generally speaking, a firm (but not viselike) grip communicates a caring attitude, whereas a weak grip communicates indifference.

Secretary of State Madeleine Albright recognizes the powerful influence of a hand-shake. She is seen here visiting refugee children from Afghanistan. (Reuters/Muzammil Pasha/Archive Photos)

2. *Degree of dryness of hands.* A moist palm is unpleasant to feel and can communicate the impression that you are nervous. A clammy hand is likely to repel most people.

3. *Duration of grip.* There are no specific guidelines for the ideal duration of a grip. Nevertheless, by extending the handshake just a little, you can often communicate a greater degree of interest in and concern for the other person.

4. *Depth of interlock.* A full, deep grip is more likely to convey friendship and strength to the other person.

5. *Eye contact during handshake.* Visual communication can increase the positive impact of your handshake. Maintaining eye contact throughout the handshaking process is important when two people greet each other.[29]

Most individuals have shaken hands with hundreds of people but have little idea whether they are creating positive or negative impressions. It is a good idea to obtain this information from those coworkers or friends who are willing to provide you with candid feedback. Like all other human relations skills, the handshake can be improved with practice.

Your Manners

The study of manners (sometimes called etiquette) reveals a number of ways to enhance our professional presence. A knowledge of good manners permits us to perform our daily work with poise and confidence. Letitia Baldrige, author of *Letitia Baldrige's New Complete Guide to Executive Manners,* provides us with a basic definition of good manners: "It's consideration and kindness and thinking about somebody other than oneself."[30] Another writer says, "Manners are the grace woven into the knotty fabric of our lives. Without them, it's all knots and thorns."[31] Practical manners suitable for the workplace represent an important key to improved interpersonal relations.

Good manners is a universal passport to positive relationships and respect. One of the best ways to develop rapport with another person is to avoid behavior that might be offensive to that individual. Although it is not possible to do a complete review of this topic, some of the rules of etiquette that are particularly important in an organizational setting are covered here.

1. *When you establish new relationships, avoid calling people by their first names too soon.* Jacqueline Thompson, author of *Image Impact,* says assuming that all work-related associates prefer to be addressed informally by their first names is a serious breach of etiquette.[32] Use titles of respect—Ms., Miss, Mrs., Mr., or Dr.—until the relationship is well established. Too much familiarity can breed irritation. When the other party says, "Call me Susan," or "Call me Roy," it is all right to begin using the person's first name. Informality should develop by invitation, not by presumption.

2. *Avoid obscenities and offensive comments or stories.* In recent years, standards for acceptable and unacceptable language have changed considerably.

> ### *Total Person Insight*
>
> *"In a society as ridden as ours with expensive status symbols, where every purchase is considered a social statement, there is no easier or cheaper way to distinguish oneself than by the practice of gentle manners."*
>
> JUDITH MARTIN
> Author

Obscenity is more permissible in everyday conversation than it was in the past. But it is still considered inappropriate to use foul language in front of a customer, a client, or, in many cases, a coworker. According to Bob Greene, syndicated columnist, an obscenity communicates a negative message to most people:

> What it probably all comes down to is an implied lack of respect for the people who hear you talk. If you use profanity among friends, that is a choice you make. But if you broadcast it to people in general, you're telling them that you don't care what their feelings might be.[33]

Never assume that another person's value system is the same as your own. Foul language and off-color stories can do irreparable damage to interpersonal relations.

3. *Watch your table manners.* Business is frequently conducted at breakfast, lunch, or dinner these days, so be aware of your table manners. When you invite a customer to lunch, do not discuss business before the meal is ordered unless the client initiates the subject. Begin eating only when the people around you have their plates. If you have not been served, however, encourage others to go ahead. Assume responsibility for making sure the conversation moves from topic to topic and person to person. No one likes to be left out. Avoid ordering food that is not easily controlled, such as ribs, chicken with bones, or lobster. Thank the server when your meal is served.

4. *Express appreciation at appropriate times.* A simple thank-you can mean a lot. Failure to express appreciation can be a serious human relations blunder. The office worker who works hard to complete a rush job for the boss is likely to feel frustrated and angry if this extra effort is ignored. The customer who makes a purchase deserves a sincere thank-you. You want your customers to know that their business is appreciated.

5. *Be familiar with meeting etiquette.* Business meetings should start and end on time. When you attend a meeting, arrive on time and don't feel obligated to comment on each item on the agenda. Yes, sometimes silence is golden. In most cases, you should not bring up a topic unless it is related to an agenda item. If you are in charge of the meeting, end it by summarizing key points, reviewing the decisions made, and recapping the responsibilities assigned to individuals during the meeting. Always start and end the meeting on a positive note.[34]

6. *Be aware of personal habits that may offend others.* Sometimes an annoying habit can be a barrier to establishing a positive relationship with someone else. Chewing gum is a habit that bothers many people, particularly if you chew gum vigorously or "crack" it. Biting fingernails, cracking knuckles, scratching your head, and combing your hair in public are additional habits to be avoided. If you wear a fragrance (cologne or after-shave lotion), apply it in moderation when going to work. Do not risk causing a client or coworker discomfort with your fragrance.[35]

Letitia Baldrige says that in the field of manners, "Rules are based on kindness and efficiency." She also believes that good manners are those personal qualities that make life at work more livable.[36] Nancy Austin, co-author of *A Passion for Excellence,* says, "Real manners—a keen interest in and a regard for somebody else, a certain kindness and at-ease quality that add real value—can't be faked or finessed."[37] Real manners come from the heart.

Professional Presence at the Job Interview

The guideline that says, "You seldom get a second chance to make a good first impression" has special meaning when you are preparing for a job interview. In most cases you are competing against several other applicants, so you can't afford to make a mistake. A common mistake among job applicants is failure to acquire background information on the employer. Without this information, it's difficult to prepare questions to ask during the interview, and decisions about what to wear will be more difficult. Let's assume you are planning to apply for a sales position at Abercrombie & Fitch, an upscale specialty chain that sells casual clothing for men and women. It would be helpful to know that the company maintains a very conservative dress code: Men are not permitted to wear necklaces or facial hair. Women cannot wear makeup or long nails. No piercing is allowed except for earrings (one for men, two for women).[38]

One of the most important objectives of a job interview is to communicate the image that you are someone who is conscientious, so be prepared. If possible, visit the place of business before your interview. Observe the people already working there; then dress one step up in terms of professional appearance. When in doubt about what to wear, opt for a more formal look. What's most important is that you show that you care enough to make a good impression.

Summary

Professional presence permits us to be perceived as self-assured and competent. These qualities are quickly perceived the first time someone meets us. People tend to form impressions of others quickly at the time they first meet them, and these first impressions tend to be preserved. In an organizational setting, the time interval for projecting a positive or negative first impression is often reduced to seconds. Positive impressions are important because they contribute to repeat business and customer referrals.

The impression you form of another person during the initial contact is made up of assumptions and facts. When meeting someone for the first time, people tend to rely heavily on assumptions. Many of your assumptions can be traced to early cultural influences. Assumptions are also based on perceptions of surface language. Surface language is a pattern of immediate impressions conveyed by appearance. The clothing and jewelry you wear, your hairstyle, and the fragrances you use all combine to make a statement about you to others.

Image consultants contend that discrimination on the basis of appearance is still a fact of life. Clothing is an important part of the image you communicate to others. Four factors tend to influence your choice of clothing for work: (1) the products or services offered by the organization, (2) the type of person served, (3) the desired image projected by the organization, and (4) the region where you work.

In addition to clothing, research indicates that facial expressions strongly influence people's reactions to each other. The expression on your face can quickly trigger a positive or negative reaction. Similarly, your entrance and carriage, voice, handshake, and manners also contribute to the image you project when meeting others. All the factors that form your image should be given attention prior to a job interview or any other situation where a positive first impression is important.

Career Corner

Q. In the near future I will begin my job search, and I want to work for a company that will respect my individuality. Some companies are enforcing strict dress codes and other policies that, in my opinion, infringe on the rights of their employees. How far can an employer go in dictating my lifestyle?

A. This is a good question, but one for which there is no easy answer. For example, most people feel they have a right to wear the fragrance of their choice, but many fragrances contain allergy-producing ingredients. In some parts of California, you will find "nonfragrance" zones. Secondhand smoke is another major issue in the workplace because some research indicates that it can be harmful to the health of workers. Rules regarding weight, hair length, and the type of clothing and jewelry that can be worn to work have also caused controversy. There is no doubt that many companies are trying to find a balance between their interests and the rights of workers. Blockbuster Entertainment Corporation has placed restrictions on the length of an employee's hair and the amount of jewelry that can be worn during work hours. The company believes employee appearance is crucial to the success of the company. The best advice I can give you is to become familiar with the employer's expectations before you accept a job. The company has a responsibility to explain its personnel policies to prospective employees, but sometimes this information is not covered until after a person is hired.

Key Terms

professional presence
primacy effect
assumptions
cultural influences
image

surface language
career apparel
wardrobe engineering
business casual

Review Questions

1. Image has been described as "more than exterior qualities such as dress and grooming." What other factors shape the image we project?
2. Define the term *primacy effect*. How would knowledge of the primacy effect help someone who works in patient care or customer service?
3. Why do people tend to rely more heavily on assumptions than on facts during the initial meeting?
4. Why should career-minded people be concerned about the image they project? Do we have control over the factors that shape the image we project? Explain.
5. What are the four factors that influence your choice of clothing for work?
6. Susan Bixler suggests that when making wardrobe decisions, you should keep in mind that three things have not changed. List and discuss these three factors.
7. What is meant by the term *business casual*? Why have some organizations established a business casual policy?
8. Describe the type of speaking voice that increases a person's effectiveness in dealing with others.
9. Provide a basic definition of good manners. Why is the study of manners important?
10. Stephen Covey says that changing outward attitudes and behaviors does very little good in the long run unless we base such changes on solid principles that govern human effectiveness. Do you agree or disagree with his views? Explain your answer.

Application Exercises

1. Harvey Mackay, president of Mackay Envelope Corporation, has designed a sixty-six-question customer profile for his sales staff. Salespeople are encouraged to complete the form for each customer they call on. The profile includes such information as birth date, current position, marital status, professional memberships, and special interests. Mackay takes the position that a salesperson cannot build long-term relationships with customers unless she or he takes a personal interest in them.

   a. Do you support the use of a customer profile to build relationships with customers or clients? Explain.

   b. What type of organization would benefit most from use of a detailed customer profile similar to the one used at Mackay Envelope Corporation?

2. The first step toward improving your voice is to hear yourself as others do. Listen to several recordings of your voice on a dictation machine, tape recorder, or VCR, and then complete the following rating form. Place a checkmark in the appropriate space for each quality.

Quality	*Major Strength*	*Strength*	*Weakness*	*Major Weakness*
Projects confidence	_____	_____	_____	_____
Projects enthusiasm	_____	_____	_____	_____
Speaking rate is not too fast or too slow	_____	_____	_____	_____
Projects optimism	_____	_____	_____	_____
Voice is not too loud or too soft	_____	_____	_____	_____
Projects sincerity	_____	_____	_____	_____

3. To survive in today's competitive climate, organizations must provide good service. Employees who have direct contact with the customer, client, or patient play a key role in the area of service. Effective front-line employees are able to express a warm, sincere greeting, display a caring attitude, and provide competent service. During the next seven days keep a record of all contacts you have with front-line people. After each contact, record your impressions of the experience. Was it positive? Negative? Briefly describe what the person said or did that caused you to view the contact as either positive or negative.

Internet Exercise

Throughout the past few years we have seen a movement toward casual dress in the workplace. Many companies have developed a casual dress code. Visit the Internet and determine what types of information are available on this topic. Using your search engine, type in the following keywords: "business casual dress" and "corporate casual dress." You may also want to visit the Web page of Levi Strauss & Company, a company that designs and sells clothes that can enhance a casual dress wardrobe. Review the available resources (such as books, articles, and training programs) related to this topic, and then prepare a written summary of your findings. Pay special attention to information that would help you develop a casual dress wardrobe.

Self-Assessment Exercise

1. For each of the following statements, circle the number from 1 to 5 that best represents your response: (1) strongly disagree (never do this); (2) disagree (rarely do this); (3) moderately agree (sometimes do this); (4) agree (frequently do this); (5) strongly agree (always do this).

   a. I project to others an image that matches my talents and aspirations.   1   2   3   4   5

   b. The clothes I wear to work and school are appropriate and project the image I want to exhibit to others.   1   2   3   4   5

   c. My entrance and carriage project total confidence.   1   2   3   4   5

   d. When I meet an acquaintance or someone new, I make eye contact and shake hands with a firm grip.   1   2   3   4   5

   e. I believe that good manners is an important key to improved human relations.   1   2   3   4   5

   Select an appropriate attitude or skill you would like to improve. Write your goal in the space provided.

   GOAL: _____

   _____

   _____

Case Problem

Etiquette 101

Should I use call waiting in my home office? When introducing a female associate and a male client, whom do I introduce to whom? Do I need to thank the server when my food is served? What do I do when a customer tells a racist joke that offends me? Many people are seeking answers to such questions because knowing rules of etiquette can help us avoid embarrassing situations. The trend toward global partnerships, increased electronic communications, and the growth of the service economy pose new challenges on the etiquette front. Judith Martin, creator of the popular *Miss Manners* advice column, featured in over 200 daily newspapers, and author of several books on etiquette, notes that the irritations of modern life are so abrasive that people ignorant of the rules of etiquette may turn to the law to regulate everyday behavior. Today people who feel offended often take legal action.

Ann Marie Sabath, founder of At East Incorporated, an etiquette consulting company in Cincinnati, says details can make or break a business relationship. She teaches her clients to extend small courtesies such as writing personalized thank-you notes, personalizing voice mail boxes, and using a person's name when speaking to him or her. Those who cannot afford to hire a consultant or to attend a seminar on etiquette often turn to books such as *Complete Business Etiquette Handbook* by Barbara Pachter and Marjorie Brody or *Business Etiquette in Brief* by Ann Marie Sabath.

Colleges and universities are giving more attention to the role of good manners in achieving career success. Howard University has developed seminars for business students on such topics as telephone etiquette, table manners, and art appreciation. Texas Christian University has a seminar that includes a six-course dinner and instructions on how to order wine.

Questions

1. Some people say the study of etiquette is not necessary because good manners is nothing more than common sense. Do you agree or disagree? Explain your answer.
2. Should colleges and universities provide instruction on the rules of etiquette? Explain your answer.
3. Some organizations provide front-line employees with etiquette training. Do you support this practice? Explain your answer.

Chapter 7

Valuing

Work Force

Diversity

Chapter Preview

After studying this chapter, you will be able to

1. Define the primary and secondary dimensions of diversity.
2. Discuss how prejudiced attitudes are formed.
3. Develop an awareness of the various forms of discrimination in the workplace.
4. Understand why organizations are striving to develop organizational cultures that value diversity.
5. Identify ways in which individuals and organizations can enhance work force diversity.
6. Discuss the current status of affirmative action programs.

THE CITY OF MINNEAPOLIS conducted an affirmative action audit of BRW, a $38 million architecture and engineering firm with 350 employees. The results showed that BRW's rates of promotion and attrition for minorities and women were not good. A few simple adjustments such as advertising for new employees in minority publications would have satisfied the city, but CEO Don Hunt chose to take a much broader look at his organization and examine how it might become more competitive.

Hunt and his partners realized that 96 percent of BRW's managers were white males—a strong contrast to their client demographics. They realized that they would be less competitive if they remained a white-male-dominated firm. Therefore, they created a thirty-five-employee diversity committee that was challenged to examine BRW's personnel systems. The committee made these recommendations:

- Require all employees to attend "diversity training" sessions that help managers recognize how their preconceived ideas about race, sex, and national origin are affecting their hiring and retention practices.
- Advertise in minority and women's publications when positions open in the firm.
- Rewrite the company handbook to reflect a more aggressive commitment to work force diversity.
- Enhance the benefits package to include flextime and health benefits for all part-time workers in order to attract more women.
- Conduct annual "Respect Week" activities to help foster mutual respect among members of the firm's diverse work force.

After implementation of the recommendations, the number of employees rose to 400, work force diversity greatly increased, and the proportion of white male managers dropped to 81 percent.[1] ∎

A growing number of progressive organizations are realizing the impact a reputation for valuing diversity in the work force can have on a company's success . . . and they are doing something about it!

THE NATURE OF DIVERSITY

E Pluribus Unum—"Out of many, one." No other country on earth is as multiracial and multicultural as the United States of America. This diversity is a popular topic and common buzzword in newspaper and magazine articles focusing on the future of American organizations.

The strength of many other nations lies in their homogeneity. Japan is mostly made up of persons of Japanese descent, and the country's economy

Total Person Insight

"Getting along with people from many backgrounds and interests is most important if you are going to be involved in society in any way. We are interdependent upon one another."

JACK PLUCKHAN

Vice President, Panasonic Corporation

and business transactions reflect this heritage. The People's Republic of China is populated mostly with persons of Chinese ancestry, and their values and culture are a major part of their global economic strength. But America has always been the "melting pot" of all the world's cultures. This diversity now represents the country's biggest crisis as well as its greatest opportunity.

The publication of *Workforce 2000,* a report prepared by the Hudson Institute for the U.S. Department of Labor, served as a powerful wake-up call for organizations throughout America. The report indicates that white males are already minorities in the labor force. Authors of the report note that the biggest gains are being made by women, minorities, and immigrants.[2] Progressive leaders are seriously considering the implications of these demographic trends toward a more diverse work force.

Ten years ago work force diversity was evident primarily in the increasing numbers of women, minorities, older workers, and immigrants. Today, diversity is about much more than visible, physical differences and demographic changes. At Pillsbury, for example, diversity is defined as "All those ways in which we differ."[3] We define **diversity** as valuing uniqueness while respecting differences and maximizing individual potentials.[4]

In the past, U.S. organizations attempted to assimilate everyone into one "American" way of doing things. The trend now, however, is to identify, respect, and value the individual differences in this new, diverse work force and to encourage every worker to make his or her full contribution. Organizations that foster the full participation of all workers will enjoy the sharpest competitive edge in the expanding global marketplace.

Dimensions of Diversity

There are primary and secondary dimensions of diversity. The **primary dimensions** are core characteristics of each individual that cannot be changed: age, race, gender, physical and mental abilities, and sexual orientation (see Figure

7.1). Together they form an individual's self-image and the filters through which each person views the rest of the world. These inborn elements are interdependent; no one dimension stands alone. Each exerts an important influence throughout life. Marilyn Loden and Judy Rosener describe individual primary dimensions in their book *Workforce America!* They say, "Like the interlocking segments of a sphere, they represent the core of our individual identities."[5]

The greater the number of primary differences between people, the more difficult it is to establish trust and mutual respect. When we add the secondary dimensions of diversity to the mix, effective human relations becomes even more difficult. The **secondary dimensions** of diversity are elements that can be changed or at least modified. They include a person's health habits, re-

FIGURE 7.1

Primary and
Secondary Dimensions
of Diversity

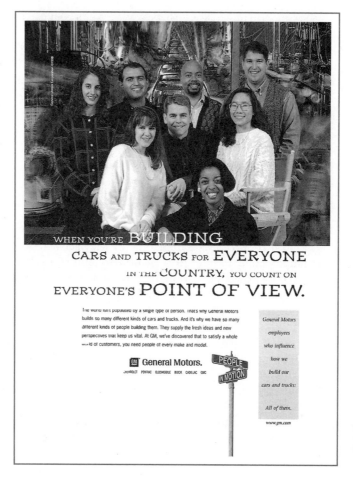

ligious beliefs, education and training, general appearance, relationship status, ethnic customs, communication style, and income (see Figure 7.1). These factors all add a layer of complexity to the way we see ourselves and others and in some instances can exert a powerful impact on our core identities. A single mother who loses her job may be severely affected by her loss of income, whereas a married woman with no children may not be as affected by a similar loss. A vocational-technical school graduate may have expectations far different from those of a four-year-college graduate. A member of the Baptist church may feel she has little in common with another woman who follows Islamic teachings.

Even though differences like these intensify the impact of particular secondary dimensions, they do not diminish the impact of primary dimensions. Instead, they add depth to the individual. This interaction of primary and secondary dimensions shapes a person's values, priorities, and perceptions throughout life.[6]

Each of us enters the work force with a unique perspective shaped by these dimensions and our own past experiences. Building effective human relationships is possible only when we learn to accept and value the differences in others. Without this acceptance, both primary and secondary dimensions of diversity can become roadblocks to further cooperation and understanding.

PREJUDICED ATTITUDES

Prejudice can be defined as a premature judgment or an opinion that is formed without examination of the facts. Throughout life we often prejudge people in light of their primary and secondary dimensions. Attitudes in favor of or against people that are based solely on these traits are prejudices. Rather than treat others as unique individuals, prejudiced people tend to think in terms of **stereotypes**—generalizations made about all members of a particular group. They uncritically accept widely held beliefs about what various racial groups, socioeconomic classes, men, women, people living in a particular geographic region, and so forth are "really like." When we bring stereotypes to the workplace, we are likely to misinterpret or devalue some primary and secondary differences even after we have been exposed to them.

Stereotyping exists, in part, because it provides an easy and convenient way of dealing with people. By accepting a stereotype, you don't have to make the effort to understand who a person really is or might become.[7] Stereotypes bring some predictability to our lives and reduce the uncertainty of dealing with other people. Stereotypes are often based on one or several real experiences a person has had in dealing with others, and they are resistant to change

---

Total Person Insight

"So long as black and white Americans see each other as stereotypes and not as people with the same dreams, ambitions and values, this nation will be frozen in suspicion and hate."

VERNON E. JORDAN, JR.

Attorney and Civil Rights Leader

because people more readily believe information that confirms their previous experience than evidence that challenges it. For example, people without a tendency to gain weight or those who have conquered a weight problem, sometimes view an overweight person as someone who lacks the self-discipline and motivation to lose weight.

Most of us object to being stereotyped but forget how often we stereotype others. Although the people most often hurt by stereotyping are women, minorities, older workers, and immigrants, white men are also victims. One dimension of the AT&T Corporation diversity program is a workshop entitled "What About White Males? Are They the Invisible Diversity Segment?" This workshop was created after many white male employees complained that conventional diversity courses perpetuated stereotypes about their supposed wealth, power, and insensitivity. More than 1,000 AT&T workers have participated in workshops aimed at dispelling myths about white men.[8]

How Prejudicial Attitudes Are Formed and Retained

Three major factors contribute to the development of prejudice: childhood experiences, ethnocentrism, and economic conditions.

Childhood Experiences Today's views toward others are filtered through the experiences and feelings of childhood. Children learn attitudes and beliefs from family, friends, and other authority figures, and they learn how to view and treat different racial, ethnic, religious, and other groups. The *emotions* of prejudice are formed in childhood. Later in life you may want to change your prejudice, but it is much easier to change your intellectual beliefs than your deep feelings.[9]

Another way we develop prejudices is by allowing our experiences with one person to color our attitude toward that individual's entire group. For example, if a company brings in Asian laborers as replacements for striking employees, those employees may thereafter regard all Asians as potential "scabs" or strikebreakers. In the same manner, a manager who discovers that one young employee is negligent or careless may generalize these attitudes to include all young workers.

Ethnocentrism The tendency to regard our own culture or nation as better or more "correct" than others is called **ethnocentrism.** The word is derived from *ethnic,* meaning a group united by similar customs, characteristics, race, or other common factors, and *center.* When ethnocentrism is present, the standards and values of our own culture are being used as a yardstick to measure the worth of other cultures.

Cultural conditioning tends to perpetuate ethnocentrism. Throughout life, we are conditioned to respond to various situations as we see others in our culture respond to them. Some cultures value emotional control and avoid open conflicts and discussions of such personal topics as money or values. Other cultures encourage a bolder, more open expression of feelings and values and accept greater levels of verbal confrontation. Tension can result when people's cultural expectations clash in the workplace.

In their book *Valuing Diversity,* Lewis Brown Griggs and Lente-Louise Louw compare ethnocentrism in an organization to icebergs floating in an ocean. We can see the tips of icebergs above the water level, just as we can see our diverse coworkers' skin color, gender, mannerisms, and job-related talents and hear the words they use and their accents. These are basically "surface" aspects of a person that others can easily learn through observation. However, just as the enormous breadth of an iceberg's base lies beneath the water's surface, so does the conditioning of people from different cultures. As icebergs increase in number and drift too close together, they are likely to clash at their base even though there is no visible contact at the water's surface.[10] As organizations increase the diversity of their work force, the potential for clashes resulting from deep-seated cultural conditioning and prejudiced attitudes also increases. These clashes will be emotional, and when they occur, effective human relations will become a challenge.

For example, a manager from one culture and his subordinate from another are talking together, and the manager begins to praise his employee for his insight and abilities. He adds that he has already told several people in the company how outstanding the employee is. This well-intentioned comment upsets the employee, who sees it as a breach of confidentiality. His deeply felt cultural conditioning has taught him to refrain from expressing any form of boastfulness in public.[11]

Economic Factors   When the economy goes through a recession or depression, and housing, jobs, and other necessities become scarce, people's prejudices against other groups often increase. If enough prejudice is built up against a particular group, members of that group will be barred from competing for jobs. The recent backlash against immigrants can be traced, in part, to a fear that the new arrivals will take jobs that would otherwise be available to local workers. Some fear that new immigrant arrivals will work for rock-bottom wages and thus depress the current workers' earning power. Prejudice based on economic factors has its roots in people's basic survival needs, and as a result, it is very hard to eliminate.

Rising income inequality is viewed by many as a serious barrier to racial harmony. Ronald Walters, University of Maryland political scientist, says, "You can only have meaningful racial reconciliation when people of roughly equal socioeconomic status can reach across the divide of race."[12] Wide gaps between rich and poor exist, and the opportunities for upward mobility for many low-skilled, low-income workers have diminished in recent years. The gap between median weekly wages of black men and white men has widened since 1990.[13]

> ## *Thinking / Learning Starters*
>
> 1. Have you ever been the object of prejudice? What were the circumstances? How did this behavior affect your self-esteem?
>
> 2. Do you carry any prejudices that are obvious carryovers from your parents? Explain.
>
> 3. Are you doing anything to overcome these prejudices? What would the benefits be if you could overcome them?

DISCRIMINATION

Discrimination is behavior based on prejudiced attitudes. If, as an employer, you believe that overweight people tend to be lazy, that is an attitude. If you refuse to hire someone simply because that person is overweight, you are engaging in discriminatory behavior.

Individuals or groups that are discriminated against are denied equal treatment and opportunities afforded to the dominant group. They may be denied employment, promotion, training, or other job-related privileges on the basis of race, lifestyle, gender, or other characteristics that have little or nothing to do with their qualifications for a job.

Gender

Discrimination based on gender has been, and continues to be, the focus of much attention. The traditional roles women have held in society have undergone tremendous changes in the past few decades. More and more women are entering the work force not only to supplement family income but also to pursue careers in previously all-male professions. Men have also been examining the roles assigned them by society and are discovering new options for themselves. Most companies have recognized that discrimination based on gender is a reality and are taking steps to deal with the problem.

Age

Discrimination based on age can apply to the older worker—40 to 70—and the younger worker—18 to 25.

Youth can be a disadvantage when potential employers show a reluctance to hire young people because of their lack of practical experience in the workplace. Such employers fail to appreciate that everyone begins his or her career with no experience and needs an opportunity to prove himself or herself. Older workers between the ages of 40 and 70 are protected against discrimination by the Age Discrimination in Employment Act. The law states that if you are fired, demoted, denied a raise given to others, or otherwise mistreated primarily because of your age, you have legal recourse.

Even though organizations can no longer require mandatory retirement at a specific age, older employees are often victims of potent though subtle forms of discrimination. They may be laid off, have their workload cut back, lose their eligibility for promotion, or be given "make-work" projects that keep them out of the mainstream of the organization.

Americans tend to have a stereotypical notion that older workers are no longer capable of effective work performance. Many employers are reluctant to hire or retrain the older worker. They feel that those educated in the 1950s and 1960s will not understand the technology and methods of the new millennium. Studies indicate, however, that older workers tend to be more dependable, to stay on the job longer, and to learn new technologies in the same amount of time required by younger workers.[14]

The fact remains that the American work force is continuing to mature: One in three Americans is over 45 years old.[15] Although it would seem logical for employers to make a commitment to skill upgrading and retraining designed to facilitate acceptance of new techniques and procedures by older workers, many are unwilling to make this investment. In most cases you must take responsibility for your own career development. Keep up with what is going on at your company, and accept change. Take the initiative in learning and using new technologies. Keep fit—a regular fitness program can help you stay energized and competitive.[16]

Race

Racial discrimination is discrimination based on traits common to a person's ethnic origin or skin color. Because people cannot change their skin color or abandon their ethnic heritage, this is often the most difficult discrimination to overcome. As DeWayne Wickman, an African American and president of Vanita Enterprises, Inc., states it, "The melting pot does not melt blacks."[17]

Few areas are more sensitive and engender more passion than issues surrounding race. Throughout history we have seen attempts to place people in racial categories and judge them as racial symbols rather than as unique individuals. Until the early decades of the twentieth century, the Irish Catholic "race" was stereotyped as lazy and violent. In the 1930s Jews in the United States were considered a separate "race" by many Christian Americans. Italians were once considered "nonwhite."[18] The use of racial categories continues in America. The following nonwhite race categories appear on U.S. Census Bureau forms (*The American Heritage Dictionary* was consulted for the description of each category):[19]

Black	Persons who descended from peoples of African origin. Many blacks have a preference for the name African American or Afro-American. Blacks represent about 12 percent of the U.S. population.
Hispanic	This is the broadest term used to encompass Spanish-speaking peoples, such as Mexican Americans, Puerto Ricans, Cubans, and South Americans. The widely used term *Latino* is generally restricted to persons of Latin American descent. Hispanics make up about 10 percent of the U.S. population.
Asian	The term *Asian* is preferred over *Oriental* for persons of South and East Asian ancestry, such as Chinese, Koreans, Japanese, Indonesians, and Filipinos. Asians make up 3 or 4 percent of the U.S. population.
Native American	This term refers to peoples indigenous to America. The term *Indian* is used as a term of pride and respect by Native Americans.

Criticism of the racial categories used by the Census Bureau and other organizations is growing. Critics say the use of these categories only intensifies and reinforces the beliefs and actions of racists. They believe that one way to break down racial barriers and promote a race-free consciousness is to get rid of racial categories. A growing number of geneticists and social scientists reject the view that "racial" differences have an objective or scientific foundation.[20] Recently the 11,000-member American Anthropological Association (AAA) took the official position that "race" has no scientific justification in human biology. The AAA position is that "There is as much genetic variability between two people from the same 'racial group' as there is between two people from any two different 'racial' groups."[21] Put another way, individual differences are much greater than group differences, regardless of how the group is defined.[22] The AAA recommended that the Census Bureau drop the term *race* and replace it with *ethnic origins,* noting that many people confuse race, ethnicity, and ancestry.

Those who oppose getting rid of racial categories hold that in order to ensure that individuals of all races and national origins are treated fairly, we must categorize people according to these characteristics. They say the current system is needed to create minority voting districts and to administer an array of federal laws and programs designed to ensure that minorities get equal housing, education, health care, and employment opportunities.[23] Groups that are working to build race pride, such as the American Indian Movement, also oppose efforts to get rid of racial categories. There is no doubt that the pros and cons of classifying individuals by race will be hotly debated in the years ahead.

Many people still have an irrational suspicion of a particular ethnic or racial group. However, because of affirmative action programs and diversity training programs (discussed later in this chapter), and the threat of legal action, blatant racism has evolved into a new, more subtle form of discrimination that is difficult to recognize and hard to combat. Strategies to combat this subtle racism should be aimed at all levels within an organization, but they must start at the top.

Disability

Employees whose work assignments are limited by their mental or physical abilities have in the past been referred to as "handicapped" or "disabled." Today, a more acceptable term is *mentally challenged* for individuals who suffer from mental retardation or a serious emotional disturbance, and *physically challenged* for individuals who have hearing, speech, visual, orthopedic, or other health impairments, including long-term obesity.

Mentally or physically challenged people find it difficult to enter the job market even though their right to do so is protected by the Americans with Disabilities Act of 1991. That law bans discrimination against workers with disabilities and requires employers to make "reasonable accommodations" so they can work. It covers a wide range of disabilities, including mental impairments, AIDS, alcoholism, visual impairments, and physical impairments that require use of a wheelchair. The law sets forth requirements for businesses with fifteen or more employees.

Is the law working? Reports on employment of the mentally and physically challenged are mixed. The Census Bureau reports that the number of these individuals has dramatically increased in recent years.[24] But studies by Louis Harris and Associates indicate that about two-thirds of working-age people with disabilities are not working.[25] This means the talents of several million disabled people are not being utilized.

Discrimination against the mentally and physically challenged takes many forms, but the most common are

- Asking a job applicant about his or her impairment
- Requiring a candidate with a disability to have a medical exam
- Reducing health insurance for an employee with a particular infirmity
- Firing a staff member who develops a disability
- Refusing to serve a customer who has a disability[26]

Mentally or physically challenged people who try to get jobs often encounter such discrimination. Some companies are exceptions, however. Du Pont Cor-

For Better or For Worse® by Lynn Johnston

© Lynn Johnston Productions, Inc. Distributed by United Features Syndicate, Inc.

poration, McDonald's, Marriott, Sears, and IBM have specific recruiting, training, and retention programs that recognize the skills and abilities of this sector of the work force.

Sexual Orientation

Discrimination based on a person's homosexual orientation is referred to as *homophobia,* an aversion to homosexuals. Not long ago, gays and lesbians went to great lengths to keep their sexuality a secret. But today many gays and lesbians are "coming out of the closet" to demand their rights as members of society. Indeed, many young people entering the work force who are used to the relative tolerance of college campuses refuse to hide their orientation once they are in the workplace. Activists want to make people aware that discrimination based on sexual orientation is as serious a problem as discrimination based on race, age, gender, or disability. And some, though not all, states have enacted laws that protect gays and lesbians from discrimination or illegal discharge from their jobs because of their sexual orientation.

An atmosphere in which gays and lesbians are comfortable being themselves is often more productive than an atmosphere in which they waste their time and energy maintaining alternate, and false, personalities. Brian McNaught, a consultant who conducts a workshop called "Homophobia in the Workplace" at the largest factory in the AT&T Corporation system, states, "Homophobia takes a toll on the ability of 10 percent of the workforce to produce."[27] He points out that it is not productive to ask gays and lesbians to completely ignore their private lives when they come to work. Heterosexuals bring their

Allan Gilmour, pictured here on the left with his partner, was the first high-ranking auto executive to be publicly identified as gay. Throughout his long career at Ford Motor Company, he rose to become the company's second-highest officer and was twice considered for the CEO position. Like many other gays and lesbians who aspire to top corporate jobs, he kept his sexual orientation a secret during his career because he feared discrimination. (Louis Psihoyos/Matrix)

personal lives to work all the time. Being unable to participate in casual conversations about weekend events or after-work activities leaves gays and lesbians feeling isolated. About 2,000 employees have attended McNaught's workshops, all voluntarily. At the end of each session, employees are offered a magnetic pink triangle—the gay logo, so to speak—if they vow to make their office or work area a "safe space" for homosexuals. Thousands of these symbols can be seen throughout the plant.[28]

The authors of *Straight Talk About Gays in the Workplace* describe what Walt Disney Company, Polaroid, Lotus, Xerox, and other companies are doing to combat homophobia.[29] Some companies have established lesbian and gay employee associations that provide a point of contact for previously invisible employees. Many companies have added sexual orientation to their anti-discrimination policies, and nationwide about 140 major public and private employers have extended medical benefits to gay and lesbian partners.

Every organization must provide workers with an environment that is safe and free of threats and intimidation. Progressive companies are taking the additional step of discovering ways in which they can provide an open, productive work atmosphere. They do not want to lose their bright, intelligent, and highly motivated lesbian and gay employees to other companies that might provide a more open environment.

Subtle Forms of Discrimination

Discrimination based on gender, age, race, or disability is prohibited under Title VII of the 1964 Civil Rights Act. This prohibition applies to discrimination in all aspects of employment, including recruitment, hiring, promotion, discharge, classification, training, compensation, and other terms, privileges, and conditions of employment.[30] A person who feels she or he has been the victim of these types of discrimination can take legal action by filing a complaint with the state office of the Equal Employment Opportunity Commission.

But the laws do not specifically protect workers from more subtle discrimination. For example, although some state laws protect gay men and lesbians from discrimination or illegal discharge from their jobs, an atmosphere that allows cruel comments and jokes about their lifestyles can nevertheless occur, adversely affecting their job performance. This lower job performance can then be used as a valid reason for dismissing the lesbian or gay person. This more subtle form of discrimination can, of course, be directed against any group and may be based on any of the secondary dimensions of diversity (religious beliefs, personal appearance, marital status). Those who are from another region of the country, speak with an accent, have too much education or too little, or possess some other personal characteristic that marks them as "different" may find themselves victims of subtle discrimination. Many people are inclined to equate a difference with a deficiency.

What Can You Do?

What can you do if you discover you are the target of discrimination? If you wish to stay in the organization, you will need to determine whether the "difference" is something you can change—your weight, the way you dress, your manner of speaking. If the difference is something you cannot or choose not to change, you may need to address the situation directly. Carefully study the assertiveness skills outlined in Chapter 8. Assertiveness by you may help change other people's attitudes and in turn alter their discriminatory behaviors. Another powerful method of eliminating subtle discrimination is to compensate for it by excelling in your work. Become an expert on the job, and work to increase your skills and your value to the organization. As your colleagues gain respect for your talents, they will change their attitudes toward you. But if your future appears blocked, investigate other workplaces where management may be more open to diversity. The important point is that you should refuse to allow discrimination to limit your personal and professional success.

Thinking / Learning Starters

1. Describe your own primary and secondary dimensions of diversity.

2. Do you hold any prejudices that might create problems for you in your career? In your personal life?

THE ISSUE OF VALUING DIVERSITY

As we look back through the previous decades, we see a pattern of workers continually struggling to be treated alike:

- Labor unions were formed to ensure that all employees would be treated the same.
- The women's movement fought for equality in the workplace.
- Many organizations implemented strategies to duplicate the Japanese management style, which rewarded teamwork rather than individual accomplishments.

The 1990s, however, brought a strong shift away from treating everyone the same and toward **valuing diversity.** In a work setting, valuing diversity means that an organization intends to make full use of the ideas, talents, experiences, and perspectives of all employees at all levels of the organization.

Organizations have traditionally valued assimilation over diversity, placing emphasis on changing people to conform to traditional norms and performance expectations. Most American organizations have been shaped primarily by the values and experiences of western European, white, heterosexual, able-bodied men. Achieving high productivity has frequently been a matter of trying to fit all workers into the same mold and rewarding those who fit best. The dominant group set and controlled the agenda of the traditional organization and expected other groups to follow, conform, or disappear. As people moved up the career ladder, the range of acceptable behavior narrowed and reverted to the traditional mold of the male founders.

However, the changing demographics of the work force brings with it the realization that organizations must break away from this traditional management approach. To remain competitive, organizations are being forced to recognize and hire the best talent available in the labor pool, regardless of skin color, gender, and cultural background. Once on board, these talented individuals will choose to stay only in an atmosphere where they are appreciated and valued. If their organization does not acknowledge their unique contribution, these diverse employees are likely to move on to an employer that does.

The Economics of Valuing Diversity

Valuing diversity is not only a legal, social, and moral issue; it is also an economic issue, because an organization's most valuable resource is its people. The price tag for *not* helping employees learn to respect and value each other is enormous in terms of lost time, wasted energy, delayed production, and increased conflict among employees.

- Highly skilled and talented employees will leave an organization that does not value diversity.
- Substantial dollars will be spent on recruiting and retraining because of high employee turnover.
- Discrimination complaints will result from mismanagement of diverse employees.
- A comment, gesture, or joke delivered without malice but received as an insult will create tension between coworkers.
- Deliberate acts of sabotage may be aimed at making coworkers who are different "look bad."

Total Person Insight

"More and more, organizations can remain competitive only if they can recognize and obtain the best talent; value the diverse perspectives that come with talent born of different cultures, races, and genders; nurture and train that talent; and create an atmosphere that values its workforce."

LEWIS BROWN GRIGGS AND LENTE-LOUISE LOUW

Authors, *Valuing Diversity: New Tools for a New Reality*

- Absenteeism associated with stress in the workplace will likely occur.
- Time will be wasted because of miscommunication and misunderstanding between diverse employees.[31]

Recognizing the value of diversity and managing it as an asset can help eliminate these negative effects and exert a positive influence on productivity and cooperation within the work force. Companies can succeed only when they have an environment that enables all employees, not just a few, to work to their full potential.

Mismanagement of employee diversity not only interferes with efficient production but also poses a significant threat to an organization's ability to provide outstanding service to its customers. In industries such as retailing, fast food, and banking, a complex set of employee transactions must take place to satisfy a customer's needs. If there is tension, infighting, disrespect, and a low level of trust among employees, there are likely to be human relations problems that stand in the way of high-quality customer service.

Thinking / Learning Starters

1. Describe how closely the student body of your school or your coworkers reflect the cultural makeup of your community.

2. Is there a disproportionate number of students of a certain race, sex, or age bracket in your college? What accounts for this situation? What effects does it have on the environment of your school?

ENHANCING DIVERSITY

By now you should be aware of the negative effects of prejudice and discrimination as well as the positive effects of valuing diversity. Many employers are no longer asking whether to diversify the work force but rather how best to manage diversity. After all, a person's differences don't create human relations problems. Other people's responses to those differences do.

What Individuals Can Do

People tend to hang on to their prejudices and stereotypes. If certain white people believe people of color are inferior, they are likely to notice any incident in which a person of color makes a mistake. But when a person of color exhibits competence and sound decision-making abilities, these same white people do not notice anything, or they attribute the positive results to other circumstances. You cannot totally eliminate prejudices that have been deeply held and developed over a long time. But you can learn to do the following:

1. *Monitor and analytically evaluate these prejudices in light of your increased personal involvement with others who are different from you.* As noted previously, it is not easy to free yourself from confining stereotypes. You need not only to change your intellectual beliefs but also to change the emotions of prejudice formed during childhood. If you feel you are prejudiced against a particular group, fine-tune your emotions by using the practices described in Chapter 8.

2. *Learn to look critically and honestly at the particular myths and preconceived ideas you were conditioned to believe about others.* Psychologists and sociologists have found that contact among people of different races, cultures, and lifestyles can break down prejudice when people join together for a common task. The more contact there is among culturally diverse individuals, the more likely it will be that stereotypes based on myths and inaccurate generalizations will not survive.

3. *Develop a sensitivity to differences.* Do not allow gender-based, racist, or antigay jokes or comments in your presence. If English is not a person's native language, be aware that this person might interpret your messages differently from what you intended. When in doubt as to the appropriate behavior, ask questions. "I would like to open the door for you because you are in a wheelchair, but I'm not sure whether that would offend you. What would you like me to do?"

4. *Use appropriate language.* In this way, you show diverse individuals your respect. For instance, the term *minority* is no longer acceptable in reference to people of color because "minority" gives the sense of less power, as in "majority versus minority." Table 7.1 offers some guidelines for appropriate terminology.

What Organizations Can Do

A well-planned and well-executed diversity program can promote understanding and defuse tensions between employees who differ in age, race, gender, religious beliefs, and other characteristics. Programs that are poorly developed and poorly executed often backfire, especially in organizations where bias and distrust have festered for years.[32] Most of the programs that fail are those that are not comprehensive and do not provide for ongoing cultural change.

TABLE 7.1

Examples of Appropriate Language

When Referring To	Instead Of	Use
Women	Girls, ladies, gals, females	Women
Black people	Negroes, minorities	African Americans, Caribbean Americans, black people, people of color
Asian people	Orientals, minorities	Asian Americans, Japanese, Koreans, Pakistanis, etc. Differentiate between foreign-born and American-born people of color.
American Indians	Minorities	Native Americans; American Indians; name of tribe, e.g., Navajo, Iroquois; people of color
People of Hispano–Latin American origin	Minorities	Latinas/Latinos, Chicanas/Chicanos. Use country of national origin, e.g., Puerto Ricans, Chileans; people of color, Hispanics
Gay men and lesbians	Homosexuals	Gay men, lesbians
People with disabilities	Handicapped, crippled, disabled	People who are physically or mentally challenged, people with (the specific disability)
White people	Anglos, WASPS	European Americans. Use country of national origin, e.g., Irish American, Polish American. White people
Older or younger adults	Geriatrics, kids, yuppies	Older adults, elderly, younger people, young adults

Source: Adapted from *Workforce America!* by Marilyn Loden and Judy Rosener, Business One Irwin, 1991, p. 85. Reprinted by permission of Richard D. Irwin, Inc.

Unfortunately, some companies view their diversity program as an *event*—a one-day workshop that promotes the advantages of a diverse work force but contains no provision for follow-up. Often these quick-fix programs create greater, not less, divisiveness among workers. Instead, organizations should approach their diversity programs as an ongoing *process*. They should include clear objectives and standards that will permit the organization to assess program outcomes. The diversity program developed by Allstate Insurance Com-

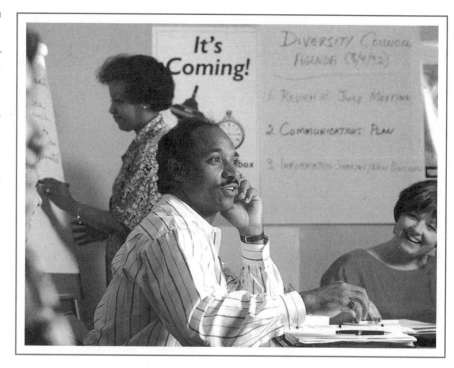

The Diversity Council at Levi Strauss & Company is seen here working on diversity and communication issues. The council is helping revamp policies, create new structures, and design a new human resource system. Like many other progressive organizations, Levi Strauss views diversity as a constructive force. (Mark Richards/ PhotoEdit)

pany is an example of an initiative that is based on accountability standards. Diversity courses are carefully evaluated, and employees who complete the courses must pass tests with specified standards. Each quarter, employees complete a survey that probes how well their manager maintains a climate that emphasizes bias-free service to customers, respect for individuals, and sensitivity. Survey results are used to develop a "diversity index." Performance on this index determines 25 percent of a manager's merit bonus.[33]

The Allstate program was implemented by a team of senior leaders. Any redesign effort must have the full support of senior management. Employees will take their cue from these leaders. If they see leaders promoting diversity at work yet joining segregated clubs, they will question how seriously top management is committed to equality. At Hoechst Celanese, the top twenty-six officers are required to join at least two organizations in which they are a minority. The company believes that managers can break out of their traditional white-male-dominated comfort zone by actually working beside people from diverse backgrounds.[34]

Adjust Employment Practices To achieve work force diversity, organizations need to seek out, employ, and develop people who have been victims of past discrimination. Some companies form partnerships with schools and colleges that have great diversity in the student body. Merrill Lynch & Co., Inc., for example, helps high schools in multiracial New Jersey prepare students for careers in the financial services area by teaching them to use personal computers and industry-specific software programs. Other companies sponsor professors' research, provide employees as guest lecturers, award scholarships, and hire students for summer jobs.[35]

Companies reviewing their standards for hiring and promoting also need to determine whether their assessment tools measure a candidate's actual abilities. Remember that many employment tests can be biased in favor of white, middle-class people. Organizations must also foster a climate for retention of women and minorities. To establish a culture that values diversity takes time. Some companies establish mentoring programs that pair each new employee with a senior employee who provides support and helps steer the new employee toward promotability. Another approach is to develop career-planning sessions for all employees so they can clearly see their future within the company.

Improve Training Organizations need training programs that give managers and employees the tools they need to work more effectively with one another regardless of their diverse backgrounds. These programs should also reduce an organization's liability for discrimination.[36]

Dallas-based Texas Instruments is often cited as a company that has distinguished itself through effective diversity training initiatives. It has been named to the honor roll of *Hispanic Magazine*'s "100 Best Companies for Hispanics" and *Black Professional* magazine's "200 Great Places to Work." The starting point is a one-day seminar to learn to value diversity and uncover unconscious behavioral patterns that could impede the progress of women and minority employees. Senior managers attend a two-day session. Follow-up courses focus on ways to foster inclusiveness at Texas Instruments and respect for the individual.[37]

Many other companies have adopted the approach used at Texas Instruments. Done well, diversity training programs can promote harmony and reduce conflict. Training courses that are poorly designed and delivered by incompetent trainers, however, can end up alienating and offending employees. Training intended to dispel discriminatory attitudes may help perpetuate them. For example, an instructor who spends a great deal of time discussing characteristics of various cultures may actually reinforce stereotypical attitudes. Focusing on certain group differences also trivializes individuality. Each person has a unique individual identity created by a blend of primary and secondary characteristics such as communication style, ethnic heritage, religion, gender, education, and family structure. Sears, Roebuck and Company takes the position that diversity is an important source of competitive advantage. Management personnel at all levels are trained to follow the guidelines for enhancing diversity shown in Figure 7.2.

"GENTLEMEN, THERE'S BEEN SOME CRITICISM FROM SOME QUARTERS ABOUT THE SUPPOSED LACK OF DIVERSITY IN THE TOP RANKS OF THIS COMPANY."

One goal of diversity training is to help employees avoid dwelling on their differences and begin to focus on what members of the organization have in common. Companies should emphasize that they have their own cultures, to which every employee can belong and in which everyone abides by the same rules. Training programs need to clearly describe unacceptable conduct and explain that the organization will not condone it. The basic rules of civil behavior should be clearly spelled out. Most people want concrete examples of behavior that will not be tolerated. For example, employees would learn that humor containing degrading racial or cultural content is unacceptable.[38] We cannot stop people from bringing prejudices to work, but we can explain that they must learn to act as though they have none.[39]

AFFIRMATIVE ACTION: YESTERDAY AND TODAY

Does affirmative action right the wrongs of the past or create new ones? This issue is being debated by some of America's best thinkers, and we are hearing strong arguments for and against this controversial program. **Affirmative action** can be defined as a program that encourages the hiring and promotion of members of groups that have been discriminated against in the past. Affirma-

FIGURE 7.2

Sears's Diversity
Guidelines

A SEARS MANAGER'S GUIDE TO DIVERSITY

☐ Give each individual—whether customer,
   associate or vendor—your uncompromising
   respect.

☐ Through selection, hiring and retention strive
   to maintain a balanced workforce that meets
   the needs of your customers and reflects the
   community in which you do business.

☐ Never treat any applicant or associate
   differently because of race, color, religion,
   gender, age, national origin, disability, citizenship
   status, sexual orientation or status as a veteran.

☐ Promote and continue Sears tradition of
   excellence in community involvement, cultural
   celebration and charitable contributions.

☐ Support vendors who understand and respect
   the importance of diversity.

☐ Recognize the diversity of your Sears
   community. Reflect it in the way your unit
   does business.

Source: *Courtesy of Sears, Roebuck and Company.*

---

tive action, in all of its various forms, amounts to a major effort to make up for
past wrongs.[40]

The Civil Rights Act of 1964, subsequent amendments, and related laws
provide employment protection for women, minorities, and other categories of
disadvantaged individuals. Affirmative action programs have attacked employment discrimination with four methods:[41]

1. Active recruitment of women and minorities
2. Elimination of prejudicial questions on employment application forms
3. Establishment of specific goals and timetables for minority hiring
4. Validation of employment testing procedures

Affirmative action was originally designed to level the playing field of employment by outlawing discrimination in hiring. Not so long ago "Whites

only" was a common hiring standard, and you could find a "Help Wanted, Female" section in your daily newspaper.[42] There is no doubt that antidiscrimination legislation was needed. Affirmative action allowed a tremendous influx of diverse individuals through the front door of thousands of schools and organizations. Many were able to work their way into advanced, top-level positions. At the same time, however, affirmative action reinforced the historical view that the members of protected groups are not qualified for various positions and therefore need assistance just to get a job.

Many people say it is time to rethink affirmative action or even eliminate it. Recent political and legal interpretations of affirmative action have stimulated a nationwide debate over the merits of any program that grants preferential treatment to specific groups. Terry Eastland, author of *Ending Affirmative Action—The Case for Color Blind Justice,* has outlined some of the most common arguments voiced by those who want to end preferential policies:[43]

- *Preferences are discriminatory.* They tend to discriminate against those who are not members of the "right" race or gender.
- *Preferences do not counter discrimination.* Efforts by a company or a government to police presumed discrimination tend to move the focus away from real instances of discrimination that should be at the heart of law enforcement efforts.
- *Preferences do not make sense, given changing demographics.* The population eligible for affirmative action continues to grow several times faster than the nonpreferred population.

Colin Powell, a distinguished African American military leader, takes a more moderate position on affirmative action. He says, "If affirmative action means programs that provide equal opportunity, then I am all for it. If it leads to preferential treatment or helps those who no longer need help, I am opposed."[44] Barbara Bergmann, professor at American University and author of *In Defense of Affirmative Action,* presents the view that affirmative action is the only practical way to rectify discrimination in hiring. She states that many companies and government agencies will not embrace fairness in hiring and promotion as long as guidelines are voluntary.[45] Historian John Hope Franklin, who was selected to lead President Clinton's advisory board on race, is one of several noted scholars who believe affirmative action policies are important to achieve full racial equality. He supports programs that open opportunities but do not lower standards.[46]

The debate about affirmative action will continue for many years. The concept and the means for implementing it are likely to be challenged in court repeatedly over the next decade. We can expect a move to focus preferences on class or socioeconomic status rather than race or gender. And voluntary efforts to establish a diverse work force will likely continue because they can influence profits. As one author noted, "Appreciating diversity isn't just a nice idea, it's a business imperative."[47]

Summary

Work force diversity has become an important issue for organizations that want to remain competitive in a global economy. These organizations are beginning to move away from focusing on prejudice and discrimination and toward valuing diversity. Two dimensions, or sets of characteristics, are the basis of every individual's diversity. Primary dimensions include gender, age, race, physical and mental abilities, and sexual orientation. Secondary dimensions include health habits, religious beliefs, ethnic customs, communication style, relationship status, income, general appearance, and education and training.

Prejudice and discrimination are major barriers to effective human relations. Prejudice is an attitude based partly on observation of others' differences and partly on ignorance, fear, and cultural conditioning. Prejudiced people tend to see others as stereotypes rather than as unique individuals. Prejudicial attitudes are formed through the effects of childhood experiences, ethnocentrism, and economic factors. Discrimination is behavior based on prejudicial attitudes. Groups protected by law from discrimination in the workplace include women, people of color, older and younger workers, and those who have disabilities. More subtle forms of discrimination include discrimination arising from personal appearance, marital status, and so on. These subtle forms of discrimination are often difficult to prove but may be offset through assertiveness, a change in the behavior that causes the discrimination, or a move to a more tolerant organization.

The issue of valuing diversity is an economic one for most organizations. The changing demographics of American society mean that the work force will soon be made up of a minority of white men and a majority of women, people of color, and immigrants. Companies cannot afford to ignore this change in the pool of human resources.

Individuals can enhance diversity by letting go of their stereotypes and learning to critically and honestly evaluate their prejudiced attitudes as they work and socialize with people who are different. They will need to develop a sensitivity to differences and use language appropriately. Organizations must develop a culture that respects and enhances diversity. Their diversity training programs should become an internal process rather than an event. They need to seek out, employ, and develop people from diverse backgrounds.

Affirmative action guidelines have helped bring fairness in hiring and promotion to many organizations. Today, however, some people believe these guidelines are discriminatory because they allow preferential treatment for the people they were designed to protect. These preferences may no longer make sense, critics say, given the changing demographics of today's work force.

Career Corner

Q. I receive phone calls at work from customers located all over the world. Most of them speak English, but because of their accents, I often have difficulty understanding what they are trying to say to me. How can I handle these calls more effectively?

A. The fact that your customers can speak two languages indicates that they are probably educated and intelligent, so treat them with respect. Statements like "I can't understand you," or "What did you say?" are rude and should be avoided. Instead, take personal responsibility for improving the communications and gently say, "I am having a little difficulty understanding you, but if you will be patient with me I am sure I will be able to help." Ask them to slow down so that you can hear all the information correctly. Listen for key words and repeat them back to the caller. Identify coworkers who are fluent in a particular language, and ask them to help when calls come in from customers who share the same culture. Remember, people with foreign accents are not hard of hearing, so don't shout.

Key Terms

diversity
primary dimensions
secondary dimensions
prejudice
stereotypes

ethnocentrism
discrimination
valuing diversity
affirmative action

Review Questions

1. Distinguish between the primary and secondary dimensions of diversity, and give examples of each.
2. Why should organizations be concerned about valuing diversity?
3. How do the changing demographics of American culture affect the human resources pool of the future? Be specific.
4. Define *prejudice* and *discrimination.* How do these two terms differ in meaning?
5. What are some of the ways in which people acquire prejudices?
6. In what ways might valuing diversity impact an organization economically?
7. How can subtle forms of discrimination hurt the victim's chances to succeed in his or her career?
8. What role does affirmative action play in today's organizations? What are some of the positive and negative outcomes of affirmative action?
9. How can organizations enhance work force diversity?
10. What flaws in diversity training programs can cause a negative backlash among participants?

Application Exercises

1. Select a professional journal, the want ads from a local or national paper, or any magazine publication. Examine the ads, articles, and pictures for evidence that the publishers and advertisers are attempting to attract and respect readers from diverse races and cultures. For example, which racial or

ethnic groups are pictured in expensive cars, offices, or homes? If your chosen career is traditionally dominated by one gender, do articles in your professional journals include references to both sexes?

2. For one week, keep a diary that records every instance in which you see actions or hear comments that reflect outmoded, negative stereotypes. For instance, watch a movie, and observe whether the villains are all of a particular race. As you read textbooks from other courses you are taking, notice whether the pictures and examples reflect any stereotypes. Listen to your friends' conversations, and notice any time they make unfair judgments about others based on stereotypes. Share your experiences with class members, and discuss what steps you can take to help rid the environment of negative stereotyping.

3. John Hope Franklin, professor of history at Duke University, was selected to lead President Clinton's advisory board on race. In an interview conducted shortly after he accepted the assignment, he noted that there are constant reminders of the deep racial divide that exists in America and that cannot easily be bridged unless people from different ethnic or racial groups begin to establish a dialogue.

Meet with someone who is a member of a racial or ethnic group different from your own, and attempt to build a relationship by discussing the things that are important to each of you. As you get to know this person, become aware of his or her beliefs and attitudes. Try not to be diverted by accent, grammar, or personal appearance; rather, really listen to the person's thoughts and ideas. Search for things you and your new acquaintance have in common, and do not dwell on your differences.

Internet Exercise

Religious beliefs represent an important secondary dimension of diversity. Unfortunately, some people do not have very much tolerance for religious beliefs and practices that differ from their own. A 19-year-old woman living in Denver showed up for work at Domino's Pizza wearing a *hijab,* the traditional muslin head scarf. The manager told her to remove the scarf or leave. She had recently converted to Islam and was not sure if the manager was being rude or intolerant of her religion. Later, company officials discovered that the manager's order was a violation of Title VII of the Civil Rights Act of 1964. The employee was then told she could wear a scarf as long as it was red and blue, the company colors.[48] Visit the Web site of one or more religious advocacy groups and find out if it provides information on religious rights at work. Examples include the Anti-Defamation League and the Council on American-Islamic Relations. You may also type in "religious rights" and "religious freedom." Prepare a written summary of your findings.

Self-Assessment Exercise

1. For each of the following statements, circle the number from 1 to 5 that best represents your response: (1) strongly disagree (never do this); (2) disagree (rarely do this); (3) moderately agree (sometimes do this); (4) agree (frequently do this); (5) strongly agree (always do this).

   a. I refuse to perpetuate negative stereotypes and   1   2   3   4   5
   accept each person as a unique individual worthy of my respect.

   b. I make every effort to identify my own preju-   1   2   3   4   5
   diced attitudes and avoid stereotypical attitudes toward people of color, older people, persons with disabilities, and others who are different from me.

   c. I work hard to combat prejudice because it has   1   2   3   4   5
   a negative impact on my self-esteem and the self-esteem of the victim.

   Select an appropriate attitude or skill you would like to improve. Write your goal in the space provided.

   GOAL: _____

   _____

   _____

Case Problem

Piscataway Township Versus Taxman

Two business education teachers began teaching the same day in Piscataway, New Jersey: Sharon Taxman was white; Debra Williams was black. In 1989 the school board was forced to reduce the ten-person business education department by one person, and school protocol demanded "last one in, first one out." Both women, however, had been hired the same day.

To preserve an element of diversity, the school board fired Ms. Taxman and retained Ms. Williams, the only minority in the department. Ms. Taxman sued the school district, claiming violation of her rights guaranteed by the affirmative action guidelines of the 1964 Civil Rights Act, which prohibits discrimination based on race. The U.S. Court of Appeals for the Third Circuit decided that affirmative action could not be used for achieving diversity. The judges wrote that affirmative action could be justified only as a remedy for precisely identified past discrimination.

People trying to preserve affirmative action argue that Title VII of the 1964 Civil Rights Act permits the use of race- and gender-based preferences. Opponents argue that the attempt to maintain a diverse work force has nothing to do with remedying past discrimination and that firing decisions based on race represent blatant discrimination. The Supreme Court agreed to hear the case in January 1998.

However, two months before the Supreme Court docket date, Taxman and her attorneys accepted an out-of-court settlement for $431,000: $186,000 in back salary and interest, plus $245,000 to cover eight years of legal fees. Opponents of affirmative action expressed disappointment as their expected victory was taken away. Supporters of affirmative action not only were relieved that the case did not go to court but also were instrumental in raising approximately 70 percent of the cash settlement through the Black Leadership Forum, a coalition of major civil rights groups, including the Urban League and the NAACP Legal Defense and Educational Fund. Jesse Jackson, leader of the Rainbow Coalition, was one of the civil rights leaders who pushed for an out-of-court settlement and helped raise the money.

Although the U.S. Court of Appeals decided that affirmative action laws could not be used to justify the firing of Sharon Taxman, this decision does not set a precedent for other states. The rest of the nation must wait for the Supreme Court to resolve the issue.

Questions

1. If you were serving on the Supreme Court, would you have upheld the rights of the fired, white teacher, or would you have voted for the right of the school board to maintain faculty diversity? Explain.
2. Polls consistently show that a majority of Americans support efforts to help people who have been excluded from basic opportunities in areas such as education and employment. However, many people oppose race and gender "preferences." In place of preferences based on race and gender, some would substitute preferences for the economically disadvantaged. What is your position on preferences based on race and gender? On economic disadvantages? Explain your answer.

Chapter 8

Strategies for Resolving Conflict and Achieving Emotional Control

Chapter Preview

After studying this chapter, you will be able to

1. List and describe some of the major causes for conflicts between people in the work setting.
2. Explain the three basic conflict resolution strategies.
3. Understand the role that assertiveness and cooperation play in personal conflict management.
4. Identify the five steps of the conflict resolution process.
5. Describe how emotions influence our thinking and behavior.
6. Understand the factors that contribute to emotional balance.
7. List and describe the major factors that influence our emotional development.
8. Learn how to deal with your anger and the anger of others.
9. Describe strategies for achieving emotional control.

TODAY WORKERS face subtle conflicts over issues that did not exist fifteen to twenty years ago. For example, most families now depend on two incomes for economic survival. As a result, working parents are demanding and getting new rights and benefits to help balance their personal and professional lives. Flextime, available at some companies, allows working parents to tailor their arrival and departure times at work to fit their child-care arrangements. Many family-friendly employers allow workers time off to attend special activities that involve their children. Some firms offer parental and maternity leave to both fathers and mothers of newborn babies. Conflicts can arise if workers who have not yet started their families or who have chosen to be child-free feel slighted when benefits and privileges are awarded to workers with children. Child-free workers in some organizations are expected to maintain regular working hours while their coworkers adjust to child-care challenges by arriving late for work or leaving early. Child-free workers may be denied personal leave time to care for a critically ill spouse while other workers have time off related to a pregnancy. And sometimes—when it comes time to work late into the evening or on weekends—child-free workers are asked or told to put forth extra effort by employers who fear they will be criticized for interfering with the "family time" of working parents. ■

What are employers to do? As organizations struggle to resolve nontraditional conflicts, traditional management-versus-labor disputes, as well as numerous other conflicts in the workplace, conflict resolution becomes a necessary human relations skill for workers and managers alike.

A key element of conflict resolution is emotional balance. This is achieved, in part, by learning to deal with your anger and the anger of others. The factors that contribute to emotional balance will be discussed later in this chapter.

A NEW VIEW OF CONFLICT

Most standard dictionaries define **conflict** as a clash between incompatible people, ideas, or interests. These conflicts are almost always perceived as negative experiences in our society. But when we view conflict as a negative experience, we may be hurting our chances of dealing with it effectively. Many books and articles imply that we must do everything in our power to eliminate the conflicts in our professional and personal lives. In reality, conflicts can serve as opportunities for personal growth if we develop and use positive, constructive conflict resolution skills.[1]

Much of our growth and social progress comes from the opportunities we have to discover creative solutions to conflicts that surface in our lives. Dudley Weeks, professor of conflict resolution at American University, says conflict

Total Person Insight

"The rapid changes of the twentieth century have increased human conflict to the point that our sensibilities toward each other are becoming numb. The human capacity for adaptation may be working against our social relationships as we passively accept conditions that are not conducive to the effective resolution of interpersonal differences. Just as we adapt to bad air, tasteless food, polluted water, congested cities, and loud noise, we are also becoming callous and indifferent to the factors in our environment that are setting us at one another's throats."

GORDON LIPPITT

Consultant, Human Resource Development

can be used to clarify a relationship, provide additional ways of thinking about the source of conflict, and open up possibilities for improving a relationship.[2]

Sometimes a difference of opinion is the first step in getting rid of outdated rules and regulations. When people work together to resolve conflicts, their solutions are often far more creative than they would be if only one person addressed the problem. Creatively managed conflict can shake people out of their mental ruts and give them new frameworks, new assumptions, and new points of view. The heart of effective human relations lies not in trying to eliminate conflict (an impossible task) but in making constructive use of the energy released by conflict.

Causes of Conflict

Conflicts among workers are caused by a wide range of factors. Some are major and need to be addressed through the legal system or labor union negotiations. Others seem relatively minor but can still have a major impact on the productivity of an organization. Here we discuss several causes of conflict that may help you anticipate, and therefore solve, people problems in your organization.

Ineffective Communication A major source of personal conflict is the misunderstanding that results from ineffective communication. In Chapter 2 we discussed the various filters that messages must pass through before effective

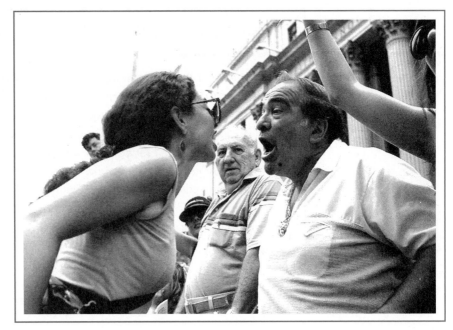

communication can occur. In the work setting, where many different people work closely together, communication breakdowns are inevitable.

Value Clashes In Chapter 4 you read that differences in values can cause conflicts between generations, among men and women, and among people with different value priorities. Consider the conflicts that might arise between "loyalists," who join their organization for life and make decisions for their own good as well as the good of the company, and "job-hoppers," who accept a job in order to position themselves for the next opportunity that might further their personal career advancement. The opportunities for value clashes are almost limitless in today's diverse organizations.

Culture Clashes For generations, culture clashes have occurred between workers not only from other countries but also from different parts of the United States. Today's diverse work force reflects a kaleidoscope of cultures, each with its own unique qualities. The individual bearers of these different cultural traditions could easily come into conflict with one another. The issues may be as simple as one person's desire to dress in ethnic fashion and a supervisor's insistence on strict adherence to the company dress code, or as complex as work ethics.

Work Policies and Practices Interpersonal conflicts can develop when an organization has arbitrary or confusing rules, regulations, and performance

---

Total Person Insight

"Everything that irritates us about others can lead us to an understanding of ourselves."

CARL JUNG, M.D.

Swiss Psychiatrist

---

standards. Workers will see little correlation between job performance and salary advancement if they discover that another worker doing the same job is making more money or is being promoted faster than they are. Conflicts over work rules or the interpretation of these rules, are quite common.

Adversarial Management   Under adversarial management, supervisors may view their employees and even other managers with suspicion and distrust and treat them as "the enemy." Employees usually lack respect for adversarial managers, resenting their authoritarian style and resisting their suggestions for change. This atmosphere makes cooperation and teamwork difficult. Supervisors who display genuine concern for both people and production and are sensitive to employee needs have far fewer conflicts than do adversarial managers.

Noncompliance   Conflict also surfaces when some workers refuse to comply with the rules and neglect their fair share of the workload. Coworkers get angry if they have to put forth extra effort to get the work done because others are taking two-hour lunch breaks, sleeping on the job, making personal phone calls during office hours, and wasting time. Now that so many organizations are organizing their work forces into teams, noncompliance has the potential for becoming a major source of conflict.

Difficult People   The focus of this book is to help you become a valued worker who is easy to get along with and productive regardless of your career path. However, you are likely to encounter coworkers who have not studied human relations. Some of them will be difficult to get along with, no matter what you do. In their book *Dealing with People You Can't Stand*, Rick Kirschner and Rick Brinkman identify ten types of difficult personalities (see Figure 8.1). They suggest four options you might consider when you work with difficult people:

1. Suffer in silence.
2. Change your attitude. You may not like the individual, but you can still work well together.

Dealing with People You Can't Stand

The Tanks: Pushy and ruthless, loud and forceful, they assume that the end justifies the means.

When under attack, hold your position, make direct eye contact, focus on breathing slowly and deeply. When they finish, say, "When you're ready to speak to me with respect, I'll be ready to discuss this matter."

The Snipers: Identify your weaknesses and use them against you through sabotage behind your back or putdowns in front of the crowd.

Stop in midsentence and focus your full attention on them. Ask them to clarify their grievance. If it is valid, take action; if invalid, express your appreciation and calmly offer new information.

The Know-It-Alls: Will tell you what they know—for hours at a time—but won't take a second to listen to your "clearly inferior" ideas.

Acknowledge their expertise and be prepared with your facts. Use plural pronouns like *we* or *us*. Present your information as probing questions rather than statements so that you are less threatening and appear willing to learn from them.

The Think-They-Know-It-Alls: They don't know much, but they don't let that get in the way. They exaggerate, brag, mislead, and distract.

Acknowledge their input, but question their facts with "I" statements, such as, "From what I've read and experienced . . ."

The Grenades: When they blow their tops, they're unable to stop. When the smoke clears and the dust settles, the cycle begins again.

When the explosion begins, assertively repeat the individual's name to get his or her attention. Then calmly address the person's first few sentences, which usually identify the real problem. Suggest taking time out to cool down, then really listen to the problem.

The Yes Persons: They are quick to agree but slow to deliver, leaving a trail of unkept commitments and broken promises.

When they say yes, ask them to summarize their commitment and write it down. Arrange a weird deadline (9:11 A.M. on Thursday) and describe the negative consequences that will result if they do not follow through.

The Maybe Persons: When faced with a crucial decision, they keep putting it off until it's too late and the decision makes itself.

List advantages and disadvantages of the decision or option. Help them feel comfortable and safe, and stay in touch until the decision is implemented.

The Nothing Persons: No verbal or nonverbal feedback. They tell you nothing and stare past you as if you're not there.

Use open-ended questions that begin with *who, what, where, when,* or *how;* use humor; describe negative results of not talking to you.

The No Persons: Doleful and discouraging, they say, "What goes up must come down." And what comes down must never be able to get back up again.

Ask them to critique your ideas. This shows you are approaching the problem realistically and with an open mind. Listen to their feedback, fix the problems, then present the plan.

The Whiners: They wallow in their woe, whine incessantly, and carry the weight of the world on their shoulders.

Listen and write down their main points. Interrupt and get specifics; identify and focus on possible solutions. If they remain in "it's hopeless" mode, walk away saying, "Let me know when you want to talk about solving the problem."

FIGURE 8.1

Source: From Rick Brinkman and Rick Kirschner, *Dealing with People You Can't Stand.* Copyright © 1994 by McGraw-Hill, Inc. Reprinted by permission of The McGraw-Hill Companies.

3. Change your behavior so that the difficult person has to learn new ways of dealing with you.

4. Look for a new job. Not all situations can be resolved.[3]

Thinking / Learning Starters

1. Have you ever experienced a conflict with a coworker? Explain. How did you handle the situation? Did you confront the other person? What were the results? Could you have handled the situation in a more productive manner? Explain.

2. Identify some of the causes of conflict in an organization in which you worked as an employee or volunteer. What types of conflict seemed to cause the most trouble among people?

DEALING WITH CONFLICT

In baseball, if two runners try to occupy the same base at the same time, there is conflict. It is an exciting situation, but if a positive solution is not found quickly, both they and their team will be losers. We must accept the fact that anytime two or more people are brought together, the stage is set for potential conflict. When conflict does occur, the results may be positive or negative, depending on how those involved choose to approach it.

When a difference of opinion has progressed to open conflict, various conflict resolution strategies may be needed to resolve the issue. When a conflict resolution strategy is applied, all opposing parties may or may not be satisfied with the outcome. Generally speaking, if any of the parties involved are dissatisfied, the conflict will probably arise again in the future.

Some of the most common approaches used to resolve conflict include withdrawing from an actual or potential dispute, smoothing it over, compromising, enforcing a solution, and confronting the situation directly. These and other approaches can be grouped into three basic conflict resolution strategies: win/lose, lose/lose, and win/win.

Win/Lose Strategy

When you rely on the **win/lose strategy,** you achieve your goals at the expense of others. Determining when to use this strategy depends on how severe the problem is and what results are desired from the solution. Although this approach may solve the conflict on a short-term basis, it usually does not address the underlying causes of the problem. When one person wins and the other loses, the loser is likely to resent the solution and may feel like a victim. In one sense, this approach simply sows the seeds for another conflict because the "loser" may seek revenge. When might the win/lose strategy be used? It can serve in situations where two factions simply cannot agree on any solution or may not even be able to talk to each other.

Lose/Lose Strategy

All parties usually lose when the **lose/lose strategy** is used. Despite the negative overtones associated with this term, the lose/lose strategy can be called on to eliminate conflicts—again, depending on the results desired. If the persons involved in the conflict are asked to compromise, then each must give up something. This sometimes happens when there is little time to find a solution through discussion and mutual problem solving.

In general, the lose/lose and win/lose strategies create a "we versus they" attitude among the people involved in the conflict rather than a "we versus the problem" approach. We versus they (or "my way versus your way") means that participants focus on whose solution is superior instead of working together to find a solution that is acceptable to all concerned.

Win/Win Strategy

The basic purpose of the **win/win strategy** is to fix the problem—not the blame! Those who use this strategy listen to all points of view, define the basic issues, and create an atmosphere of trust among all involved. Everyone must believe that the problem will be settled on the merits of the case rather than through political or personal influence. Those involved in the win/win process should be flexible, sensitive, patient, and calm. No one should feel threatened or humiliated. The result of the win/win strategy will be a solution to the problem that caused the conflict—one that meets individual needs, results in mutual benefits, and strengthens the relationship.

Assertiveness: A Personal Strategy for Resolving Conflict

Assertiveness is based on rights. **Assertive behavior** involves standing up for your rights and expressing your thoughts and feelings in a direct, appropriate way that does not violate the rights of others. It is a matter of getting the

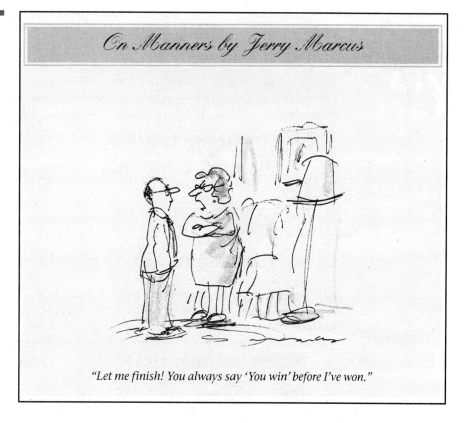

On Manners by Jerry Marcus

"Let me finish! You always say 'You win' before I've won."

other person to understand your viewpoint.[4] People who exhibit assertive behavior skills are able to handle their conflicts with greater ease and assurance while maintaining good interpersonal relations. Use assertive behaviors when you sense someone is taking advantage of you, ignoring your needs, or disregarding your point of view.

Some people do not understand the distinction between being aggressive and being assertive. **Aggressive behavior** involves expressing your thoughts and feelings and defending your rights in a way that violates the rights of others. Aggressive people may interrupt, talk fast, ignore others, and use sarcasm or other forms of verbal abuse to maintain control. They do not view conflict resolution as a strategy for improving relationships.

People who attempt to avoid conflict by simply ignoring things that bother them are exhibiting **nonassertive behavior.** Nonassertive people often give in to the demands of others, and their passive approach makes them less likely to make their needs known. If you fail to take a firm position when such action is appropriate, colleagues may take advantage of you, and management may question your ability to lead.[5] Table 8.1 may give you a clearer understanding

> ## Total Person Insight
>
> *"Any method of negotiation may be fairly judged by three criteria: It should produce a wise agreement if agreement is possible. It should be efficient. And it should improve or at least not damage the relationship between the parties."*
>
> ROGER FISHER AND WILLIAM URY
>
> Authors, *Getting to Yes*

of how assertive, aggressive, and nonassertive individuals respond when confronted with conflict situations.

How to Become More Assertive   If you are aggressive, nonassertive, or less assertive than you would like to be in certain situations, do not be discouraged. With practice, you can acquire the sense of well-being that comes with knowing that you can communicate your wants, dislikes, and feelings in a clear, direct manner without threatening or attacking others. Entire books have been written describing assertiveness skills, so it is impossible to explain the various techniques within the context of this short chapter. Nevertheless, we can offer you practical guidelines that may help you develop assertiveness skills.

1. *In the beginning, take small steps.* Being assertive may be difficult at first, so start with something that is easy. You might decline the invitation to keep the minutes at the weekly staff meeting if you feel others should assume this duty from time to time. If you are tired of eating lunch at Joe's Diner (the choice of a coworker), suggest a restaurant that you would prefer. If someone insists on keeping the temperature at a cool 68 degrees and you are tired of being cold all the time, approach the person and voice your opinion. Keeping other people from getting what they want, while asking that your desires be considered, is not necessarily a bad thing.[6]

2. *Use communication skills that enhance assertiveness.* A confident tone of voice, eye contact, firm gestures, and good posture create nonverbal messages that say, "I'm serious about this request." Using "I" messages can be especially helpful in cases where you want to assert yourself in a nonthreatening manner. If you approach the person who wants the thermostat set at 68 degrees and say, "You need to be more considerate of others," the person will likely become defensive. However, if you say, "I feel uncomfortable when the temperature is so cool," you will start the conversation on a more positive note.

TABLE 8.1

Behaviors Exhibited
by Assertive,
Aggressive, and
Nonassertive Persons

	Assertive Person	Aggressive Person	Nonassertive Person
In conflict situations	Communicates directly	Dominates	Avoids the conflict
In decision-making situations	Chooses for self	Chooses for self and others	Allows others to choose
In situations expressing feelings	Open, direct, honest, while allowing others to express their feelings	Expresses feelings in a threatening manner; puts down, inhibits others	Holds true feelings inside
In group meeting situations	Direct, clear, "I" statements: "I believe that . . ."	Clear but demeaning "you" statements: "You should have known better . . ."	Indirect, unclear statements: "Would you mind if . . ."

3. *Be soft on people and hard on the problem.* The goal of conflict resolution is to solve the problem but avoid doing harm to the relationship. Of course, relationships tend to become entangled with the problem, so there is a tendency to treat the people and the problem as one. Your coworker Terry is turning in projects late every week, and you are feeling a great deal of frustration each time it happens. You must communicate to Terry that each missed deadline creates serious problems for you. Practice using tact, diplomacy, and patience as you keep the discussion focused on the problem, not on Terry's personality traits.

Conflict Resolution Styles

Depending on personality and past experiences in dealing with conflict in the workplace, individuals naturally develop their own conflict resolution styles. Through training in assertiveness and conflict resolution, individuals can learn to recognize their own style as well as the styles of others. They can learn how and when to adapt their behavioral style to deal effectively with conflict situations.

Robert Maddux has proposed a conflict resolution model that combines two factors: degree of assertiveness and degree of cooperation (see Figure 8.2). He suggests that there are five different styles resulting from various combinations of assertiveness and cooperation. Maddux takes the position that differing styles may be appropriate in different situations. He says, for example, if you must win at any cost, then the *win/lose style* may be your best option. If your goal is to maximize cooperation, even at the expense of personal goals, then the *accommodating style* would be your best choice.

Avoidance Style (Uncooperative/Nonassertive)   This style is appropriate when the conflict is too minor or too great to resolve. Any attempt to resolve

FIGURE 8.2

Conflict Resolution Styles

Source: Adapted from Robert B. Maddux, *Team Building: An Exercise in Leadership,* Crisp Publications, Inc., Menlo, CA, 1986, p. 53. Reprinted by permission of the publisher.

the conflict might result in damaging a relationship or simply wasting time and energy. Avoidance might take the form of diplomatically sidestepping an issue or postponing your response until a more appropriate time.

Accommodating Style (Cooperative/Nonassertive) This style is appropriate when resolving the conflict is not worth risking damage to the relationship or general disharmony. Individuals who use this approach relinquish their own concerns to satisfy the concerns of someone else. Accommodating might take the form of selfless generosity or blind obedience to another's point of view.

Win/Lose Style (Uncooperative/Aggressive) This style may be appropriate when the conflict involves "survival of the fittest," when you must prove your superior position, or when your opinion is the most ethically or professionally correct. This power-oriented position allows you to use whatever means seem appropriate when it is time to stand up for your rights.

Compromising Style (Moderately Aggressive/Moderately Cooperative) This style is appropriate when no one person or idea is perfect, when there is more than one good way to do something, or when you must give to get what you want. Compromise attempts to find mutually acceptable solutions to the conflict that partially satisfy both sides. Never use this style when unethical activities are the cause of the conflict.

Problem-Solving Style (Assertive/Cooperative) This style is appropriate when all parties openly discuss the issues and a mutually beneficial solution can be found without anyone making a major concession. Problem solvers attempt to uncover underlying issues that may be at the root of the problem and then focus the discussion toward achieving the most desirable outcome. They seek to replace conflict with collaboration.

Thinking / Learning Starters

1. Imagine and describe the human relations atmosphere in an organization where win/lose strategies are consistently applied.

2. Briefly describe the most recent conflict you had with another person. How assertive were you? How assertive was the other person? Who won? Who lost? How might you have changed your conflict resolution style to better handle the situation?

CONFLICT RESOLUTION PROCESS

In the past, the responsibility for conflict resolution was often given to supervisors, department heads, team leaders, shop stewards, mediators, and other individuals with established authority and responsibility. Today, the picture is changing as more companies are organizing workers into teams. The trend toward increased worker participation in decision making and problem solving (employee empowerment) is also having an impact on conflict resolution practices. Many progressive organizations want employees to resolve their own conflicts whenever possible. This means that every employee needs to possess conflict resolution skills. The **conflict resolution process** consists of five steps that can be used in both work and family situations.

Step One: Decide Whether You Have a Misunderstanding or a True Disagreement

David Stiebel, author of *When Talking Makes Things Worse!*, says a misunderstanding is a failure to accurately understand the other person's point. A disagreement, in contrast, is a failure to agree that would persist despite the most accurate understanding. In a true disagreement, people want more than your explanation and further details; they want to change your mind.[7] When we fail to realize the distinction between these two possibilities, a great deal of time and energy may be wasted. Consider the following conflict situation.

As Sarah entered the driveway of her home, she could hardly wait to share the news with her husband, Paul. Late that afternoon she had met with her boss and learned she was the number-one candidate for a newly created supervisory position. Sarah entered the house and immediately told Paul about the promotion opportunity. In a matter of seconds, it became apparent that he was not happy about the promotion. He said, "We don't need the extra money, and you do not need the headaches that come with a supervisory position." Having expected a positive response, Sarah was very disappointed. In the heat of anger, Sarah and Paul both said things they would later regret.

If Sarah and Paul had asked each other a few questions, this conflict might have been avoided. Prior to arriving home, Sarah had already weighed the pros and cons of the new position and decided it was not a good career move; however, she wanted her husband's input before making the final decision. This conflict was not a true disagreement, in which one person tries to change the other person's mind; it was a misunderstanding that was the result of incomplete information. If Sarah and Paul had fully understood each other's position, it would have become clear that a true disagreement did not exist.

Step Two: Define the Problem and Collect the Facts

The saying "A problem well defined is a problem half solved" is not far from the truth. It is surprising how difficult this step can be. Everyone involved needs to focus on the real cause of the conflict, not on what has happened as a result of it. At this stage, it is helpful to have everyone write a one- or two-sentence definition of the problem. When everyone is allowed to define the problem, the real cause of the conflict will often surface.

As you begin collecting information about the conflict, it may be necessary to separate facts from opinions. Ask questions that focus on who is involved in the conflict, what happened, when, where, and why. What policies and procedures were involved? Collection of all the facts may be impossible in a particular case, but as long as the major points are identified, the process can keep moving.

Step Three: Clarify Perceptions

Your perception is your interpretation of the facts surrounding the situations you encounter. Perceptions can have a tremendous influence on your behavior. In a conflict situation, it is therefore very important that you clarify all parties' perceptions of the problem. You can do this by attempting to see the situation as others see it. Take the case of Laura, a sales representative who was repeatedly passed over for a promotion even though her sales numbers were among the best in the department.

Over a period of time Laura became convinced that she was the victim of gender discrimination. She filed charges with the Equal Employment Opportunity Commission (EEOC), and a hearing was scheduled. When Laura's boss was given a chance to explain his actions, he described Laura as someone who was very dedicated to her family. He said, "It's my view that she would be unhappy in a sales management position because she would have to work longer hours and travel more." He did not see his actions as being discriminatory. Laura explained that she valued the time she spent with her husband and children but achieving a management position was an important career goal. Laura and her boss's perceptions of the same situation were totally different.

Dudley Weeks says there are some important questions to be asked as you clarify perceptions of the conflict. What does each party think the conflict is about? Is the conflict over deeply held values or just preferences? Is the conflict over goals or methods? The answers to these questions can be important components of the conflict resolution process.[8]

Step Four: Generate Options for Mutual Gain

Once the basic problem has been defined, the facts surrounding it have been brought out, and everyone is operating with the same perceptions, everyone involved in the conflict should focus on generating options that will fix the problem. Some people, however, do not consider generating options to be part of the conflict resolution process. Rather than broadening the options for mutual gain, some individuals want to quickly build support for a single solution. The authors of the best-selling book *Getting to Yes* say, "In a dispute, people usually believe that they know the right answer—their view should prevail."[9] This is where brainstorming comes in. **Brainstorming** is a process that encourages all those involved in the conflict to generate a wide variety of ideas and possibilities that will lead to the desired results. No one should be allowed to evaluate, judge, or rule out any proposed solution. Each person is encouraged to tap his or her creative energies without fear of ridicule or criticism. Once all options are on the table, you will need to eliminate those that will not lead to the desired results and settle on the most appropriate ones.

Step Five: Implement Options with Integrity

The final step in the conflict resolution process involves finalizing an agreement that offers win/win benefits to those in conflict. Sometimes, as the conflict resolution process comes to a conclusion, one or more parties in the conflict may be tempted to win an advantage that weakens the relationship. This might involve hiding information or using pressure tactics that violate the win/win spirit and weaken the relationship. Even the best conflict solutions can fail unless all conflict partners serve as "caretakers" of the agreement and the relationship.[10]

Establish timetables for implementing the solutions, and provide a plan to evaluate their effectiveness. On a regular basis, make a point to discuss with others how things are going to be sure that old conflict patterns do not resurface. Conflict resolution agreements must be realistic and effective enough to survive as the challenges of the future confront them. Avoid the temptation to implement quick-fix solutions that may prove to be unsatisfactory in a few weeks.[11]

Beware of Defensive Behaviors

Progress toward conflict resolution is often slowed or sidetracked completely by defensive behaviors that surface when individuals are faced with unwarranted criticism, reminders of their shortcomings, or threats to their security. When one person in a conflict situation becomes defensive, others may mirror this behavior. In a short time, progress is slowed because people stop listening and begin thinking about how they can defend themselves against the other person's comments.

ACHIEVING EMOTIONAL CONTROL

An **emotion** can be thought of as a feeling, such as jealousy, fear, love, joy, and grief, that influences our thinking and behavior. It is not an exaggeration to say that much of the human behavior we observe every day springs from feelings. An emotional experience often alters thought processes by directing attention toward some things and away from others.

Throughout each day our feelings are activated by a variety of events (see Figure 8.3). You might feel a sense of joy after learning that a coworker has just given birth to a new baby. You might feel tremendous grief after learning that your supervisor was killed in an auto accident. Angry feelings may surface when you discover that someone borrowed a tool without your permission. Once your feelings have been activated, your mind interprets the event. In some cases, the feelings trigger irrational thinking: "No one who works here can be trusted!" In other cases, you may engage in a rational thinking process: "Perhaps the person who borrowed the tool needed it to help a customer with an emergency repair." The important point to remember is that we can choose how we behave.

Feelings provide us with knowledge of our current emotional condition and the energy to act out our beliefs.[12] For example, after an argument with a coworker you may experience anger over your coworker's comments or regret about your own. Feelings serve as communication links with your emotions.

Emotional Intelligence

Daniel Goleman, author of the best-selling book *Emotional Intelligence,* challenges the traditional view of the relationship between IQ and success. He says there are widespread exceptions to the rule that IQ predicts success: "At best,

FIGURE 8.3

Behavior Is Influenced
by Activating Events

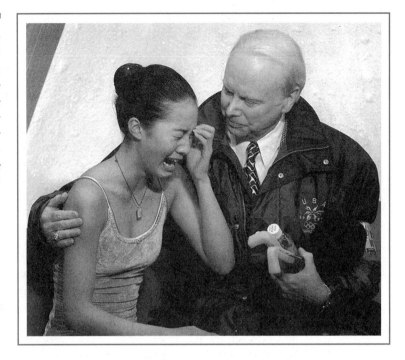

We often see a variety of emotions expressied at sporting events. Here we see Michelle Kwan, Olympic ice skater, crying after completing her silver medal performance. (AP/Wide World Photos)

IQ contributes about 20 percent to the factors that determine life success, which leaves 80 percent to other forces."[13] Goleman's book focuses on the human characteristics that make up what he describes as *emotional intelligence*. The ability to keep distressing emotions in check is a fundamental aspect of emotional intelligence, according to Goleman.[14]

Emotional Balance

We carry inside us a large array of emotions that have been with us since birth and will be with us until death. However, we sometimes suffer from a lack of emotional balance because we learn to inhibit the expression of certain emotions and to overemphasize the expression of others. Some families, for example, discourage the expression of love and affection. Some people are taught from an early age to avoid expressing anger. Others learn that a public display of grief (crying, for example) is a sign of weakness. If as a child you were strongly encouraged to avoid the expression of anger, fear, love, or some other emotion, you may repress or block these feelings as an adult.[15]

Emotional imbalance also develops if we become fixated on a single emotion. The high incidence of violent crime in America has motivated some people to become almost totally infused with the emotion of fear. One writer

---

Total Person Insight

"All of our technology is underutilized and will remain so until we put the emotion of doing business onto parity with the logical and rational aspects of performance improvement."

JAMES C. GEORGES

Chief Executive Officer, The Par Group

---

noted that people who are preoccupied with fear may be intensifying the problem: "We have a habit of keeping ourselves overwhelmed, through the news media, with bad and scary things that have happened all over the world each day; and then the chronic pattern of worrying about which of these bad things might happen to us in the future."[16] To focus on one emotion to the exclusion of others creates a serious imbalance within us. A person obsessed with hatred toward a specific minority group will find it difficult to display compassion toward persons who are members of that group. The emotion of hatred can overpower and extinguish the emotion of love.

FACTORS THAT INFLUENCE OUR EMOTIONS

The starting point in achieving greater emotional control is to determine the source of emotional difficulties. Why do we sometimes display indifference when the expression of compassion would be more appropriate? Why is it so easy to put down a friend or coworker and so hard to recognize that person's accomplishments? Why do we sometimes worry about events that will never happen? To answer these and other questions, it is necessary to study the factors that influence our emotional development.

Temperament

Temperament refers to a person's individual style and frequency of expressing needs and emotions; it is biological and genetically based. It reflects a contribution by nature to the beginning of an individual's personality.[17] Researchers have found that certain temperamental characteristics are apparent in children at birth and remain somewhat stable over time. For example, the traits associated with extroversion and introversion can be observed when a baby is born.

Of course, many events take place between infancy and adulthood to alter or shape a person's temperament. Personality at every age reflects the interplay of temperament and of environmental influences, such as parenting.[18]

Subconscious Influences

The **subconscious mind** is a vast storehouse of forgotten memories, desires, ideas, and frustrations, according to William Menninger, founder of the famed Menninger Foundation.[19] He noted that the subconscious mind can have a great influence on behavior. It contains memories of past experiences as well as memories of feelings associated with past experiences. The subconscious is active, continuously influencing conscious decision-making processes.

Cultural Conditioning

A professor at Dartmouth College said, "Culture is what we see and hear so often that we call it reality. Out of culture comes behavior."[20] A number of cultural influences are currently having a dramatic impact on the emotional health of American children and adults. According to the National School Boards Association, U.S. schools are being hit by an epidemic of violence. About one-quarter of all students say they have been victims of violence in or near their public schools.[21]

The rate of interpersonal violence in the United States is the highest among all industrialized countries. Americans of all ages are preoccupied with violence and encounter fictionalized violence in movies, TV programs, and video games. Research indicates that by the time most Americans reach the age of 18, they will have seen 40,000 made-for-TV murders and 200,000 acts of violence. The negative effects of televised violence appear to be increased aggression—both immediate and long term—in children and adults.[22] In addition to mass media violence, there is the real violence in sports as fights occur more frequently during games.

We are just beginning to understand the extent and seriousness of family violence in America. It appears to be far more common than most experts imagined. The authors of *No Safe Haven*, a major report on violence against women by an American Psychological Association task force, notes that as many as 4 million women experience a severe or life-threatening assault from a male partner in an average twelve-month period.[23] Domestic abuse is the leading cause of injury to women in this country. Many people—both men and women—are victims of verbal aggression, which may take the form of insults or swearing. Verbal aggression can affect people in ways similar to physical aggression, and it is also sometimes the first step toward physical aggression.[24]

Azim Khamisa (second from left) and Ples Felix, with students at Birney Elementary School in San Diego, organized the first Violence Impact Forum—a program aimed at ending the culture of gang violence. After Khamisa's only son was killed by Felix's grandson, the two men put aside their differences and decided to join together to try to prevent further violence. (James Aronovsky)

COPING WITH YOUR ANGER AND THE ANGER OF OTHERS

In the presence of disagreement or conflict we often experience primary feelings such as frustration, hurt, embarrassment, guilt, or insecurity. These feelings are often followed by the secondary feeling of anger. If someone strongly criticizes your work in front of coworkers, you may experience shame, alarm, or insecurity, which are primary feelings. Later, in the privacy of your office or home, you may begin to feel a strong sense of anger. You may say to yourself, "She didn't have to criticize my work in front of everybody!"

Anger may be defined as the thoughts, feelings, physical reactions, and actions that result from unacceptable behavior by others.[25] The negative emotion of anger often triggers hostility. Learning to deal effectively with anger is a key to a healthy relationship and to your physical and mental health. The authors of *Anger Kills* say that about 20 percent of the general population have levels of hostility high enough to be dangerous to health, another 20 percent have very low levels, and the rest of the population fall somewhere in between.[26] Learning to deal with your anger, and the anger of other people, is one of the most sophisticated and mature skills people are ever required to learn. Intense anger takes control of people and distorts their perceptions, which is why angry people often make poor decisions.[27]

Taking Control of Your Anger

When anger surfaces, we usually have several options. If another driver pulls out in front of your car and almost causes an accident, you will likely feel fear (a primary feeling) followed by anger (a secondary feeling). One option is to suppress the angry feelings. Another is to give way to irrational thinking and act out your angry feelings. You may be tempted to pull alongside the other driver and make a threatening gesture or shout obscenities. The consequences of this action may be quite negative. The other person may respond with further threats, and conflict may evolve to a point where violence takes place. Even if no such response takes place, you may experience feelings of guilt or embarrassment after acting out your anger in a destructive manner.

Appropriate expressions of anger can reduce your anxiety and help you get rid of unhealthy stress. An expression of anger may also improve communication, because the other person learns exactly how you feel. In deciding whether to express your anger, consider these factors:

1. *Try to determine what impact your message will have on the self-esteem of the other person.* Is this person able to hear and understand your feelings without feeling threatened, inferior, or defensive?
2. *Consider the stability of the relationship between yourself and the other person.* Is the relationship strong enough to withstand the impact of your anger? Will your expression of anger evoke defensiveness, resentment, or violence?
3. *Reflect on your need to express anger.* Would it be unhealthy to suppress this anger? Are there less risky outlets for your anger? For example, your anger might dissipate after you discuss the problem with a close friend or colleague who is a good listener.[28]

It is often a good idea to engage in a quick self-examination before you express your anger. Try to pinpoint what triggered the anger. Are you relying on rational or irrational thinking? Anger is often the result of not having our needs met, so reflect on the source of the anger. Can it be traced to unfulfilled needs for belonging? For recognition? For security?

Effective Ways to Express Your Anger

Buddha said, "You will not be punished for your anger, you will be punished by your anger." Intense anger that is suppressed will linger and become a disruptive force in your life unless you can find a positive way to get rid of it. Expressing feelings of anger can be therapeutic, but many people are unsure about the best way to self-disclose this emotion. To express anger in ways that will improve the chances that the other person will receive and respond to your message, consider these suggestions:

1. *Avoid reacting in a manner that could be seen as emotionally unstable.* If others see you as reacting irrationally, you will lose your ability to influence them.[29] Failure to maintain your emotional control can damage your image.
2. *Do not make accusations or attempt to fix blame.* It would be acceptable to begin the conversation by saying, "I felt humiliated at the staff meeting this morning." It would not be appropriate to say, "Your comments at the morning staff meeting were mean spirited and made me feel humiliated." The latter statement invites a defensive response.[30]
3. *Express your feelings in a timely manner.* The intensity of anger can actually increase with time. Also, important information needed by you or the person who provoked your anger may be forgotten or distorted with the passing of time.
4. *Be specific as you describe the factors that triggered your anger, and be clear about the resolution you are seeking.* The direct approach, in most cases, works best.

In some cases the person who triggers your anger may be someone you cannot confront without placing your job in jeopardy. For example, one of your best customers may constantly complain about the service he receives. You know he receives outstanding service, and you feel anger building inside you each time he complains. But any display of anger may result in loss of his business. In this situation you rely on your rational thinking power and say to yourself, "This part of my work is very distasteful, but I can stay calm each time he complains." Similarly, if the person who triggers your anger is your

---

Total Person Insight

"We all want to live sufficiently free from anger so that it isn't a problem, so that it doesn't prevent us from living successfully and harmoniously with other people and at peace within ourselves. This requires not just a philosophy, or a way of looking at things; it requires some skill-building."

KIMES GUSTIN

Author, *Anger, Rage, and Resentment*

boss, and you cannot confront her without risking the loss of your job, you may have to defuse your anger in some other way. You might practice deep breathing, going for a long walk after work, or taking a few minutes out of your work to meditate.[31]

How to Handle Other People's Anger

Dealing with other people's anger may be the most difficult human relations challenge we face. Most of us are not well prepared to deal with our own anger or the anger of others. The following skills can be learned and applied to any situation where anger threatens to damage a relationship.

1. *Recognize and accept the other person's anger.* The simple recognition of the intense feelings of someone who is angry does a lot to defuse the situation.[32] In a calm voice you might say, "I can see that you are very angry," or "It's obvious that you are angry."

2. *Encourage the angry person to vent his or her feelings.* By asking questions and listening carefully to the response, you can encourage the person to discuss the cause of the anger openly. Try using an open-ended question to encourage self-disclosure: "What have I done to upset you?" or "Can you tell me why you are so angry?"

3. *Do not respond to an angry person with your own anger.* To express your own anger or become defensive will only create another barrier to emotional healing. When you respond to the angry person, keep your voice tone soft. Keep in mind the old biblical injunction, "A soft answer turns away wrath."[33]

4. *Give the angry person feedback.* After venting feelings and discussing specific details, the angry person will expect a response. Briefly paraphrase what seems to be the major concern of the angry person, and express a desire to find ways to solve the problem. If you are at fault, accept the blame for your actions and express a sincere apology.

Thinking / Learning Starters

1. Try to recall a situation where you overexpressed your feelings of anger. How did your behavior affect the other person?

2. Think about the last time someone expressed his or her anger to you. Were you able to respond in an appropriate way? Was the relationship between you and the angry person damaged?

STRATEGIES FOR ACHIEVING EMOTIONAL CONTROL

We live our lives in two distinct worlds—one of fact and certainty and one of emotions and ambiguity. The world of certainty is that part of our lives that deals with objects and our rational side; the world of ambiguity deals with people and our feeling, or emotional, side—our human world. Too often we try to handle our human world in the same way that we handle our factual world.[34] Most of us are better prepared to deal with the rational side of our life because most of our previous education (formal and informal) emphasized this area. In this, the final part of the chapter, we share with you some practical suggestions for achieving greater control of the emotions that affect your life. Although emphasis is on the emotion of anger, the information presented here will help you deal with other emotions, such as fear, jealousy, hurt, and grief.

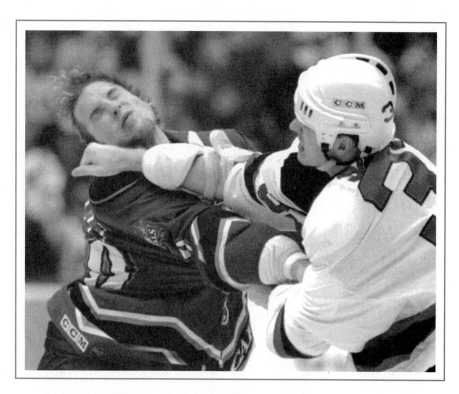

New Jersey hockey player Reid Simpson (right) lands a punch to the jaw of Washington's Brendan Witt. Each of us must learn to take control of our anger. (AP / Wide World Photos)

Identifying Your Emotional Patterns

We could often predict or anticipate our response to anger if we would take the time to study our emotional patterns—to take a running inventory of circumstances that touch off our anger and our response to anger. An easy way to do this is to record your anger experiences in a diary or journal, noting such details as when, where, with whom, and to what degree you became angry. How did you respond to the anger? How long did the feelings of anger last? If you expressed your angry feelings to the person who upset you, how did you feel afterward? These journal entries can provide a path to greater self-awareness and help you determine changes you want to make in your emotional style.

Tamra Reed, a graphic designer employed by a large newspaper, felt anger and frustration every time a coworker delivered material late. New to her position, Tamra was hesitant to discuss her feelings with the offending person, but she did record them in a journal. She recorded not only her conscious feelings, such as anxiety, but also other feelings in her body—a knot in her stomach and muscle tension when material arrived late. Tamra soon began to identify some patterns. The late arrival of the material meant she had less time to work on the final design, so her completed work often fell short of the high-quality standards she set for herself.

The journal entries helped Tamra become aware of ways to cope with her problem. She discovered that she had lost touch with the power of her own resources. Each time she accepted late material, she gave her power to the offending person. This was followed by feelings of anger toward herself and toward the person who turned in the material late. She finally resolved to stop accepting late material and made her intentions known to those who were missing deadlines.

If you don't feel comfortable with journal writing, consider setting aside some quiet time to reflect on your emotional patterns. Try to answer some specific questions about the way you deal with anger. What makes you angry? Have others learned which "buttons" to push in order to make you angry? What is your typical response to strong feelings of anger? Do you feel guilty after expressing anger? Do you find it hard to let go of resentment? A period of quiet reflection will help you focus your thoughts and impressions. Becoming a skilled observer of your own emotions is one of the best ways to achieve greater emotional control.

In addition to journal writing and quiet reflection, there is one more way to discover emotional patterns. At the end of the day, construct a chart of your emotional landscape. Make a chart (see Table 8.2) of the range of emotions you experienced and expressed during the day.[35] Your first entry might be "I woke up at 6:00 A.M. and immediately felt _____." The final entry might be "I left the office at 5:30 P.M. with a feeling of _____." What emotions surfaced throughout your workday? Resentment? Creative joy? Anxiety? Boredom? Contentment? Anger? Satisfaction? Reflect on the completed

TABLE 8.2

Charting Your
Emotional Landscape

Time	Circumstance	Emotion
6:00 A.M.	Alarm goes off. Mind is flooded by thoughts of all the things that must be done during the day.	Anxiety
7:10 A.M.	Depart for work. Heavy traffic interferes with plan to arrive at work early.	Anger and helplessness
8:00 A.M.	Thirty-minute staff meeting scheduled by the boss lasts fifty minutes. No agenda is provided. Entire meeting seems a waste of time.	Anger and frustration
9:35 A.M.	Finally start work on creative project.	Contentment
10:15 A.M.	Progress on project interrupted when coworker enters office, sits down, and starts sharing gossip about another coworker.	Anger and resentment
11:20 A.M.	Progress is made on creative project.	Contentment
1:45 P.M.	Creative project is complete and ready for review.	Joy and contentment
2:50 P.M.	Give project to boss for review. She says she will not be able to provide any feedback until morning. This delay will cause scheduling problems.	Frustration
4:00 P.M.	Attend health insurance update seminar sponsored by human resources department. No major changes are discussed.	Boredom
5:40 P.M.	Give up on a search for a missing document, turn off computer, and walk to parking lot.	Relief and fatigue

chart and try to determine which patterns need to be changed. For example, you might discover that your behavior is too often influenced by irrational thinking. Repeat this process over a period of several days in order to identify your unique emotional patterns.

Fine-Tuning Your Emotional Style

Once you have completed the process of self-examination and have identified some emotional patterns you want to change, it is time to consider ways to fine-tune your emotional style. Getting rid of emotional imbalances can help you to live a fuller, more satisfying life. Here are four things you can begin doing today.

Total Person Insight

"It's unfortunate that we're never really taught how to show emotion in ways that help our relationships. Instead, we're usually told what we should not do. However, too little emotion can make our lives seem empty and boring, while too much emotion, poorly expressed, fills our interpersonal lives with conflict and grief. Within reason, some kind of balance in the expression of emotion seems to be called for."

GERARD EGAN

Author, *You and Me*

- *Take responsibility for your emotions.* How you view your emotional difficulties will have a major influence on how you deal with them. If your anger is triggered by thoughts such as "I can never make my boss happy" or "Things always go wrong in my life," you may never find an effective way to deal with this emotion. By shifting the blame to other people and events, you cannot achieve emotional control.

- *Put your problems into proper perspective.* Why do some people seem to be at peace with themselves most of the time while others seem to be in a perpetual state of anxiety? People who suffer from an emotional imbalance often are unable or unwilling to look at problems realistically and practically, and they view each disappointment as a major catastrophe. Some things are not worth getting upset about. When faced with unpleasant events, pause and ask yourself, "Is this problem worth getting angry about?"

- *Take steps to move beyond anger and resentment.* Some people are upset about things that happened many years ago. Some even nurse grudges against people who have been dead for years. The sad thing is that the anger remains long after we can achieve any positive learning from it.[36] Studies of divorce, for example, indicate that anger and bitterness can linger a long time. Distress seems to peak one year after the divorce, and many people report that it takes at least two years to move past the anger.[37] When anger dominates one's life, whatever the reason, therapy or counseling may provide relief. Membership in a support group is often helpful.

- *Give your feelings some exercise.* Several prominent authors in the field of human relations have emphasized the importance of giving our feelings some exercise. Leo Buscaglia, author of *Loving Each Other,* says, "Exercise feelings. Feelings have meaning only as they are expressed in action."[38] Sam Keen, author of *Fire in the Belly,* said, "Make a habit of identifying your feelings and expressing them in some appropriate way."[39] If you have offended someone, how about sending that person a letter of regret? If someone you work with has given extra effort, why not praise that person's work? If you have been nursing a grudge for some time, how about practicing forgiveness?

Every day of our personal and work life we face some difficult decisions. One option is to take only actions that feel good at the moment. In some cases, this means ignoring the feelings of customers, patients, coworkers, and supervisors. Another option is to behave in a manner that is acceptable to the people around you. If you choose this option, you will have to make some sacrifices. You may have to be warm and generous when the feelings inside you say, "Be cold and selfish." You may have to avoid an argument when your feelings are insisting, "I'm right and the other person is wrong!" To achieve emotional control often requires restructuring our ways of feeling, thinking, and behaving.

Summary

Conflicts among people in organizations happen every day and can arise because of poor communications, value and culture clashes, confusing work policies and practices, or adversarial management. Often, however, conflicts come from coworkers who refuse to carry their fair share of the workload or have a difficult personality. While unresolved conflicts can have a negative effect on an organization's productivity, a difference of opinion sometimes has a positive effect by forcing team members toward creative and innovative solutions to the problem.

There are several approaches for dealing with conflict: win/lose, lose/lose, and win/win. Using the win/win strategy can not only resolve a conflict but also preserve effective human relations. Regardless of the strategy implemented, your ability to display assertiveness and cooperation behaviors are key factors in the effective resolution of conflicts with others. There are five steps in the conflict resolution process.

We carry inside us a vast array of emotions that come into play when we encounter a conflict situation. An emotion can be thought of as a feeling that influences our thinking and behavior. We sometimes experience emotional imbalance because we learn to inhibit the expression of certain emotions and overemphasize the expression of others.

Our emotional development is influenced by temperament (the biological shaper of personality), our subconscious mind, and cultural conditioning. Throughout the long process of emotional development we learn different ways to express our anger. Appropriate expressions of anger contribute to improved interpersonal relations, help us reduce anxiety, and give us an outlet for unhealthy stress. We must also learn how to handle other people's anger. It takes a great deal of effort to learn how to deal with our own anger and the anger of others.

Emotional control is an important dimension of emotional style. The starting point in developing emotional control is to identify your current emotional patterns. One way to do this is to record your anger experiences in a diary or journal. Once you have completed the process of self-examination, you should consider appropriate ways to fine-tune your emotional style.

Career Corner

Q. I am in my mid-40s, have spent twenty-two years working my way up to supervisor of my department in a major department store, and love my job. The new 31-year-old store manager has started to exclude me from memos and weekly management meetings, saying, "There's no reason for you to attend." Many of my coworkers are much younger than I, dress in jeans instead of professional suits, and seem to lack the traditional work ethic. Those of us over 40 are finding it difficult to keep our mouths shut. Any suggestions?

A. It is obvious your conflict stems from a values clash that sometimes develops between older and younger workers. There also seems to be a breakdown in communication. Your younger coworkers and the store manager may be consciously or unconsciously building an "us versus them" scenario in relation to the more experienced members of the team. You need to establish communication with your store manager. Openly discuss your concerns and assertively seek an explanation for the changes that have taken place. When you allow others to ignore your needs and disregard your point of view, you display passive behaviors that will get you nowhere.

Key Terms

conflict
win/lose strategy
lose/lose strategy
win/win strategy
assertive behavior
aggressive behavior

nonassertive behavior
conflict resolution process
brainstorming
emotion
temperament
subconscious mind
anger

Review Questions

1. What are some of the major causes of conflicts between people in organizations?
2. Discuss the positive aspects of conflict in an organization.
3. What results might you expect when you implement the win/lose strategy? The lose/lose strategy? The win/win strategy?
4. How does assertive behavior differ from aggressive behavior?

5. How does a misunderstanding differ from a true disagreement?
6. What is the relationship between feelings and emotion? What role do feelings play in our life?
7. What is meant by the term *emotional balance?* What factors create an emotional imbalance?
8. What four steps can improve the chances that another person will receive and respond to your feelings of anger?
9. List four skills that can be used effectively to handle anger in other people.
10. List and briefly describe four ways to fine-tune your emotional style.

Application Exercises

1. Recall the last time you were angry with another person or were the victim of a situation that made you angry. For example, a housemate or roommate refuses to pay her share of the grocery bill, or your manager accuses you of wrongdoing without knowing all the facts. Then answer the following questions:
   a. Did you express your anger verbally, physically, or emotionally?
   b. Did you suppress any of your anger? Explain.
   c. What results did you experience from the way you handled this situation? Describe both positive and negative results.
   d. If the same situation arose again, would you do anything differently? Explain.
2. To develop your assertiveness skills, find a partner who will join you for a practice session. The partner should assume the role of a friend, family member, or coworker who is doing something that causes you a great deal of frustration. (The problem can be real or imaginary.) Communicate your dislikes and feelings in a clear, direct manner without threatening or attacking. Then ask your partner to critique your assertiveness skills. Participate in several of these practice sessions until you feel confident that you have improved your assertiveness skills.

Internet Exercise

As noted at the beginning of this chapter, workers today are faced with subtle conflicts over issues that did not exist fifteen or twenty years ago. Effective conflict management strategies are needed in every type of work setting. Visit the Internet to discover what information is available on this topic. Using your search engine, type in the following keywords:

conflict resolution

conflict management

conflict resolution process

Review the available resources (such as books, articles, and training programs), and identify information that would be helpful as you attempt to resolve conflicts in your life. Prepare a written report of your findings.

For each of the following statements, circle the number from 1 to 5 that best represents your response: (1) strongly disagree (never do this); (2) disagree (rarely do this); (3) moderately agree (sometimes do this); (4) agree (frequently do this); (5) strongly agree (almost always do this).

a. When I experience conflict with others I strive to determine how much assertive behavior and how much cooperative behavior to display.   1   2   3   4   5

b. In my attempts to resolve conflict I strive for a solution that all parties can accept.   1   2   3   4   5

c. I am able to solve problems and make decisions in a logical manner without allowing my emotions to interfere.   1   2   3   4   5

d. My relationships with people at home, school, and work do not suffer because of my expressions of anger or impatience.   1   2   3   4   5

e. I have developed effective ways to cope with my own anger and the anger of others.   1   2   3   4   5

f. I am familiar with, and can apply, several strategies for achieving emotional control.   1   2   3   4   5

Case Problem

Personal Assertiveness Pays Off

JO Browning, a 5-foot-5-inch, 115-pound, soft-spoken daughter of an Air Force medic, never took up causes or ran for office in high school. In 1984, when she applied for a job building tires at Uniroyal-Goodrich, men in the plant took bets she wouldn't last and predicted, "That little skinny one ain't gonna be worth ————." But for twelve years, she proved her worth, married a coworker, gave birth to Whitney, then worked back-to-back shifts while her husband cared for their daughter. The couple had little time together, and Jo learned to live on three hours of sleep a day.

The global economy forced Uniroyal to cancel stable weekday and weekend work schedules and convert to rotating shifts in order to lower costs and improve quality control. The new scheduling plan involved the rotation of four factory crews among four cycles that combined eight- and twelve-hour shifts. The delicate balance Jo had established for her family was shattered. None of the 73 child-care providers she called was willing to give weekend care.

Jo turned her bitterness and anger into action. She researched child care at the library, contacted advocacy groups, informed management personnel about the problem when no one else in the plant would, and keynoted a union-hall child-care meeting. She learned that Uniroyal had joined a nineteen-employer child-care alliance and was planning a joint study with the local nonprofit child-care resource center. She badgered human resource managers to speed up the study and hand-carried the surveys to each worker. The results confirmed child-care problems among 86 percent of the parents. Child Care Systems of America saw the study and created a plan for an innovative seven-days-a-week child-care center. More hurdles put Jo in front of a city planning meeting, urging zoning approval for the center. The center, funded by parent fees, is now open in a sparkling three-bedroom house.

Jo Browning's coworkers recognized her efforts and elected her secretary of her local 1,325-member steelworkers' union. The first woman to hold officer status in her union, Jo is determined to make child care an issue at the bargaining table.

Questions

1. What role did assertiveness play in Jo Browning's approach to this conflict resolution?
2. Which steps of the conflict resolution process detailed in this chapter did she follow?
3. Was the result of this personal approach to conflict resolution a lose/lose, win/lose, or win/win solution? Explain.

Chapter 9

A Life Plan

for Effective

Human Relations

Chapter Preview

After studying this chapter, you will be able to

1. Define success by standards that are compatible with your needs and values.
2. Learn how to better cope with life's uncertainties and disappointments.
3. Understand the forces that are influencing work/life balance.
4. Discuss the meaning of *right livelihood*.
5. Describe four nonfinancial resources that can enrich your life.
6. Provide guidelines for developing a healthy lifestyle.
7. Develop a plan for making needed changes in your life.

FOR YEARS CHARLES "ROCKY" RHODES worked seven-day weeks. As a cofounder and chief engineer of Silicon Graphics, he could pick among cutting-edge research and development projects at his company. He loved his work, but as the years passed, he felt the need for greater balance between work and family. One day Rhodes and his wife decided to take a hard look at their lives and develop some priorities. After much deliberation, they scribbled on a Post-it note the four priorities they agreed were most important: God, family, exercise, and work, in that order. They put the note on the refrigerator door, where it would be a daily reminder of what was really important in their lives. To reduce the tension between work and family, Rhodes gradually reduced his working hours. In the area of new product development, he assumed an advisory role that did not require full-time work. Today he works half-time and allocates the other hours to his family, volunteer work, and his church.[1] ■

No amount of training or education can fully prepare you for some of the experiences you will face in your career. There will usually be some unexpected rewards and a few major disappointments. Consider the experience of Lisa Latno, who found that a full-time job at Unum Life Insurance and a daily three-hour commute created major work/life tensions. She needed more time to raise her 2-year-old son and do the other things required of someone who blends work and family. Her request to work ten fewer hours a week was turned down by her supervisor, but another department manager invited Latno to take a thirty-hour-a-week job in her department.[2] Job flexibility helps many workers, men and women, achieve work/life balance.

The experiences of Rocky Rhodes and Lisa Latno remind us that our personal life and our work life are very much intertwined. The problems we experience at home (conflict with other family members, rebellion by a teenager, divorce) often have an influence on our performance at work. And a negative experience at work may influence how we feel and act away from the job.

In this chapter we help you construct a life plan that will enhance your relationships with people in your personal life and in your work life. This plan will also help you better manage the relationship you have with yourself. We discuss the meaning of success and suggest ways to cope with major disappointments such as losing your job or being passed over for a promotion. You will learn how to avoid being trapped by a lifestyle that offers financial rewards but little else. This chapter also helps you define your relationship with money and describes four nonfinancial resources that give meaning to life.

TOWARD A NEW DEFINITION OF SUCCESS

Most of us have been conditioned to define success in narrow terms. Too frequently we judge our own success, and the success of others, by what is accomplished at work. Successful people are described as those who have a "good job" or have "reached the top" in their field. We sometimes describe the person who has held the same job for many years as successful. We do not stop to consider that such a person may find work boring and completely devoid of personal rewards.

From early childhood on we are taught to equate progress with pay increases and promotions. Amy Saltzman, author of *Downshifting,* notes that many people tend to set goals and measure success along a vertical career path that is often described as the "career ladder" or the "fast track." Saltzman says, "One is not successful, according to this school of thought, unless one is consistently moving up the ladder in some clearly quantifiable way."[3] Too often the person who is striving to achieve an immediate career goal (one more rung on the career ladder, for example) is forced to give up everything else that gives purpose and meaning to life. This may mean spending less time with family members and friends, spending less time keeping physically fit, abandoning vacation plans, and spending weekends at work.

Of course, the fast track is no longer an option for many employees. Today there are fewer rungs on the corporate ladder. One major goal of downsizing is to reduce the number of layers of management. The flattening of organizations will likely continue into the year 2000 and beyond.[4]

For those persons who have defined success in terms of larger paychecks earned by working overtime, the picture seems to be changing. Giving up time with friends and family, or giving up that part in the local community theater

---

Total Person Insight

"When it comes to defining a successful life in American Society, today's career professionals seem stuck between two ultimately dissatisfying extremes: dropping out completely and creating their own vision of a better world, or working within the system and speeding up their pace on the success treadmill."

AMY SALTZMAN

Author, *Downshifting: Reinventing Success on a Slower Track*

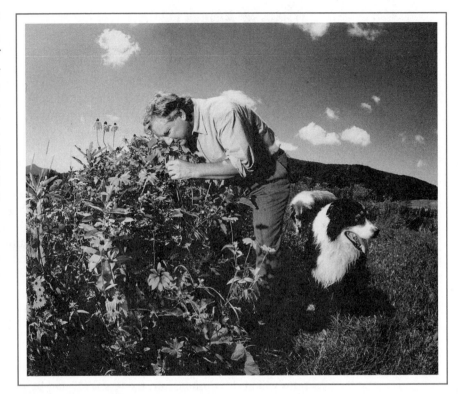

Here we see Tom Peters, noted author of best-selling business books, taking time to smell the flowers. Leisure time can provide us with the opportunity to relax and get rid of work-related stress. (Rafael Fuchs/Outline Press)

production, in return for more money is less appealing to some workers today. Juliet Schor, Harvard economist and author of *The Overworked American*, believes that during the next decade workers will give up income in exchange for more leisure time. She says, "People are very interested in issues like personal development, family, home and those kinds of things, so they are starting to want more from a job than just a paycheck; they're wanting flexibility, and that usually involves time."[5]

The Need for a New Model of Success

In recent years, a growing number of people are angry, disillusioned, and frustrated because they had to abruptly change their career plans. They gave their best efforts to an employer for ten, fifteen, or twenty years, and then the company eliminated their jobs. For years the firm said, "Take care of business and we'll take care of you," but then the situation changed. Under pressure from new global competition, hostile takeovers, and the need to restructure, companies started getting rid of loyal workers. The unwritten and unspoken contract between the company and the employee was broken. Many of the people who lost their jobs during the past decade were once told that if they had ambition and worked tirelessly to achieve their career goals, success would be their reward. But the "reward" for many people has been loss of a job, loss of self-esteem, and increased anxiety about the future.

We should certainly feel sympathy for persons who have lost their jobs and watched their dreams dissolve. But there is another group of people who also merit our concern. These are the persons who put in long hours, climbed the ladder of success, and still have a job but have discovered that something is missing from their lives. These people have a good job, a regular paycheck, and in some cases an impressive title, but they do not *feel* successful. How should we feel about the person who invested ten, fifteen, or twenty years in a

Total Person Insight

"If I had only...
Forgotten future greatness
and looked at the green things and the buildings
and reached out to those around me
and smelled the air
and ignored the forms and the self-styled obligations
and heard the rain on the roof
and put my arms around my wife
... and it's not too late"

HUGH PRATHER

Poet; Author, *Notes to Myself: My Struggle to Become a Person.* Copyright © 1970. by
Real People Press. Used by permission of Bantam Books, a division of Random
House, Inc.

job, gave up all or most of his or her leisure time, gave up quality time with
friends and family, reached the top rung on the career ladder, and then discovered that life was empty and unfulfilling?

The traditional success model is slowly breaking down. This model defined
success almost exclusively in terms of work life. The model emphasized working long hours, accomplishing work-related goals, and meeting standards often
set by others. Lynn Lannon, president of the Lannon Group, a San Francisco–based consulting firm, says the old model results in "judging one's success by the standards of others, never feeling quite good enough and often
feeling dissatisfied."[6]

The old model of success required us to be "one-dimensional" people for
whom work is the single dimension. In the life of such a person, everything
that has meaning seems to be connected to the job. When a person defines
himself or herself by a job and then loses that job, what does that person have
left? People who are able to broaden their perspectives, develop interests beyond their jobs, and put balance in their lives usually not only achieve more
self-fulfillment but also become more valuable as employees.[7]

Loss of Leisure Time

Many Americans are beginning to understand that "all work and no play" is
not good for their long-term mental and physical health. People who work too

many hours often lose their ability to relate effectively to coworkers and family members. Some of America's best-managed companies are beginning to realize the negative consequences of long hours on the job and loss of leisure time. Perry Christensen, director of human resource strategy and planning for Merck and Company, says, "You can't build an effective company on a foundation of broken homes and strained personal relationships."[8]

In previous chapters we noted two trends that tend to erode leisure time: The number of hours people work per week has steadily increased over the years, and the use of pagers, fax machines, and cellular phones makes it increasingly difficult for people to escape the day-to-day demands of the workplace. The number of people who hold down more than one job has also increased.[9] U.S. workers work longer hours and spend less time on vacation than do workers in most other industrialized countries.

Developing Your Own Life Plan

The goal of this chapter is to help you develop a life plan for effective relationships with yourself and others. The information presented thus far has, we hope, stimulated your thinking about the need for a life plan. We have noted that personal life can seldom be separated from work life. The two are very much intertwined. We have also suggested that it is important for you to develop your own definition of success. Too frequently people allow others (parents, teachers, counselors, a spouse) to define success for them. Judging your success by the standards established by someone else may lead to a life of frustration.

Many people today are discovering that true success is a combination of achievements. Becoming too focused on one narrow goal may not provide the self-satisfaction you are seeking. One author makes this observation: "Everyone wants to be successful. But each person must have a personal definition of what success will feel like, and understand that true success rarely means having just one goal."[10] A narrow definition of success may actually prove to be counterproductive if it means giving up everything else that adds meaning to life.

Because work is such an important part of life, we now move to a discussion of items that will help you in your career planning. We discuss the concept of "right livelihood."

TOWARD RIGHT LIVELIHOOD

Visit Sena Plaza in downtown Santa Fe and you will see a public garden that is a wonderland of color and texture. The person responsible for this beautiful garden is Barbara Fix, a graduate of Stanford Law School who chose gardening over a high-powered law career. She says, "I've been offered many jobs in my life. I could have been on Wall Street making six figures, but the only job I ever hustled for was this one—six dollars an hour as the gardener at Sena Plaza."[11]

Barbara Fix is an example of someone who appears to have achieved "right livelihood." The original concept of right livelihood apparently came from the teachings of Buddha. In recent years, the concept has been described by Michael Phillips in his book *The Seven Laws of Money* and by Marsha Sinetar in her book *Do What You Love . . . The Money Will Follow*. **Right livelihood** is work consciously chosen, done with full awareness and care, and leading to enlightenment. When Jason Wilson gave up a challenging business career to become a carpenter, he embraced the concept of right livelihood. He later started his own home construction business.[12] Ronald Sheade, once a vice president at a Fortune 1,000 company, now teaches eighth-grade science in a suburb of Chicago. He doesn't make big money anymore, but he loves teaching and now gets to spend more time with his family.[13] There are three characteristics to right livelihood.

Right Livelihood Is Based on Conscious Choice

Marsha Sinetar says, "When the powerful quality of conscious choice is present in our work, we can be enormously productive."[14] She points out that many people have learned to act on what others say, value, and expect and thus find conscious choice very difficult:

> It takes courage to act on what we value and to willingly accept the consequences of our choices. Being able to choose means not allowing fear to inhibit or control us, even though our choices may require us to act against our fears or against the wishes of those we love and admire.[15]

To make the best choices, you must first figure out what you like to do, as well as what you are good at doing. What you like doing most is often not obvious. It may take some real effort to discover what really motivates you. Students often get help from career counselors or explore a career option during a summer internship. If you are employed, consider joining a temporary project team. A team assignment may give you the opportunity to work closely with experts in such diverse areas as finance, marketing, or manufacturing.[16] If the team option is not available to you, seek a temporary assignment in some other department, or create a job that does not currently exist.

Right Livelihood Places Money in a Secondary Position

People who embrace this concept accept that money and security are not the only rewards in life. Michael Phillips explains that "right livelihood has within itself its own rewards; it deepens the person who practices it."[17] For example, people who work in the social services usually do not earn large amounts of money, but many receive a great deal of personal satisfaction from their work. Barbara Fix does not make much money as a gardener, but the work provides enormous personal satisfaction. In her words, "Working in here is a privilege beyond measure. It's calming to the soul."[18]

Many people who once viewed success in terms of wealth, material possessions, and status are realizing that something is missing from their lives. They do not *feel* successful. They once felt pressured to "have it all" but now feel disappointed that their achievements have not brought them real happiness.

Right Livelihood Recognizes That Work Is a Vehicle for Self-Expression

Most of us spend from forty to sixty hours each week at work. Ideally, we should not have to squelch our real abilities, ignore our personal goals, and forget our need for stimulation and personal growth during the time we spend at work.[19] John Naisbitt and Patricia Aburdene, authors of *Re-Inventing the Corporation,* state that "in their hearts, people know that work should be fun and that it should be related to the other parts of their lives."[20] Most employees know intuitively that work should fulfill their need for self-expression, but this message has not been taken seriously by many leaders. Too few organizations truly empower workers and give them a sense of purpose.

Marsha Sinetar says that although their jobs may differ, bicycle repair people, furniture makers, physicians, salespersons, and artists can use work as a means of self-expression and gain the satisfaction of growth and self-understanding.[21] In recent years, many people have abandoned secure, well-paying corporate jobs to start their own businesses. These entrepreneurs often report that their new businesses are a vehicle for self-expression.

For a growing number of people, right livelihood involves work/life balance. To achieve this balance, you will need the following skills:[22]

- *Clarify and act on your values.* This skill, discussed in Chapter 4, should be developed *before* you interview for a job. Mark Buzek, a recent graduate of Ohio State, decided not to take a job that would require frequent relocation and excessive travel. Although he is not married, he has strong ties with his parents, two sisters, and a brother in Ohio. Staying close to family members is an important value in his life.[23]
- *Build trusting relationships at work.* What will be the reaction of coworkers if you take parental leave, leave work early to attend events that involve your children, refuse to work weekends? You are more likely to get support from those who know what is important in your life, value your friendship, and trust you to do the right thing.
- *Ask for what you need from bosses and family members.* Talk about your desire to maintain work/life balance. Be open and frank about what is important to you. Many people keep silent on work/life balance issues for fear of being seen as "uncommitted" to the job.
- *Learn to accept from yourself less than 100 percent some of the time.* Liz Landon, an employee of Andersen Consulting, recalls some advice she received from her boss: "Don't get crispy fried in the business. The insidious suction of achievement could leave you with no soul."[24] Do your best, but do not let the demands you place on yourself create major work/life tensions.

Thinking / Learning Starters

1. Do you agree that many people define success in terms that are too narrow? Reflect on your personal knowledge of friends and family members before answering this question.

2. In your opinion, does the concept of right livelihood seem realistic? Is right livelihood an option for everyone, or only a select few? Explain.

Defining Your Relationship with Money

Money is a compelling force in the lives of many people. It often influences selection of a career and the amount of time and energy invested in that career.
Many people are pursuing money with the misguided belief that it is the key to
happiness, and a significant number believe money is the only meaningful
measure of success.[25] Melvyn Kinder, author of *Going Nowhere Fast,* says many
people are on a money treadmill: "The money treadmill is built on a miscon-
ception about what money is, what it does, and what it means. We have been
brainwashed into thinking money itself, once we amass it sufficiently, will
bring us happiness and an end to insecurity."[26]

The money treadmill can be a trap, especially when you do not know what
amount of money is enough. If you think that having *more* money is going to
produce happiness or peace of mind, will you ever earn enough? Many people
accept the "myth of scarcity." They have a mind-set or belief that "I don't
have enough _____ ." Money becomes the lightning rod for the
scarcity notion.[27] With this mind-set, any extra money earned is quickly spent on
the things you think you do not have enough of. What might have been "wants"
in the past (a big-screen TV set, a bigger home, a new car) now become "needs."
Once you turn your wants into needs, then the need to work more overtime,
hold down a second job, or continue a dual-earner arrangement intensifies.[28]

Many Americans are locked into a work-and-spend cycle. As debts increase,
people give up leisure time to make more money. As the treadmill continues to
roll, some people become too tired to enjoy active leisure activities such as hik-
ing, swimming, or playing a round of golf. The alternative is involvement in
less satisfying activities such as sitting passively in front of the television set.

Competence in managing your personal finances is no less important than
competence in managing your career. What matters most is not how much
you earn but how much you keep. It is difficult to take career risks (leaving a
job you dislike) unless you are able to build a financial cushion. Here are some
tips on how to manage your personal finances:

- *Determine where your income is going.* With a simple record-keeping system,
  you can determine how much you spend each month on food, housing,
  clothing, transportation, and other things. Search for spending patterns you
  may want to change.
- *Spend less than you earn.* To do this, you may need to get rid of some credit
  cards, eat fewer meals at restaurants, use public transportation instead of
  driving your car, or make some other lifestyle change.
- *Maintain a cash cushion.* If you lost your job today, how long could you
  live on your current cash reserves? Financial consultants suggest that cash reserves should be equal to the amount you earn during a two-month period.
- *Develop a personal financial plan.* With a financial plan, you are more likely
  to achieve your financial goals. Without a plan, you will likely follow a haphazard approach to management of your finances.

Com-Corp Industries, a manufacturing plant based in Cleveland, Ohio, sees personal money management skills as one key to reducing conflict in the workplace. Employees who cannot live within their means are often under great stress and are more likely to experience interpersonal problems at work and at home. The company provides employees with classes on such subjects as developing a household budget and wise use of credit.[29]

Nonfinancial Resources

If you become totally focused on your financial resources, if you are caught up in the work-and-spend cycle, then chances are you have ignored your **nonfinancial resources.** And it is often the nonfinancial resources that make the biggest contribution to a happy and fulfilling life. A strong argument can be made that the real wealth in life comes in the form of good health, peace of mind, time spent with family and friends, learning (which develops the mind), and healthy spirituality. Paul Hwoschinsky, author of *True Wealth,* makes this observation about nonfinancial resources: "If you are clear about who you are, and clear about what you want to do, and bring your financial and nonfinancial resources together, it's extraordinary what can happen. I encourage people to really honor their total resources, and magical things happen. New options occur."[30] If you focus most or all of your attention on work, and you suffer a major work-related disappointment, then the result will likely be feelings of depression and despair. Thoughts such as "Now I have lost everything" can surface when you fail to get a promotion, find out that you were not selected to be a member of a special project team, or learn that your job has been eliminated. If you fully understand the power of your nonfinancial resources, then work-related disappointments are easier to cope with. The starting point is to realize that *most* of your resources are nonfinancial. During periods of great uncertainty, it is especially important that you think about your nonfinancial

---

Total Person Insight

"Keep in mind that there is no harder work than thinking—really thinking—about who you are and what you want out of life. Figuring out where your goals and your skills match up is a painful, time-consuming process."

JULIE CONNELLY

Contributing Editor, *Fortune*

assets and consider ways to enhance them. We briefly discuss four nonfinancial resources that can enrich your life: physical and mental health, education and training (intellectual growth), leisure time (time for family, socializing, recreation), and healthy spirituality (see Figure 9.1).

Physical and Mental Health Is the statement "Health means wealth" just a worn-out cliché, or is this slogan a message of inspiration for people who want to get more out of life? If good health is such an important nonfinancial asset, then why are so many people flirting with self-destruction by eating the wrong foods, drinking too much, exercising too little, and generally choosing unhealthy lifestyles? The answer to the second question may be lack of awareness of the benefits of physical fitness. Susan Smith Jones, a fitness instructor at UCLA and author of "Choose to Be Healthy," offers these benefits of good health:

- There is an interrelationship between health and outlook on life. For example, when the physical body is fit, toned, and strong, this condition has a positive effect on the mind. We are more likely to experience higher levels of self-esteem, feel a greater sense of self-confidence, and have a more positive outlook on life.
- Poor health tends to interfere with everything else in life: family harmony, work schedules, and relationships.
- Regular exercise and a healthy diet produce greater mental clarity, a higher energy level, and a more youthful appearance.[31]

Jones states that good health is something you must *choose* to have. She says, "Regardless of the lifestyle you've lived until now, you can, at any moment, choose differently."[32] If your breakfast is currently five cups of coffee and a danish, you can choose to change your diet. If you are spending thirty to forty

FIGURE 9.1

Put Balance In
Your Life

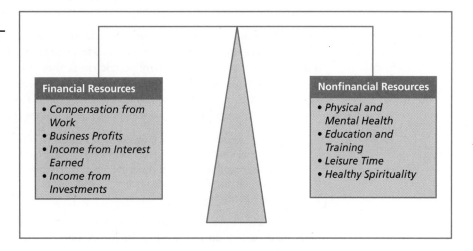

Financial Resources
- *Compensation from Work*
- *Business Profits*
- *Income from Interest Earned*
- *Income from Investments*

Nonfinancial Resources
- *Physical and Mental Health*
- *Education and Training*
- *Leisure Time*
- *Healthy Spirituality*

hours a week sitting in front of a TV set, you can choose to spend that time in a different way. Your current level of health is the result of many choices you made in the past. Later in this chapter we discuss ways to form new habits that will help you achieve vibrant health.

Education and Training (Intellectual Growth)   It is sometimes easy to take for granted the time and energy required to earn a high school diploma, a certificate of completion in a technical field, a college degree, or some other form of recognition of achievement in education and training. We should view these achievements as important nonfinancial assets.

Throughout life we must continue to acquire this important resource. The time when you could achieve career success with just hard work and loyalty has passed. Today, employees are likely to be judged and rewarded on the basis of performance. Michael Hammer, co-author of *Re-Engineering the Corporation,* says, "You have to get results, and you have to continually update, train and develop yourself so that you're ready for tomorrow's jobs."[33] The expression "never stop learning" has never had more relevance than it does today. Here are some tips on how to acquire the skills and abilities you need:

- *Think of yourself as a unique product.* To maintain value in the marketplace, you must stay up-to-date. What skills and capabilities do you need to maintain or increase your value?[34]
- *Be selective in what you learn.* Learning often requires large amounts of time and energy, so consider carefully what unit of knowledge or skill will generate the most improvement.[35]
- *Take advantage of various learning pathways.* It helps to think of your job as a learning resource. Take full advantage of instructional programs offered by your employer. Volunteer for assignments that will provide new learning opportunities. And look outside the company at community college classes or programs offered by Toastmasters, Dale Carnegie, or other organizations.[36]

Leisure Time   Leisure time can provide an opportunity to relax, get rid of work-related stress, get some exercise, spend time with family and friends, or simply read a good book. Many people think they want more leisure time, but when it is available, they do not know what to do. Some people even feel guilty when they are not working. In her book *Downshifting,* Amy Saltzman talks about the problems Americans have with leisure time:

> The fact is, leisure today has something of a negative connotation. Having too much leisure implies we are wasting time and not working hard enough to get ahead. With so little time and so much of it devoted to professional pursuits, spending a Saturday afternoon on the front porch reading a book, talking to the neighbors or writing a letter to a friend is out of the question.[37]

If you are working for someone who is on the fast track, someone who may have given up all or most of his or her leisure time, you may be pressured to work at the same pace. If your boss is constantly trying to meet impossible deadlines and deal with last-minute rushes, you may feel the need to give up time for recreation or family. If this happens, try to identify the consequences of being overworked. Look at the situation from all points of view. If you refuse to work longer hours, what will be the consequences for your relationship with the boss, your relationship with other employees, your future with the organization?[38] You have choices, but they may be difficult ones. If it looks as though the pressure to work longer hours will never end, you may want to begin searching for another job.

Is it worth taking some risks to protect the leisure time you now have? Should you increase the amount of leisure time available in your life? Consider the following benefits of leisure time:

- Maintaining social connections with friends and family can be good for your health. A growing number of studies show that if you have strong and fulfilling relationships, you may live longer, decrease your chances of becoming sick, and cope more successfully when illness strikes.[39] Time spent with friends and family can be a powerful source of mental and physical renewal.
- One of the best ways to feel satisfied about your work is to get away from it when you begin to feel worn out. People who take time off from work often return with new ideas, a stronger focus, and increased energy. When you discover that end-of-the-week exhaustion is still hanging around Monday morning, it's time to take some vacation or personal days.[40]
- An excellent way to increase your social connections and improve your own health is to become a volunteer. Research indicates that volunteers experience pleasurable physical sensations such as feelings of warmth, well-being, and calmness, and increased energy levels.[41]

If you want more leisure time, then you must establish your priorities and set your goals. This may mean saying no to endless requests to work overtime or rejecting a promotion. Achieving success does not always require seven-day workweeks and time away from family and friends. Sometimes you must pull back from the endless demands of work and "get a life."

Healthy Spirituality   A discussion of nonfinancial resources would not be complete without an introduction to healthy spirituality. To become a "whole" or "total" person requires movement beyond the concrete, material aspects of life to the spiritual side of the human experience. Healthy spirituality can bring a higher degree of harmony and wholeness to our lives and move us beyond self-centeredness.

Spirituality can be defined as an inner attitude that emphasizes energy, creative choice, and a powerful force for living. It frees us to become positive, caring human beings.[42]

Spirituality encompasses faith, which can be described as what your heart tells you is true when your mind cannot prove it. For some people, faith exists within the framework of a formal religion; for others it rests on a series of personal beliefs such as "Give others the same consideration, regard, kindness, and gentleness that you would like them to accord you."[43]

An understanding of the many aspects of spirituality can give us an expanded vision of what it means to be human. Although spirituality is often associated with religion, it should be viewed in broader terms. Robert Coles of Harvard Medical School likes a definition of spirituality given to him by an 11-year-old girl:

> I think you're spiritual if you can escape from yourself a little and think of what's good for everyone, not just you, and if you can reach out and be a good person—I mean live like a good person. You're not spiritual if you just talk spiritual and there's no action. You're a fake if that's what you do.[44]

The words of this young girl remind us that one dimension of spirituality involves showing concern and compassion for others. It means turning away from rigid individualism and investing some time and energy in helping others. It means in some cases rolling up our sleeves and getting involved. We can enhance our spirituality through volunteer work, taking the time to listen to a coworker who is trying to resolve a serious personal problem, helping a stranded motorist, or simply writing a personal note of appreciation to someone at work who has given us assistance.

In many ways, large and small, work can be made more spiritual. Some of America's most successful business leaders have made this discovery. J. C. Penney, who built one of the nation's largest retail chains, adopted the golden rule as a key operating principle of his company. The philosophy of Worthington Industries is expressed in a single sentence: "We treat our customers, employees, investors and suppliers as we would like to be treated."[45] Hudson Food Inc. hired a chaplain to provide support and counseling to troubled employees.[46] Lotus Development Corporation formed a "soul" committee to examine the company's management practices and values. The company wants to find ways to make the work environment as humane as possible.[47] Edward Bednar teaches Zen Buddhist meditation techniques to employees working in the Wall

Total Person Insight

"Not only is it possible to unite the worlds of business and spirituality, the resulting synergy creates benefits for both worlds."

FRED HUYGHUE

President, SSiM Group

Street area. He is attempting to help them live a more contemplative life.[48] At the Hazelwood, Missouri, Ford Motor plant a nondenominational prayer group meets regularly.[49]

Spirituality is present in people who have a zest for life and are enthusiastic about experiencing its richness. Visiting an art gallery, listening to a concert, or walking near the ocean can stimulate healthy spirituality.

Healthy spirituality can often serve as a stabilizing force in our lives. The various twelve-step programs (Alcoholics Anonymous is one example) emphasize the need for a spiritual connection. "Working the steps" means, among other things, turning life over to a higher power. This spiritual connection seems to give hope to persons who feel a sense of loneliness and isolation. Although the spiritual component of twelve-step programs has not been fully explained by the scientific community, it is viewed as an important part of the healing process.

For many people, a commitment to a specific religion is an important dimension of spirituality. Active membership in a religious group provides an opportunity to clarify spiritual values and achieve spiritual direction. If you do not attend the services of some religious group at a church, synagogue, temple, mosque, or other place of worship—investigate one that seems compatible with your general orientation and attend a few times. If this experience tends to nurture your spiritual life, try to incorporate the core beliefs into your life.[50] For many people, membership in a religious community provides social connections—an extended family that they can depend on for social support.[51]

Healthy spirituality can be a positive, enlightening force in our lives. It can grow during quiet times when we reflect on the meaning of life, meditate, pray, or enjoy nature during a long walk in the woods. These activities draw our focus away from ourselves and the anxieties in our lives. We are more likely to experience healthy spirituality when we avoid self-pity and self-criticism and stay connected to others.

As more companies accept the whole person in the workplace, healthy spirituality will grow in importance. Hyler Bracey, consultant and author of *Managing from the Heart,* said, "We used to check our feelings, health, sexuality,

---

Total Person Insight

"Take time for nurturing your wellness. If you don't take time for wellness, you are going to have to make time for sickness."

SUSAN SMITH JONES

Fitness Instructor; Author, "Choose to Be Healthy and Celebrate Life" spirituality and family problems at the door of the workplace. We've matured enough to get beyond that. The unspeakable is now acceptable."[52]

DEVELOPING A HEALTHY LIFESTYLE

Earlier in this chapter we noted that a healthy lifestyle can provide a higher energy level, a greater sense of self-confidence, and generally a more positive outlook on life. People who maintain good health usually have more endurance, spend less time feeling tired or ill, and miss less work than persons who are not physically fit. Good health is receiving greater attention today because many Americans are investing more time and energy in their work. They are being asked to work longer hours and do more in less time. Good health can help combat stress and tension at work and at home.

There is another important reason to adopt a healthy lifestyle. Throughout the past decade, the cost of health care has steadily increased, and several million Americans have lost their health insurance.[53] The old saying "I can't afford to get sick" is on the minds of many workers today.

The first step toward adopting a healthy lifestyle is to become well informed—to read, study, and learn what can be done to maintain your current level of health or improve your health. In this section we offer guidelines that form the framework for a good diet and a good exercise program. The second

For a growing number of people, meditation is an important key to achieving a healthy lifestyle. Here we see a Hatha Yoga class at Yoga Works in Santa Monica, California, where people learn breathing techniques. (A. Ramey/ PhotoEdit)

step is to determine what changes you need to make in your lifestyle and then make those changes. For many people, step one does not automatically lead to step two. Present-day Americans have access to more information about nutrition and exercise than any previous generation, but many refuse to give up poor eating habits and adopt an exercise program.

Guidelines for a Healthy Diet

Eating the right foods can improve your health, boost your energy level, and in some cases extend your life. The link between health and diet is quite clear. Although we do not know enough about nutrition to identify the "ideal diet" for every person (food needs differ depending on age, body size, gender, physical activity, and other conditions), we can rely on dietary guidelines that are suitable for most Americans.[54]

Eat a Variety of Foods   Eating a variety of foods is important because you need more than forty different nutrients for good health: vitamins and minerals, amino acids (from proteins), essential fatty acids (from fats and oils), and sources of energy (calories from carbohydrates, fats, and proteins).[55] If you eat a variety of foods, you are more likely to maintain a well-balanced diet, because most foods contain more than one nutrient (see Figure 9.2).

Cut Down on Fatty Foods   The foods that are popular with many Americans are relatively high in fat, especially saturated fat, which contributes to high blood cholesterol levels. Many restaurant foods are high in fat because it gives menu items the flavor people often seek when eating out (see Table 9.1). Heart disease and certain kinds of cancer are byproducts of a high-fat diet.

Although diet is the most important factor in lowering cholesterol, exercise can help. About ninety minutes of aerobic exercise per week along with dietary changes has been found to lower total cholesterol.

Eat Foods with Adequate Starch and Fiber   Foods high in starch, such as breads made with whole grains, dry beans and peas, and potatoes, contain many essential nutrients. Many starches also add dietary fiber to your diet. A growing number of scientists believe that high-fiber diets can help reduce the odds of getting cancer of the colon. Some cereals and most fruits and vegetables are good sources of fiber.

Avoid Too Much Sodium   A common byproduct of excess sodium is high blood pressure. In the United States, where sodium-rich diets are very common, about one in four adults has elevated blood pressure. In populations with low sodium intakes, high blood pressure is very uncommon.[56] The recommended daily intake of sodium is 1,100 to 2,400 milligrams.

FIGURE 9.2

Recommended Food
Groups and Amounts
Necessary for a
Healthy Diet

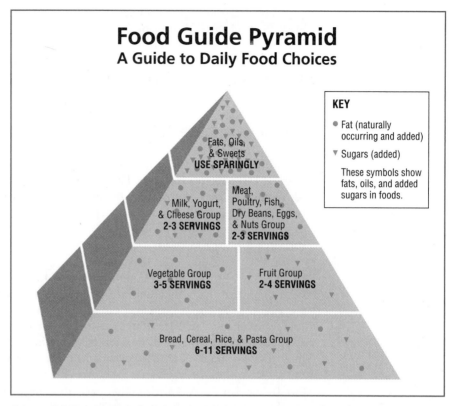

Source: U.S. Department of Agriculture/U.S. Department of Health and Human Services.

If You Drink Alcohol, Do So in Moderation Alcoholic beverages are high in calories and low in nutrients and cause serious health risks when used in excess. When alcohol is consumed in excess of one or two drinks per day, there tends to be a strong relationship between alcohol intake and high blood pressure. Excessive alcohol consumption has been linked to liver damage and certain types of cancer.[57]

With the help of these healthy diet guidelines, you can develop your own plan for achieving a healthful diet. Keep in mind that good nutrition is a balancing act. You want to select foods with enough vitamins, minerals, protein, and fiber but avoid too much fat and sodium. You want to consume enough calories to maintain the energy level required in your life but avoid weight gain.

Improving Your Physical Fitness

With regard to exercise, people often choose one of two extreme positions. Some adopt the point of view that only high-intensity activities (marathon

TABLE 9.1

Food Choices That Are
High in Fat and
Sodium

	Fat (grams)	Sodium (milligrams)	Calories
Sara Lee Bran Muffin (large)	22	470	440
Taco Bell's Taco Salad	61	910	905
Hot Pockets Ham 'n' Cheese	15	840	340
Long John Silver's Caesar with Chicken Wrap	73	3,710	1,450
Burger King's Double Whopper with Cheese	61	1,245	935

Source: *University of California at Berkeley Wellness Letter,* January 1998, p. 3; *University of California at Berkeley Wellness Letter,* July 1997, p. 3; *Tufts University Diet & Nutrition Letter;* Denise Webb, "Nutrition Now—Eat Right at a Fast-Food Restaurant," *Redbook Magazine,* July 1991.

running, high-impact aerobics) increase physical fitness. These people believe in the "no-pain, no-gain" fitness approach. The other extreme position is to become a "couch potato" and avoid all forms of exercise. Both positions should be avoided.

Physical fitness can be defined as the ability to perform daily tasks vigorously and have enough energy left over to enjoy leisure activities. It is the ability to endure difficult and stressful experiences and still carry on. Physical fitness, which involves the performance of the lungs, heart, and muscles, can also have a positive influence on mental alertness and emotional stability.[58] Research indicates that we can achieve and maintain physical fitness with a moderate exercise program. For most people, a program that involves regular physical activity at least three times a week and includes sustained physical exertion for twenty to thirty minutes during each activity period is adequate.[59] This modest investment of time and energy will give you a longer and healthier life.

You do not need to become an obsessive fitness fanatic to achieve lifesaving benefits from exercise. Start slowly with an aerobic fitness activity you feel you will enjoy. Walking, swimming, running, low-impact aerobics, and jogging are aerobic exercise. When we engage in aerobic exercise, the body is required to improve its ability to handle oxygen.[60] These exercises strengthen the heart, burn up calories, increase stamina, and help release tension.

If you are younger than 35 and in good health, you probably do not need to see a doctor before beginning an exercise program. If you are older than 35 and have been inactive for several years, consult your doctor before engaging in vigorous exercise.[61]

PLANNING FOR CHANGES IN YOUR LIFE

Throughout this book we have emphasized the concept that you can control your own behavior. In fact, during these turbulent times changes in your behavior may be one of the few things under your control. If making changes in your life seems to be a logical course of action at this point, then it is time to do some planning. The starting point is to clearly identify the personal growth goals that can make a difference in your life. What are some behaviors you can adopt (or alter) that will make an important positive change in your life? Once you have identified these behaviors, you can set goals and do what is necessary to achieve them. At the end of Chapter 1 you were encouraged to complete the self-assessment exercise at the end of each chapter. If you completed these exercises, then you no doubt gained awareness of your strengths and a better understanding of those abilities you want to improve.

The Power of Habits

Before we discuss specific goal-setting methods, let us take a look at the powerful influence of habits. Some habits, like taking a long walk three or four times a week, can have a positive influence on our well-being. Simply saying "Thank you" when someone does a favor or pays a compliment can be a habit. Other habits, such as smoking, never saying no to requests for your time, feeling jealousy, or constantly engaging in self-criticism, are negative forces in our lives. Stephen Covey, author of *The 7 Habits of Highly Effective People,* makes this observation: "Habits are powerful factors in our lives. Because they are consistent, often unconscious patterns, they constantly, daily, express our character and produce our effectiveness . . . or ineffectiveness."[62]

Breaking deeply embedded habits, such as impatience, procrastination, or criticism of others, can take a tremendous amount of effort. The influences supporting the habit, the actual root causes, are often repressed in the subconscious mind and forgotten.[63] How do you break a negative habit or form a positive habit? The process involves five steps.

Motivation   Once you are aware of the need to change, you must develop the willingness or desire to change. After making a major commitment to change, you must find ways to maintain your motivation. The key to staying motivated is to create a sense of urgency that is so intense you feel compelled to act on your desire to change. You must continually remind yourself why you want to change a bad habit or form a new habit.[64] If you are trying to break the habit of overeating, for example, try to visualize all of the benefits that will come from a change in your eating habits.

Knowledge   Once you clearly understand the benefits of breaking a habit or forming a new one, you must acquire the knowledge you need to change. Seek information, ask for advice, or learn from the experiences of others. This may involve finding a mentor, joining a group, or gathering sufficient material and teaching yourself. For example, suppose you decide you need to lose weight. Your first step might be to visit a bookstore and buy one or two books on weight reduction practices. Let's assume the books help but you discover that reading is not enough. Your next step might be to talk with others who share the same goal. You might consider joining a support group or talking to a counselor or an expert in nutrition. In the process of acquiring information, you are actually gaining a better understanding of the habit you want to learn or unlearn.

Practice Information is only as useful as you make it. This means that to change your behavior you must *practice* what you have learned. If you are a shy person, does this mean you need to volunteer to make a speech in front of several hundred people? The answer is no. Although there is always the rare individual who makes a major change seemingly overnight, most people find that the best and surest way to develop a new behavior is to do so gradually. This is particularly true if you feel a lot of anxiety about changing. Take your time. Allow yourself to ease into your new behavior until you feel comfortable with it.

Feedback Whenever you can, ask for feedback as you attempt to change a habit. Your progress will be much faster than it would be if you used only the trial-and-error method. Everyone has blind spots, particularly when trying something new. You will often need to rely on the feedback of others to tell you when you are off course or when you have really changed—sometimes you are too close to the process to tell.

Reinforcement When you see yourself exhibiting the type of behavior you have been working to develop—or when someone mentions that you have changed—reward yourself! The rewards can be simple, inexpensive ones—treating yourself to a movie, a bouquet of flowers, a favorite meal, or a special event. This type of reinforcement is vital when you are trying to improve old behaviors or develop new ones. Do not postpone rewarding yourself until the goal is reached. Intermediate success is just as important as the final result.

The Goal-Setting Process

Many years ago J. C. Penney, founder of the large retail chain, made a strong statement regarding the value of having goals: "Give me a stock clerk with a goal, and I will give you a man who will make history. Give me a man without a goal, and I will give you a stock clerk."[65] Penney recognized that goals give direction to our lives. Setting and achieving personal goals contributes to emotional well-being. It gives us a sense of personal control and a greater feeling of confidence in ourselves.[66] With the awareness of self-control comes the strength to accept more responsibility for our own life.

Goals should be an integral part of your plan to break old habits or form new ones. You will need an assortment of goals that address the different needs of your life. After a period of serious reflection, you may be facing unlimited goal-setting possibilities. Where do you begin? We hope that reading the previous chapters in this book, completing the self-assessment exercises, and reviewing the material in this chapter will help you narrow the possibilities.

The goal-setting process requires that you be clear about what you want to accomplish. If your goal is too general or vague, progress toward achieving that goal will be difficult to observe. Goals such as "I want to be a success" or "I desire good health" are much too general. The more specific the goal, the easier it will be for you to achieve.[67]

A very important step in the goal-setting process is to put the goal in writing. Kazuo Wada, chair of the retail giant Yaohan International Group, strongly recommends written goals. He says, "If you write down a goal, it becomes part of your consciousness."[68] His approach is to put his goals in writing again and again until he achieves them. Although the power of written goals is widely recognized, many people do not put their goals in writing. A written goal, reviewed daily, is much more likely to be achieved. Achieving your goals will usually require hard work and effort over a period of time. The process of achieving your goals, however, can be very rewarding.

THE CHOICE IS YOURS

Are you ready to develop a life plan for effective human relations? We hope the answer is yes. One of the positive aspects of personal planning is that you are making your own choices. You decide what kind of person you want to be and then set your own standards and goals. The results can mean not only career advancement and financial benefits but also the development of strong, satisfying relationships with others. These relationships may be the key to future opportunities, and you in turn may be able to help others achieve their goals.

In the opening chapter of this text, we talked about the total person approach to human relations. By now, we hope you realize that you are someone special! You have a unique combination of talents, attitudes, values, goals, needs, and motivation—all in a state of development. You can decide to tap your potential to become a successful, productive human being, however *you* understand those terms. We hope this book helps you to develop your human relations skills and become what you want to be. You can turn the theories, concepts, and guidelines presented here into a plan of action for your own life and career. We wish you the best!

Summary

The traditional definitions of success that most of us know are too confining. They view success almost entirely in terms of measurable job achievements. These definitions leave out the intangible successes to be had in private and in professional life.

Many people today are discovering that true success is a combination of achievements. Achieving right livelihood is one important dimension of success. Right livelihood is work consciously chosen, done with full awareness and care, and leading to enlightenment. Right livelihood is based on conscious choice. Although right livelihood recognizes that work is a vehicle for self-expression, it is a concept that places money in a secondary position. People who choose right livelihood are more likely to have high self-esteem, are self-disciplined, and have established meaningful goals.

A person's nonfinancial resources make one of the biggest contributions to a happy and fulfilling life. Each of us has four nonfinancial resources that can enrich our lives: physical and mental health, education and training (intellectual growth), leisure time (time for family, socializing, recreation), and healthy spirituality. These nonfinancial resources can be acquired throughout our lives.

Many Americans are working to achieve healthy lifestyles. Healthy lifestyles can give us a higher energy level, a greater sense of self-confidence, and generally a more positive outlook. People who maintain good health usually have more endurance, spend less time feeling tired or ill, and miss less work than persons who are not physically fit.

Planning for changes in your life often requires breaking negative habits or forming positive habits. The process of breaking habits and forming new ones involves five steps: motivation, knowledge, practice, feedback, and reinforcement. Goal setting is also an integral part of a successful plan to make changes. Unspecified or vague goals, goals that are not put in writing, are harder to reach and contribute less than they could to a productive, enriching life.

Career Corner

Q. I work for a large company and have a terrific job. Because of downsizing, all of us in the office are working sixty-hour weeks to get the work done. I take work home and do the work four people used to do. By the end of the week my mind is numb, my productivity is down, and I am exhausted. This not only is hard on my family but is bad for the company. It seems that if the work can't be handled during a normal workweek, then we need to hire more people to do the job. What do you suggest?

A. If you can get another job with no trouble, do it! If you feel lucky to have your job, then let your boss know that you need help. Gather your colleagues together and present your case. Set limits at work and quit taking work home. Perhaps this will allow you to be more productive at work. Don't accept an unreasonable amount of work because you are afraid you will be laid off. A job that is causing you to burn out is not worth it.

Key Terms

right livelihood
nonfinancial resources

spirituality
physical fitness

Review Questions

1. What have been the traditional criteria used to measure success? What are some of the reasons we need a new model for success in our society?
2. Explain the reasons many Americans have experienced a decline in leisure time.
3. What does the term *right livelihood* mean? What are the common characteristics of right livelihood?
4. What is the work-and-spend cycle?
5. List and describe four nonfinancial resources.
6. Julie Connelly in the Total Person Insight says there is no harder work than thinking about who you are and what you want out of life. Do you agree or disagree with her point of view? Explain.
7. What are the major reasons we should adopt a healthy lifestyle?
8. List and describe the guidelines for a healthy diet.
9. Provide a brief description of physical fitness. Why is physical fitness so important in the life of a typical worker?
10. What are the five steps involved in breaking a negative habit or forming a positive habit?

Application Exercises

1. In recent years, it has become popular for organizations to develop a mission statement that reflects their philosophy and objectives. The Lotus Operating Principles prepared by Lotus Development Corp. (see Chapter 4) provide an example. Prepare a personal mission statement that reflects your goals and aspirations for a successful life. Your mission statement should cover the roles of financial and nonfinancial resources in your life.
2. Throughout this chapter you were encouraged to take control of your life and establish your own definition of success. This chapter has a strong "all development is self-development" theme. Can we really control our own destinies? Can we always make our own choices? Mike Hernacki, author of the book *The Ultimate Secret of Getting Absolutely Everything You Want*, says yes:

   To get what you want, you must recognize something that at first may be difficult, even painful to look at. You must recognize that *you alone* are the source of all the conditions and situations in your life. You must recognize that whatever your world looks like right now, you alone have caused it to look that way. The state of your health, your finances, your personal relationships, your professional life—all of it is *your* doing, yours and no one else's.[69]

Do you agree with this viewpoint? Take a position in favor of or in opposition to Hernacki's statement. Prepare a short one- or two-paragraph statement that expresses your views.

3. There are many ways to deepen and extend your spirituality. One way is to begin placing a higher value on silence, tranquillity, and reflection. If your life is extremely busy, you may not be taking time for thought or reflection. If you are accustomed to living in the presence of noise throughout the day, quiet times may make you feel uncomfortable at first. Over a period of one week, set aside a few minutes each day for your own choice of meditation, prayer, contemplation, or reflection. Try to find a quiet place for this activity. At the end of the week, assess the benefits of this activity, and consider the merits of making it part of your daily routine.[70]

Internet Exercise

Dale Carnegie Training offers human relations training programs to people in seventy different countries. Access the company's Web site, and review the information provided. Examine information about the company, and then review the books and courses available. Read the course description for *The Dale Carnegie Course*. Does it appear that this company offers courses and materials that would be of interest to you at some future date? Prepare a one-page summary of your views.

Self-Assessment Exercise

For each of the following statements, circle the number from 1 to 5 that best represents your response: (1) strongly disagree (never do this); (2) disagree (rarely do this); (3) moderately agree (sometimes do this); (4) agree (frequently do this); (5) strongly agree (almost always do this).

a. I try to maintain balance in my life by avoiding addiction to work and by engaging in leisure-time activities.

    1   2   3   4   5

b. I envision my existence in a larger context and view healthy spirituality as a positive, enlightening force in my life.

    1   2   3   4   5

c. I avoid rigid individualism (self-centered behavior) by investing time and energy in helping others.

    1   2   3   4   5

d. I seek advice and counsel from   1   2   3   4   5
friends, coworkers, and professionals
in order to cope with life's problems.

e. I stay connected with family and friends   1   2   3   4   5
and monitor the development of my
nonfinancial resources carefully.

f. I have established well-thought-out, realistic   1   2   3   4   5
goals for my life, and these goals are tied
to my values.

Select an appropriate attitude or skill you would like to improve. Write
your goal in the space provided.

GOAL: _____

_____

_____

Case Problem   It's a Matter of Choice

As one of the top-ranking women builders in the nation, Julia Stasch insists
that women be given the same chance as men to succeed or fail on the
job. Her company has completed over $775 million worth of projects since
1990, and it employs about three times as many construction women as the
industry average. Stasch's professional career spans jobs such as being a Vista
volunteer on a Native American tribal reservation, a high school history
teacher, a secretary, and now the president of Stein & Co., a major Chicago
development firm. Along the way she and her husband, a professor at Loyola
University, made the conscious decision not to have any children. "I wouldn't
be where I am today if I'd made the decision to have a family," Stasch says.

Many men seeking a more nontraditional role are placing their relationship
with their children on a par with, or even above, their career goals. They may
delay career advancement while their children are young to be able to spend
more time with them. Magazine editor Robert Barker chose to cut his workweek and paycheck by two-fifths to share child-care responsibilities for his
infant daughter with his working wife. He joined the slower-paced "daddy-
track." After one year, the announcement of his wife's second pregnancy, and
a reorganization at work, he returned to his job full time only to find his career
goals and mind-set had been permanently altered. When offered a promotion,
he turned it down, knowing he wanted to be able to spend more time with his
family.

Newspaper editor Mary Newsom discovered a richer life after the birth of her daughter and during her subsequent maternity leave. She found time in the grocery store to speak to strangers who stopped to admire her baby and spent leisurely afternoons with neighbors and their infants. As she began to acknowledge this slower pace, she admitted, "Not once did I hear a droning deep in my head, the insistent buzz of tasks undone.... Time had become a sweetly flowing river, not the downhill rapids I once knew.... Only because I hadn't poured the last ounce of my spirit into my job was I able to make those simple connections with people."

Questions

1. How do you feel about the choices each of these individuals made? Do you believe you would feel the same way if you were placed in similar situations?
2. Under what circumstances would you say no to professional demands in favor of family demands?
3. Discuss the comment Mary Newsom made about pouring your last ounce of spirit into your job. How might this degree of dedication affect your human relationships at home and at work?

Notes

Chapter 1

1. Mary Scott, "Interview with Howard Schultz," *Business Ethics,* November/December 1995, p. 28.
2. Kate Berry, "Starbucks Opens First Stores in Miami, Hoping to Woo Lovers of Cuban Coffee," *Wall Street Journal,* March 31, 1997, p. A9; Jennifer Reese, "Starbucks—Inside the Coffee Cult," *Fortune,* December 9, 1996, pp. 190–198.
3. John A. Byrne, "The Pain of Downsizing," *Business Week,* May 9, 1994, pp. 60–69.
4. "The Secret Purpose of Downsizing," *Business Ethics,* November/December 1996, p. 13.
5. Gene Koretz, "The Downside of Downsizing," *Business Week,* April 28, 1997, p. 26.
6. "Now Renting: Attorneys and Rocket Scientists," *Training,* February 1997, p. 10.
7. Hal Lancaster, "Managing Your Career," *Wall Street Journal,* February 18, 1997, p. B1.
8. Frederick F. Reichheld, "Solving the Productivity Puzzle," *Wall Street Journal,* March 4, 1996, p. 14.
9. Stephen B. Shepard, "Defining the Q-Word," *Business Week* (Quality Edition), 1991, p. 4.
10. "Questing for the Best," *Business Week* (Quality Edition), 1991, p. 8.
11. Bernard Avishai, "Companies Can't Make Up for Failing Schools," *Wall Street Journal,* July 28, 1996, p. A12.
12. Jeff Pettit, "Team Communication: It's in the Cards," *Training & Development,* January 1997, p. 12.
13. Marilyn Loden and Judy B. Rosener, *Workforce America!* (Homewood, Ill.: Business One Irwin, 1991), p. 23.
14. "Miles Traveled, More to Go," *Business Week* (Quality Edition), 1991, p. 71.
15. Haidee Allerton, "Working Life," *Training & Development,* August 1995, p. 72.
16. Joseph Pereira, "Employers Confront Domestic Abuse," *Wall Street Journal,* March 2, 1995, p. B1.
17. Maggie Jackson, "Dads Speak Up About Work-Family," *Roanoke Times,* June 15, 1997, p. B1.
18. Shawn Tully, "America's Healthiest Companies," *Fortune,* June 12, 1995, p. 276.
19. "Who Wins and Why," *Inc.,* April 1987, p. 103.
20. Robert Kreitner, *Management,* 7th ed. (Boston: Houghton Mifflin, 1998), p. 263.
21. David Stamps, "Relaxed Fit," *Training,* October 1996, pp. 90–100.
22. David Stamps, "Going Nowhere: Culture Change at the Postal Service Fizzles," *Training,* July 1996, pp. 26–34.
23. Chris Lee, "The Vision Thing," *Training,* February 1993, p. 27.
24. William W. Arnold and Jeanne M. Plas, *The Human Touch* (New York: Wiley, 1993), pp. 1 and 2.
25. D. R. Hampton, C. E. Summer, and R. A. Webber, *Organizational Behavior and the Practice of Management* (Glenview, Ill.: Scott, Foresman, 1973), p. 215.
26. J. David McCracken and Ana E. Falcon-Emmanuelli, "A Theoretical Basis for Work Values Research in Vocational Education," *Journal of Vocational and Technical Education,* Spring 1994, p. 7.
27. Betsy Jacobson and Beverly Kaye, "Balancing Act," *Training & Development,* February 1993, p. 26.
28. Roy W. Walters, "Improving Man/Machine Interface for Greater Productivity," *BNAC Communicator,* Summer 1982, p. 13.
29. Jacobson and Kaye, "Balancing Act," pp. 24–26.
30. Sue Shellenbarger, "Dad Takes Home a Tough Day at Work," *Wall Street Journal,* June 29, 1994, p. B3.
31. Sue Shellenbarger, "It's the Type of Job You Have That Affects the Kids, Studies Say," *Wall Street Journal,* July 31, 1996.
32. Rochelle Sharpe, "Labor Letter," *Wall Street Journal,* September 13, 1994, p. 1.
33. Sue Shellenbarger, "Keeping Workers by Reaching Out to Them," *Wall Street Journal,* June 1, 1994, p. B1.
34. Robert Levering and Milton Moskowitz, *The 100 Best Companies to Work for in America* (New York: Currency-Doubleday, 1993), p. 211.
35. Bradley J. Rieger, "Lessons in Productivity and People," *Training & Development,* October 1995, pp. 56–58.
36. For a detailed examination of the Hawthorne criticisms and the legacy of the Hawthorne research, see David A. Whitsett and Lyle Yorks, *From Management Theory to Business Sense* (New York: American Management Association, 1983).
37. Jim Collins, "The Classics," *Inc.,* December 1996, p. 55.
38. Thomas J. Peters and Robert H. Waterman, Jr., *In Search of Excellence: Lessons from America's Best-Run Companies* (New York: Harper & Row, 1982), p. 14.

39. John R. Diekman, *Human Connections* (Englewood Cliffs, N.J.: Prentice-Hall, 1982), p. xii.

40. Hal Lancaster, "Re-Engineering Authors Reconsider Re-Engineering," *Wall Street Journal,* January 17, 1995, p. B1.

41. Stephen R. Covey, *The 7 Habits of Highly Effective People* (New York: Simon & Schuster, 1989), pp. 66–67.

42. Richard Koonce, "Emotional IQ, a New Secret of Success," *Training & Development,* February 1996, p. 19.

43. Denis Waitley, *Empires of the Mind* (New York: Morrow, 1995), p. 133.

44. H. Jackson Brown, Jr., *Live and Learn to Pass It On* (Nashville, 1992), poster.

45. Harold H. Bloomfield and Robert K. Cooper, *The Power of 5* (Emmaus, Pa.: Rodale Press, 1995), p. 61.

Chapter 2

1. Robert Levering and Milton Moskowitz, *The 100 Best Companies to Work for in America* (New York: Currency-Doubleday, 1993), p. 419.

2. "The Open Book Revolution," *Inc.,* June 1995, cover story.

3. Levering and Moskowitz, *The 100 Best Companies to Work for in America,* p. 421.

4. Alex Markels, "Memo 4/8/97, FYI: Messages Inundate Offices," *Wall Street Journal,* April 7, 1997, p. B1.

5. "Effective Listening Skills," *Women in Business,* March–April 1994, p. 28.

6. John Stewart and Gary D'Angelo, *Together—Communicating Interpersonally* (New York: Random House, 1988), p. 5.

7. Patricia A. Galagan, "On Being a Beginner," *Training & Development,* November 1992, p. 36.

8. Mike France and Tim Smart, "The Ugly Talk on the Texaco Tape," *Business Week,* November 18, 1996, p. 58.

9. "Tom Chappell—Minister of Commerce," *Business Ethics,* January–February, 1994, p. 18.

10. David Shenk, *Data Smog—Surviving the Information Glut* (San Francisco: Harper Edge, 1997), p. 54.

11. Sy Lazarus, *Loud and Clear* (New York: AMACOM, 1974), p. 3.

12. Brian Hickey, "Throwing the Book at Legalese," *TWA Ambassador,* June 1990, p. 86.

13. "Memos from Hell," *Fortune,* February 3, 1997, p. 120.

14. Roger E. Axtell, ed., *Do's and Taboos Around the World,* compiled by Parker Pen Company, 3d ed. (New York: Wiley, 1993), p. 155.

15. Deborah Tannen, *You Just Don't Understand* (New York: Ballantine Books, 1991), p. 42.

16. Judith C. Tingley, *Genderflex: Men and Women Speaking Each Other's Language at Work* (New York: AMACOM, 1994), p. 33.

17. Ginger Trumfio, "More Than Words," *Sales & Marketing Management,* April 1994, p. 55.

18. "Server Posture Affects How We Tip," *The Menninger Letter,* November 1993, p. 5.

19. Phyllis Mindell, "The Body Language of Power," *Executive Female,* May/June 1996, p. 48.

20. Axtell, *Do's and Taboos Around the World,* p. 46.

21. Ibid., p. 47.

22. Ibid., p. 49.

23. William B. Gudykunst, Stella Ting-Toomey, Sandra Sudweeks, and Lea Stewart, *Building Bridges: Interpersonal Skills for a Changing World* (Boston: Houghton Mifflin, 1995), pp. 315–316.

24. Cheryl Hamilton, *Communicating for Results* (Belmont, Calif.: Wadsworth, 1990), p. 48.

25. Camille Wright Miller, "Working It Out," *Roanoke Times & World-News,* May 8, 1994, p. F4.

26. C. Glenn Pearce, "How Effective Are We as Listeners?" *Training & Development,* April 1993, pp. 79–80.

27. Gary Blake, "How to Become an 'Active Listener,'" *Fluid Power Journal,* January 1995, p. 6.

28. Donna Deepose, "Listen Your Way to Better Management," *Supervisory Management,* May 1993, pp. 7–8.

29. Stephen R. Covey, *The Seven Habits of Highly Effective People* (New York: Simon & Schuster, 1989), pp. 240–241.

30. C. Glenn Pearce, "Learning How to Listen Empathically," *Supervisory Management,* September 1991, p. 11.

31. James G. Carr, "Dare to Share," *Pace,* June 1988, p. 22.

32. Hendric Weisinger and Norman Lobsenz, *Nobody's Perfect—How to Give Criticism and Get Results* (Los Angeles: Stratford Press, 1981), p. 39.

33. Kenneth Labaich, "Rethinking Almost Everything," *Fortune,* May 13, 1996, p. 179.

34. "Business Being Built Without Bricks, Mortar," *Springfield News-Leader,* April 28, 1994, p. 1B.

35. Ginger Trumfio, "Liberty, Equality, E-Mail!" *Sales & Marketing Management,* March 1994, p. 38.

36. Charlene Marmer Solomon, "Global Operations Demand That HR Rethink Diversity," *Personnel Journal,* July 1994, p. 44.

37. Ibid.

38. Ibid., p. 40.

39. "Growing Your Business by Going Global," *Inc.,* January 1994, p. 65.

40. "Don't Be an Ugly-American Manager," *Fortune,* October 16, 1995, p. 225.

41. Lennie Copeland, "Training Americans to Do Business Overseas," *Training,* July 1983, p. 12.

42. Andy Cohen, "Small World, Big Challenge," *Sales & Marketing Management,* June 1996, p. 72.

Chapter 3

1. Sue Shellenbarger, "What Does Your Job Tell a Crystal Burch About Fulfillment?" *Wall Street Journal,* April 24, 1996, p. B1.
2. L. B. Gschwandtner, "Creating a Champion," *Personal Selling Power,* March 1992, pp. 57–60.
3. Nathaniel Branden, *The Six Pillars of Self-Esteem* (New York: Bantam, 1994), p. 7.
4. California State Department of Education, *Toward a State of Esteem* (Sacramento: Department of Education, January 1990), p. 19.
5. Quoted in A. H. Maslow, "A Theory of Human Motivation," in *Psychological Foundations of Organizational Behavior,* ed. Barry M. Stow (Santa Monica, Calif.: Goodyear Publishing, 1977), pp. 7–8.
6. David E. Shapiro, "Pumping Up Your Attitude," *Psychology Today,* May/June 1997, p. 14.
7. Richard Laliberte, "Self-Esteem Workshop," *Self,* May 1994, p. 201.
8. Branden, *The Six Pillars of Self-Esteem,* p. 39.
9. Laliberte, "Self-Esteem Workshop," p. 201.
10. Tim Simmons and Ruth Sheehan, "Even in Earliest Years, Brain Is 'Wiring' for Life," *News & Observer,* February 16, 1997, p. 1A.
11. Madeleine J. Nash, "Fertile Minds," *Time,* February 3, 1997, pp. 51–52.
12. Simmons and Sheehan, "Even in Earliest Years, Brain Is 'Wiring' for Life," p. 1A.
13. Amy Bjork Harris and Thomas A. Harris, *Staying OK* (New York: Harper & Row, 1985), p. 24.
14. Margaret Henning and Ann Jardim, *The Managerial Woman* (New York: Anchor Books, 1977), pp. 106–107.
15. Ellen Graham, "Leah: Life Is All Sweetness and Insecurity," *Wall Street Journal,* February 9, 1995, p. B16.
16. "The New American Body," *University of California at Berkeley Wellness Letter,* December 1993, p. 1.
17. Mary Pipher, *Reviving Ophelia* (New York: Ballantine Books, 1994), p. 23.
18. Stephanie Mehta, "Photo Chain Ventures Beyond Big Hair," *Wall Street Journal,* May 13, 1996, p. B1.
19. Ellen Uzelac, "In a Daughter's Voice," *Common Boundary,* September/October 1995, p. 49.
20. Emmett E. Miller, *The Healing Power of Happiness* (Emmaus, Pa.: Rodale Press, 1989), pp. 12–13.
21. Amy Saltzman, *Down-Shifting* (New York: Harper-Collins, 1990), pp. 15–16.
22. Miller, *The Healing Power of Happiness,* pp. 12–13.
23. Belleruth Naparstek, "About Face," *Common Boundary,* July/August 1996, p. 64.
24. Richard Ringer, David Balkin, and R. Wayne Boss, "Matching the Feedback to the Person," *Executive Female,* November–December 1993, p. 11.
25. Hyrum W. Smith, *The 10 Natural Laws of Successful Time and Life Management* (New York: Warner Books, 1994), p. 178.
26. Branden, *The Six Pillars of Self-Esteem,* p. 48.
27. Ibid., p. 33.
28. California State Department of Education, *Toward a State of Esteem,* pp. 23–24.
29. Robert J. Kriegel, with Louis Platier, *If It Ain't Broke . . . Break It!"* audiocassette produced by Barr Audio, Irwindale, Calif., 1992.
30. Arnold A. Lazarus and Clifford N. Lazarus, *The 60-Second Shrink* (San Luis Obispo, Calif.: Impact Publishers, 1997), p. 40.
31. Cheri Burns, "The Extra Edge," *Savvy,* December 1982, p. 42.
32. Hal Lancaster, "It's Harder, but You Still Can Rise Up from the Mail Room," *Wall Street Journal,* June 18, 1996, p. B1.
33. Chip R. Bell, "Making Mentoring a Way of Life," *Training,* October 1996, p. 138; Lin Standke, review of *Managers as Mentors: Building Partnerships for Learning,* by Chip Bell, *Training,* April 1997, pp. 64–65.
34. Hal Lancaster, "You Might Need a Guide to Lead You Around Career Pitfalls," *Wall Street Journal,* July 30, 1996, p. B1.
35. Ibid.
36. Hal Lancaster, "How Women Can Find Mentors in a World with Few Role Models," *Wall Street Journal,* April 1, 1997, p. B1.
37. Lazarus and Lazarus, *The 60-Second Shrink,* pp. 3, 4.
38. Shakti Gawain, *Creative Visualization* (San Rafael, Calif.: Whatever Publishing, 1978), p. 14.
39. Lazarus and Lazarus, *The 60-Second Shrink,* p. 3.
40. L. B. Gschwandtner, "Mary Lou Retton," *Personal Selling Power,* 15th Anniversary Issue, 1995, p. 99.
41. Denis Waitley, "The Winning Generation Video Series," Advanced Learning, Inc., Cedar Falls, Iowa.
42. Lazarus and Lazarus, *The 60-Second Shrink,* pp. 1, 2.
43. Herb Kindler, "Working to Change Old Habits," *Working Smart,* May 1992, p. 8.
44. Julia Flynn Siler, "The Corporate Woman: Is She Really Different?" *Business Week,* June 25, 1990, p. 14.
45. Sheila Ostrander and Lynn Schroeder, *Superlearning* (New York: Dell Publishing, 1979), pp. 87–109.
46. Roy J. Blitzer, Colleen Petersen, and Linda Rogers, "How to Build Self-Esteem," *Training & Development,* February 1993, pp. 58–60.
47. Pipher, *Reviving Ophelia,* p. 183.

Chapter 4

1. O. C. Ferrell and John Fraedrich, *Business Ethics* (Boston: Houghton Mifflin, 1997), pp. 267–274.

2. Dennis Levine, "The Inside Story of an Inside Trader," *Fortune,* May 21, 1990, p. 82.

3. Kathleen Morris and Lisa Sanders, "Professor Milken's Lesson Plan," *Business Week,* August 4, 1997.

4. "The Strength of Character," *Royal Bank Letter* (Royal Bank of Canada) May–June 1988, p. 1.

5. "Practicing What You Preach," *The Pryor Report,* vol. 10, no. 1a.

6. Richard Brookhiser, "Why Virtue Is in Short Supply," *New York Times Book Review,* March 3, 1996, p. 12.

7. Stephen R. Covey, *The Seven Habits of Highly Effective People* (New York: Simon & Schuster, 1989), p. 92.

8. Joseph Josephson and Ednah Josephson, *Character Counts Wallet Card* (Marina del Ray, Calif.: Josephson Institute of Ethics, 1994).

9. Hyrum W. Smith, *The 10 Natural Laws of Successful Time and Life Management* (New York: Warner Books, 1994), pp. 14–15.

10. J. David McCracken and Ana E. Falcon-Emmanuelli, "A Theoretical Basis for Work Values Research in Vocational Education," *Journal of Vocational and Technical Education,* Spring 1994, p. 4.

11. Smith, *The 10 Natural Laws of Successful Time and Life Management,* pp. 66–67.

12. Sue Shellenbarger, "Some Top Executives Are Finding a Balance Between Job and Home," *Wall Street Journal,* April 23, 1997, p. B1.

13. Kevin A. Wilson, "Halo Car," *Autoweek,* April 7, 1997.

14. Katherine Paterson, "Family Values," *New York Times Book Review,* October 15, 1995, p. 32.

15. Tom Pickens, "Ethics: Easy as A-B-C?" *Creative Living,* vol. 22, no. 4, p. 8.

16. "Put First Things First," *Inc.,* December 1987, p. 168.

17. Chris Lee and Ron Zemke, "The Search for Spirit in the Workplace," *Training,* June 1993, p. 21.

18. Stanley M. Elam, Lowell C. Rose, and Alec M. Gallup, "The 26th Annual Phi Delta Kappa/Gallup Poll of the Public's Attitudes Toward the Public Schools," *Phi Delta Kappan,* September 1994, p. 49.

19. Sonia L. Nazario, "Schoolteachers Say It's Wrongheaded to Try to Teach Students What's Right," *Wall Street Journal,* April 6, 1990, p. B1.

20. Sanford N. McDonnell, "A Virtuous Agenda for Education Reform," *Wall Street Journal,* February 18, 1997, p. A22.

21. Andrew Stark, "What's the Matter with Business Ethics?" *Harvard Business Review,* May–June 1993, p. 38.

22. William J. Bennett, *The Index of Leading Cultural Indicators: Facts and Figures on the State of American Society* (New York: Simon & Schuster, 1994), p. 103.

23. Richard S. Dunham and Michael O'Neal, "Gunning for the Gangstas," *Business Week,* June 19, 1995, p. 41.

24. Roy Furchgott, "Howard Stern's Battle of Richmond," *Business Week,* June 17, 1996, p. 6.

25. Morris Massey, *The People Puzzle* (Reston, Va.: Reston Publishing, 1979).

26. James C. Collins, "Change Is Good but First, Know What Should Never Change," *Fortune,* May 29, 1995, p. 141.

27. Jeffrey L. Seglin, "Playing by the Rules," *Inc.,* November 1996, p. 39.

28. Neal Donald Walsch, *Conversations with God, Book 1 Guidebook* (Charlottesville, Va.: Hampton Roads, 1997), p. 71.

29. "Newsbreakers," *Inc.,* October 1990, p. 25.

30. Joan E. Rigdon, "Some Workers Gripe Bosses Are Ordering Too Much Overtime," *Wall Street Journal,* September 29, 1994, pp. A1, A6.

31. "McDonnell Douglas Executive Ousted," Associated Press, *Springfield News Leader,* October 27, 1996, p. A1.

32. Sue Shellenbarger, "In Real Life, Hard Choices Upset Any Balancing Act," *Wall Street Journal,* April 19, 1995.

33. Smith, *The 10 Natural Laws of Successful Time and Life Management,* pp. 68–69.

34. Vivian Arnold, B. June Schmidt, and Randall L. Wells, "Ethics Instruction in the Classrooms of Business Educators," *Delta Pi Epsilon Journal,* vol. 38, no. 4, Fall 1996, p. 185.

35. "Workers Cut Ethical Corners, Survey Finds," *Wall Street Journal,* March 10, 1995, p. A2.

36. "Nearly Half of Workers Take Unethical Actions—Survey," *Des Moines Register,* April 7, 1997, p. 18B.

37. Paula Ancona, "How to Handle Unethical Situations in the Office," *San Jose Mercury News,* July 9, 1995, p. 1PC.

38. Sherwood Ross, "The Thief on the Payroll," *San Jose Mercury News,* April 14, 1996, p. 1PC.

39. Marian Wright Edelman, *The Measure of Our Success* (Boston: Allyn & Bacon, 1992), pp. 502–503.

40. "Long-Distance Services Target Customers' Values," *Springfield NewsLeader,* June 25, 1996, p. C1.

41. Eric D. Randall, "Money No Longer Tops for MBAs," *USA Today,* May 25, 1994, p. 5B.

42. Dawn Anfuso, "Soul-Searching Sustains Values at Lotus Development," *Personnel Journal,* June 1994, pp. 54–61.

43. Sue Shellenbarger, "Some Workers Find Bosses Don't Share Their Family Values," *Wall Street Journal,* July 12, 1995, p. B1.

44. Betsy Weisendanger, "Doing the Right Thing," *Sales & Marketing Management,* March 1991, p. 82.

45. M. Scott Peck, *The Road Less Traveled* (New York: Simon & Schuster, 1978), p. 19.

46. Michael H. Mescon and Timothy S. Mescon, "And Then Some . . . ," *Sky,* August 1989, p. 92.

47. George Kegley, "Broker with a Difference: A. G. Edwards, Chairman," *Roanoke Times & World-News,* April 13, 1990, p. B6.

48. Krystal Miller, "Former Honda Executives Plead Guilty to Charges Tied to Bribes from Dealers," *Wall Street Journal,* March 15, 1994, p. A4; Holman W. Jenkins, Jr., " 'Tis the Season of Sin at Honda," *Wall Street Journal,* December 17, 1996, p. A23.

49. Leslie Scism, "Prudential's New Chief Is Finding It Difficult to Avoid the Rock," *Wall Street Journal,* January 24, 1997, p. A1.

50. Richard Behar, "Skimming the Cream," *Time,* August 2, 1993, p. 49.

51. Mary Ellen Egan, "Old Enough to Know Better," *Business Ethics,* January/February 1995, p. 19.

52. Bob Filipczak, "The Soul of the Hog," *Training,* February 1996, pp. 38–42.

53. Andrew Stark, "What's the Matter with Business Ethics?" *Harvard Business Review,* May–June 1993, p. 38.

54. "Tom Chappell—Minister of Commerce," *Business Ethics,* January/February 1994, p. 17.

55. "Ethical Programs and Personal Values Are Still Not Enough," *Business Ethics,* May/June 1996, p. 12.

56. Joshua Hyatt, "How to Hire Employees," *Inc.,* March 1990, p. 2.

57. Claudia H. Deutsch, "You Want This Job? Pass the Integrity Test," *San Jose Mercury News,* February 25, 1990, p. 2.

58. "Honesty Tests: The Defense Rests," *Training,* May 1991, p. 12.

59. Phillip Barnhart, "The Ethics Game," *Training,* June 1993, pp. 65, 66.

60. Ellen Neuborne, "Whistle-Blowers Pipe Up More Frequently," *USA Today,* July 22, 1996, p. 2B.

61. Paul M. Sherer, "North American and Asian Executives Have Contrasting Values, Study Finds," *Wall Street Journal,* March 8, 1996, p. B12.

62. John Bussey and James McGregor, "What, Why, and How," *Wall Street Journal,* December 19, 1993, p. R19.

63. Chris Hill and Toby Hanlon, "26 Simple Ways to Change How You Feel," *Prevention,* August 1993, p. 126.

Chapter 5

1. Ron Zemke, "Custom Service as a Performing Art," *Training,* March 1993, p. 40.

2. Robert Levering and Milton Moskowitz, *The 100 Best Companies to Work for in America* (New York: Currency-Doubleday, 1993), p. 398.

3. Alex Taylor III, "Bla Car, Bad Book," *Fortune,* November 29, 1993, p. 17.

4. "What Matters Most to Employers?" *Inc.,* June 1995, p. 90.

5. Thomas Pelzinger, Jr., "How Lynn Mercer Manages a Factory That Manages Itself," *Wall Street Journal,* March 7, 1997, p. B1.

6. Ken Gepfert, "As Wage Edge Shrinks, Workers' Attitude Shines," *Wall Street Journal,* May 28, 1997, p. S2.

7. "A Matter of Attitude," *Royal Bank Letter,* May–June 1994, p. 2.

8. Wayne F. Cascio, *Costing Human Resources* (Boston: PWS-Kent Publishing, 1991), p. 130.

9. Ibid., p. 131.

10. Tom Lopp, "Attitude Makes the Difference," *Vocational Education Journal,* January 1996, p. 8.

11. Bernie S. Siegel, *Love, Medicine and Miracles* (New York: Harper & Row, 1986), p. 26.

12. Jerome Kagan, *Psychology: An Introduction* (New York: Harcourt Brace Jovanovich, 1984), p. 548.

13. "Tailored Health Plans Take Off," *Fortune,* June 27, 1994, p. 12.

14. Henry Labalme, "Breaking the Chains of Addiction to Television," *Roanoke Times,* April 23, 1996, p. A5.

15. William F. Schoell and Joseph P. Guiltinan, *Marketing,* 5th ed. (Boston: Allyn & Bacon, 1992), pp. 166–167; William M. Pride and O. C. Ferrell, *Marketing,* 10th ed. (Boston: Houghton Mifflin, 1997), p. 146.

16. Eamonn Fingleton, "Jobs for Life—Why Japan Won't Give Them Up," *Fortune,* March 29, 1995, pp. 119–125.

17. Michael R. Quinlan, "How Does Service Drive the Service Company?" *Harvard Business Review,* November–December 1991, p. 156.

18. John Case, "Corporate Culture," *Inc.,* November 1996, pp. 42–53.

19. Thomas E. Ricks, "New Marines Illustrate Growing Gap Between Military and Society," *Wall Street Journal,* July 27, 1995, p. A1.

20. Shawn Cavence, "Spiritual Doctor Sets Up Shop," *Collegiate Times,* February 20, 1990, p. A6.

21. Timothy G. Hatcher, "The Ins and Outs of Self-Directed Learning," *Training & Development,* February 1997, pp. 35–39.

22. Anthony P. Carnevale, Leila J. Gainer, and Ann S. Meltzer, *Workplace Basics Training Manual* (San Francisco: Jossey-Bass, 1990), p. 3.

23. David Holzman, "When Workers Run the Show," *Working Woman,* August 1993, p. 74.

24. Nancy L. Mueller, "Wisconsin Power and Light's Model Diversity Program," *Training & Development,* March 1996, p. 57.

25. Patricia Sellers, "Now Bounce Back!" *Fortune,* May 1, 1995, pp. 49–62.

26. Martin Seligman, *Learned Optimism* (New York: Knopf, 1991), p. 4.

27. Redford Williams and Virginia Williams, *Anger Kills* (New York: Harper Perennial, 1993), p. 12.

28. Phil Catalfo, "Buckminster Fuller—the 50-Year Experiment," audiotape (San Francisco: New Dimensions Foundation, 1988).

29. Robert F. Mager, *Developing Attitudes Toward Learning* (Belmont, Calif.: Fearon-Pitman, 1968), p. 47.

30. Quoted in Nancy W. Collins, Susan K. Gilbert, and Susan Nycum, *Women Leading: Making Tough Choices on the Fast Track* (Lexington, Mass.: Stephen Greene Press, 1988), p. 1.

31. "Walking in Your Customers' Shoes," *Training,* February 1995, p. 16.

32. Matt Rothman, "Into the Black," *Inc.,* January 1993, pp. 59–65.

33. "Work Week," *Wall Street Journal,* January 7, 1997, p. A1.

Chapter 6

1. Kevin Helliker, "Smile: That Cranky Shopper May Be a Store Spy," *Wall Street Journal,* November 30, 1994, p. B1.

2. Hal Kahn, "Secrets of a Mystery Shopper," *San Jose Mercury News,* September 22, 1996, pp. 1E, 2E.

3. Stephen R. Covey, *The 7 Habits of Highly Effective People* (New York: Simon & Schuster, 1989), pp. 22, 34.

4. Susan Bixler, *Professional Presence* (New York: G. P. Putnam's Sons, 1991), p. 16.

5. "Author: Success Pivots on First Impressions," *San Jose Mercury News,* November 8, 1992, p. 2 PC.

6. Douglas A. Bernstein, Alison Clarke-Stewart, Edward J. Roy, and Christopher D. Wickens, *Psychology,* 4th ed. (Boston: Houghton Mifflin, 1997), p. 241.

7. "Dress Codes for Presidential Candidates," *Parade Magazine,* November 5, 1995, p. 17.

8. Malcolm Fleschner, with Gerhard Gschwandtner, "Power Talk," *Personal Selling Power,* July/August 1995, p. 14.

9. Leonard Zunin and Natalie Zunin, *Contact—The First Four Minutes* (New York: Ballantine Books, 1972), p. 17.

10. Clyde Haberman, "No Offense," *New York Times Book Review,* February 18, 1996, p. 11.

11. Diane E. Lewis, "Some Firms in a Twist over Braids," *San Jose Mercury News,* May 25, 1997, p. 1 PC.

12. Haberman, "No Offense," p. 11.

13. James Gray, Jr., *The Winning Image* (New York: American Management Association, 1982), pp. 3–5.

14. Ibid., p. 6.

15. Robert L. Simison, "GM Is Spending $25 Million to Teach Good Olds Guys to Be Even Friendlier," *Wall Street Journal,* May 11, 1994, p. B5.

16. John T. Molloy, *Dress for Success* (New York: Peter H. Wyden, 1975); and John T. Molloy, *The Woman's Dress for Success Book* (New York: Warner Books, 1977).

17. Bixler, *Professional Presence,* p. 141.

18. Michael Solmon, "Standard Issue," *Psychology Today,* December 1987, pp. 30–31.

19. Haidee E. Allerton, "Dress Code Backlash," *Training & Development,* August 1997, p. 8.

20. Dave Knesel, "Image Consulting—A Well-Dressed Step Up the Corporate Ladder," *Pace,* July–August 1981, p. 74.

21. Haidee Allerton, "Working Life," *Training & Development,* April 1993, p. 96.

22. Bill Saporito, "Unsuit Yourself—Management Goes Informal," *Fortune,* September 20, 1993, p. 118.

23. "HR Shows Its Fall Collection." *Training,* August 1996, p. 14.

24. Janet G. Elsea, *The Four-Minute Sell* (New York: Simon & Schuster, 1984), p. 34.

25. Susan Bixler, *The Professional Image* (New York: Perigee Books, 1984), p. 217.

26. Ibid., p. 219.

27. Martha Sherrill Dailey, "The Way We Sound," *Roanoke Times & World-News,* May 8, 1988, p. 1.

28. Marc Hequet, "Giving Good Feedback," *Training,* September 1994, p. 74.

29. Adapted from Zunin and Zunin, *Contact,* pp. 102–108; "Handshake 101," *Training & Development,* November 1995, p. 71.

30. Amy Gamerman, "Lunch with Letitia: Our Reporter Minds Her Manners," *Wall Street Journal,* March 3, 1994, p. A14.

31. Barbara Lazear Ascher, "Mind and Manners," *Self,* May 1994, p. 129.

32. Jacqueline Thompson, *Image Impact* (New York: Ace Books, 1981), p. 8.

33. Bob Greene, "Why Must We Say Things Like . . . and . . . ?" *Roanoke Times & World-News,* April 27, 1980, p. 7.

34. Ann Marie Sabath, "Meeting Etiquette: Agendas and More," *DECA Dimensions,* January–February 1994, p. 8.

35. Susan Bixler, "Your Professional Presence," *Training Dimensions,* vol. 9, no. 1, 1994, p. 1.

36. Letitia Baldrige, *Letitia Baldrige's Complete Guide to Executive Manners* (New York: Rawson Associates, 1985), p. 13.

37. Nancy K. Austin, "What Do America Online and Dennis Rodman Have in Common?" *Inc.,* July 1997, p. 54.

38. Laura Bird, "No Detail Escapes the Attention of Abercrombie & Fitch's Chief," *Wall Street Journal,* October 7, 1997, p. B1.

Chapter 7

1. Donna Fenn, "More than Just Affirmative Action," *Inc.,* July 1995, p. 93.
2. Sharon Nelton, "Nurturing Diversity," *Nation's Business,* June 1995, p. 25.
3. "Diversity—Making the Business Case," *Business Week,* December 9, 1996, n.p.
4. Adapted from a definition developed by 3M Company published in Michael L. Wheeler, *Diversity: Business Rationale and Strategies* (New York: Conference Board, 1995), p. 9.
5. Marilyn Loden and Judy B. Rosener, *Workforce America!* (Homewood, Ill.: Business One Irwin, 1991), p. 18.
6. Ibid., p. 21.
7. Dudley Weeks, *The 8 Essential Steps to Conflict Resolution* (New York: G. P. Putnam's Sons, 1992), pp. 114–115.
8. Joann S. Lublin, "Companies Rethink Diversity Training," *Wall Street Journal,* June 16, 1995, p. B5A.
9. Daniel Goleman, *Emotional Intelligence* (New York: Bantam Books, 1995), pp. 156–157.
10. Lewis Brown Griggs and Lente-Louise Louw, *Valuing Diversity* (New York: McGraw-Hill, 1995), pp. 3–4, 150–151.
11. Ibid., p. 151.
12. Susan Garland, "Going Beyond Rhetoric on Race Relations," *Business Week,* June 23, 1997, p. 40.
13. Aaron Bernstein, "Is America Becoming More of a Class Society?" *Business Week,* February 26, 1996, pp. 86–91.
14. "Fifty-Something," *Training & Development,* May 1994, p. 143.
15. Griggs and Louw, *Valuing Diversity,* p. 17.
16. Haidee Allerton, "Not Older, Just Better," *Training & Development,* August 1995, p. 72.
17. Sam Fulwood III, "Black Still Isn't the Color of Money," *Venture,* March 1988, p. 32.
18. James Q. Wilson, "A Long Way from the Back of the Bus," *New York Times Book Review,* November 16, 1997, p. 10; Orlando Patterson, "Why Conduct a Racial Census?" *News & Observer,* July 13, 1997, p. 29A.
19. *American Heritage Dictionary,* 3d ed. (Boston: Houghton Mifflin, 1992), pp. 108, 195, 856, 918.
20. Robert S. Boynton, "Color Us Invisible," *New York Times Book Review,* August 17, 1997, p. 13.
21. Stephen Magagini, "A Race Free Consciousness," *News & Observer,* November 23, 1997, pp. 25a–26a.
22. Wilson, "A Long Way from the Back of the Bus," p. 10.
23. Lawrence Lindsey, "This Is a Political Matter," *Wall Street Journal,* December 26, 1996, p. 16A.
24. Gene Koretz, "A Law That Put People to Work," *Business Week,* February 10, 1997, p. 28.
25. "More of the Disabled Are Unemployed," *San Jose Mercury News,* August 18, 1996, p. 2 PC.
26. Deborah L. Jacobs, "The Americans with Disabilities Act," *Your Company* (Milwaukee, Wis.: Northwestern Mutual Life Insurance Co., Summer 1994), p. 10.
27. Thomas A. Stewart, "Gay in Corporate America," *Fortune,* December 16, 1991, p. 44.
28. Thomas Petzinger, Jr., "AT&T Class Teaches an Open Workplace Is Profitably Correct," *Wall Street Journal,* November 10, 1995, p. B1.
29. "Gays in the Workplace," *Inc.,* January 1996, p. 86.
30. U.S. Commission on Civil Rights, *Promise and Perceptions: Federal Efforts to Eliminate Employment Discrimination Through Affirmative Action* (Washington, D.C.: U.S. Government Printing Office, October 1981), p. 17.
31. Loden and Rosener, *Workforce America!,* p. 12.
32. Alex Markels, "A Diversity Program Can Prove Divisive," *Wall Street Journal,* January 30, 1997, p. B1.
33. Lisa Lucadamo and Scott Cheney, "Learning from the Best," *Training & Development,* July 1997, pp. 25–26.
34. Faye Rice, "How to Make Diversity Pay," *Fortune,* August 8, 1994, p. 82.
35. Ibid., p. 84.
36. Stan Crock and Michele Galen, "A Thunderous Impact on Equal Opportunity," *Business Week,* June 26, 1995, p. 37.
37. Stephen M. Paskoff, "Ending the Workplace Diversity Wars," *Training,* August 1996, p. 44.
38. Cathleen Watson, "Making Diversity Work," *Executive Female,* September/October 1996, p. 42.
39. Paskoff, "Ending the Workplace Diversity Wars," pp. 46–47.
40. Joanne L. Symons, "Is Affirmative Action in America's Interest?" *Executive Female,* May/June 1995, p. 52.
41. Robert Kreitner, *Management,* 7th ed. (Boston: Houghton Mifflin, 1998), pp. 325–326.
42. Symons, "Is Affirmative Action in America's Interest?" p. 52.
43. Terry Eastland, "Endgame for Affirmative Action," *Wall Street Journal,* March 28, 1996, p. A15.
44. Michael K. Frisby, "Powell Reshapes Debate on Affirmative Action, Deepening Divisions Among Black Republicans," *Wall Street Journal,* August 13, 1996, p. A14.
45. Paul Berman, "Redefining Fairness," *New York Times Book Review,* April 14, 1996, p. 16.
46. Beth Baker, "Forcing America to Keep Faith," *AARP Bulletin,* vol. 38, no. 8, 1997, p. 8.
47. Geoffrey Brewer, "Why We Can't All Get Along," *Sales & Marketing Management,* December 1995, p. 32.

48. Katherine Roth, "God on the Job," *Working Woman,* February 1998, pp. 65–66.

Chapter 8

1. Dudley Weeks, *The Eight Essential Steps to Conflict Resolution* (New York: G. P. Putnam's Sons, 1992), p. 7.
2. Ibid., pp. 7–8.
3. "Surviving the Office Jerk Takes Patience," *Springfield News-Leader,* November 6, 1994, p. 2E.
4. "Assertiveness: More than a Forceful Attitude," *Supervisory Management,* February 1994, p. 3.
5. Stephen Ash, "How to Make Assertiveness Work for You," *Supervisory Management,* p. 8.
6. Albert Ellis, *Effective Self-Assertion, Psychology Today* audiotape, 1985.
7. David Stiebel, *When Talking Makes Things Worse!* (Dallas: Whitehall & Nolton, 1997), p. 17.
8. Weeks, *The Eight Essential Steps to Conflict Resolution,* pp. 90–101.
9. Roger Fisher and William Ury, *Getting to Yes* (New York: Penguin Books, 1981), p. 59.
10. Weeks, *The Eight Essential Steps to Conflict Resolution,* p. 228.
11. Ibid., p. 223.
12. Willard Gaylin, *Feelings* (New York: Ballantine Books, 1979), p. 1.
13. Daniel Goleman, *Emotional Intelligence* (New York: Bantam Books, 1995), p. 34.
14. Daniel Goleman, "The Educated Heart," *Common Boundary,* November/December 1995, p. 27.
15. John Selby, *Conscious Healing* (New York: Bantam Books, 1989), p. 32.
16. Ibid.
17. Douglas A. Bernstein, Edward J. Roy, Alison Clark-Stewart, and Christopher D. Wickens, *Psychology,* 4th ed. (Boston: Houghton Mifflin, 1997), p. 403.
18. Ibid.
19. William C. Menninger and Harry Levinson, *Human Understanding in Industry* (Chicago: Science Research Associates, 1956), p. 29.
20. Donella H. Meadows, "We Are, to Our Harm, What We Watch," *Roanoke Times & World-News,* October 16, 1994, p. G3.
21. "Schools Hit by Epidemic of Violence," *Roanoke Times & World-News,* January 6, 1994, p. A1.
22. "Reducing TV Violence May Curb Antisocial Behavior," *Menninger Letter,* October 1995, p. 4.
23. Tori DeAngelis, "Women's Safety Illusory When Males Turn Violent," *APA Monitor,* September 1994, p. 1.
24. Jan E. Stets and Debra A. Henderson, "Contextual Factors Surrounding Conflict Resolution While Dating: Re-

sults from a National Study," *Family Relations,* January 1991, pp. 29–36.
25. Harold H. Bloomfield and Robert K. Cooper, *The Power of 5* (Emmaus, Pa.: Rodale Press, 1995), p. 334.
26. Redford Williams and Virginia Williams, *Anger Kills* (New York: HarperCollins, 1993), p. 3.
27. Kimes Gustin, *Anger, Rage, and Resentment* (West Caldwell, N.J.: St. Ives' Press, 1994), p. 1.
28. Helen Hall Clinard, *Winning Ways to Succeed with People* (Houston: Gulf Publishing, 1985), p. 82.
29. Susan Bixler, *Professional Presence* (New York: G. P. Putnam's Sons, 1991), pp. 190–191.
30. Rolland S. Parker, *Emotional Common Sense* (New York: Barnes & Noble Books, 1973), pp. 80–81.
31. Jane Brody, "Turning Anger into Useful Force," *Roanoke Times & World-News,* November 30, 1993, p. E1.
32. Gustin, *Anger, Rage, and Resentment,* p. 37.
33. Les Giblin, *How to Have Confidence and Power in Dealing with People* (Englewood Cliffs, N.J.: Prentice-Hall 1956), p. 37.
34. William J. Crockett, "Our Two Worlds," *Training & Development,* May 1982, p. 60.
35. Sam Keen, *Fire in the Belly—On Being a Man* (New York: Bantam Books, 1991), p. 242.
36. Borysenko *Minding the Body, Mending the Mind,* p. 169.
37. Ellen Safier, "Our Experts Answer Your Questions," *Menninger Letter,* May 1993, p. 8.
38. Leo F. Buscaglia, *Loving Each Other* (Thorofare, N.J.: Slack, 1984), p. 160.
39. Keen, *Fire in the Belly,* p. 242.

Chapter 9

1. Sue Shellenbarger, "Software Ace Turns His Life Upside Down, and Is Happier for It," *Wall Street Journal,* January 31, 1996, p. B1.
2. Keith H. Hammonds, "Balancing Work and Family," *Business Week,* September 16, 1996, p. 80.
3. Amy Saltzman, *Downshifting* (New York: HarperCollins, 1991), p. 16.
4. Marc Heguet, "Flat and Happy?" *Training,* April 1995, pp. 29–34.
5. Robert Kuttner, "No Time to Smell the Roses Anymore," *New York Times Book Review,* February 2, 1992, pp. 1, 21.
6. Lynn Lannon, "Giving Back: The Secret of Creating Success," *Training & Development,* April 1990, p. 58.
7. Robert McGarvey, "Softening the Blow," *U.S. Air,* September 1991, p. 18.
8. Sue Shellenbarger, "Keeping Your Career a Manageable Part of Your Life," *Wall Street Journal,* April 12, 1995, p. B1.

9. Kuttner, "No Time to Smell the Roses Anymore," p. 21; Gene Koretz, "Those Educated Moonlighters," *Business Week,* August 4, 1997, p. 22.

10. "When Success Fails to Make You Happy," *Working Smart,* September 1991, p. 1.

11. Marsha McEuen, "A Natural Art," *Santa Fean,* August 1997, pp. 104–107.

12. Interview conducted on February 8, 1992.

13. Ronald Henkoff, "So You Want to Change Your Job," *Fortune,* January 15, 1996, p. 52.

14. Marsha Sinetar, *Do What You Love . . . The Money Will Follow* (New York: Dell, 1987), p. 11.

15. Ibid., pp. 11–12.

16. Anne Fisher, "Six Ways to Supercharge Your Career," *Fortune,* January 13, 1997, pp. 46–48; John Epperheimer, "If It Feels Good, Do It and Change Your Career," *San Jose Mercury News,* July 17, 1996, p. 7G.

17. Michael Phillips, *The Seven Laws of Money* (Menlo Park, Calif.: Word Wheel and Random House, 1997), p. 9.

18. McEuen, "A Natural Art," p. 105.

19. Sinetar, *Do What You Love,* pp. 14–15.

20. John Naisbitt and Patricia Aburdene, *Re-Inventing the Corporation* (New York: Warner Books, 1985), p. 5.

21. Sinetar, *Do What You Love,* p. 15.

22. Sue Shellenbarger, "Keeping Your Career a Manageable Part of Your Life," p. B1.

23. Sue Shellenbarger, "New Job Hunters Ask Recruiters, Is There a Life After Work? *Wall Street Journal,* January 29, 1997, p. B1.

24. Patricia Sellers, "Don't Call Me Slacker!" *Fortune,* December 12, 1994, p. 196.

25. Howard Gleckman, "Generation $ Is More Like It," *Business Week,* November 3, 1997, p. 44.

26. Melvyn Kinder, *Going Nowhere Fast* (Englewood Cliffs, N.J.: Prentice-Hall, 1990), p. 76.

27. Michael Toms, "The Soul of Money—A Conversation with Lynne Twist," *New Dimensions,* January–February 1997, pp. 7–8.

28. Ibid., p. 8.

29. Teri Lammers Prior, "If I Were President . . . ," *Inc.,* April 1995, pp. 56–60.

30. Michael Toms, "Money: The Third Side of the Coin" (interview with Joe Dominguez and Vicki Robin), *New Dimensions,* May–June 1991, p. 7.

31. Susan Smith Jones, "Choose to Be Healthy and Celebrate Life," *New Realities,* September–October 1988, pp. 17–19.

32. Ibid., p. 18.

33. Hal Lancaster, "Re-Engineering Authors Reconsider Re-Engineering," *Wall Street Journal,* January 17, 1995, p. B1.

34. Derwin Fox, "Career Insurance for Today's World," *Training & Development,* March 1996, pp. 63–64.

35. Ibid., p. 63.

36. Ibid., p. 64.

37. Saltzman, *Downshifting,* p. 23.

38. Jay T. Knippen, Thad B. Green, and Kurt Sutton, "Asking Not to Be Overworked," *Supervisory Management,* February 1992, p. 6.

39. Art Ulene, *Really Fit Really Fast* (Encino, Calif.: Health-Points, 1996), pp. 198–199.

40. Marilyn Chase, "Weighing the Benefits of Mental-Health Days Against Guilt Feelings," *Wall Street Journal,* September 9, 1996, p. B1.

41. Ulene, *Really Fit Really Fast,* p. 199.

42. Leo Booth, "When God Becomes a Drug," *Common Boundary,* September/October 1991, p. 30.

43. Harold H. Bloomfield and Robert K. Cooper, *The Power of 5* (Emmaus, Pa.: Rodale Press 1995), p. 484.

44. "Making the Spiritual Connection," *Lears,* December 1989, p. 72.

45. Robert Bolton and Dorothy Grover Bolton, *People Styles at Work* (New York: AMACOM, 1996), pp. 110–111.

46. Barnaby J. Feder, "Clergymen on the Job to Help Workers Deal with Problems," *Roanoke Times,* October 13, 1996, p. A-6.

47. G. Paul Zachary, "The New Search for Meaning in Meaningless Work," *Wall Street Journal,* January 9, 1997, p. B1.

48. Judith Valente, "Some Employ Faith to Get the Job Done," *USA Today,* June 16, 1995, p. B1.

49. Ibid., p. B2.

50. Redford Williams and Virginia Williams, *Anger Kills* (New York: HarperCollins, 1993), p. 181.

51. Ibid., p. 182.

52. Chris Lee and Ron Zemke, "The Search for Spirit in the Workplace," *Training,* June 1993, p. 25.

53. "Wellness Facts," *University of California at Berkeley Wellness Letter,* November 1995, p. 1.

54. *Dietary Guidelines for Americans* (Washington, D.C.: U.S. Department of Health and Human Services, December 1995), pp. 3–21.

55. Ibid., p. 5.

56. Ibid., p. 36.

57. Ibid., p. 40–41.

58. Ulene, *Really Fit Really Fast,* pp. 20–21.

59. "One Small Step . . . ," *University of California at Berkeley Wellness Letter,* January 1991, p. 1; Kenneth Blanchard, D. W. Edington, and Marjorie Blanchard, *The One Minute Manager Gets Fit* (New York: Morrow, 1986), p. 36.

60. Robert A. Gleser, *The Healthmark Program for Life* (New York: McGraw-Hill, 1988), p. 147.

61. *Fitness Fundamentals* (Washington, D.C.: Department of Health and Human Services, 1988), p. 2.

62. Stephen R. Covey, *The 7 Habits of Highly Effective People* (New York: Simon & Schuster, 1989), p. 46.

63. James Fadiman, *Be All That You Are* (Seattle: Westlake Press, 1986), p. 25.

64. David L. Mortellaro, Response to question and answer interview, *Roanoke Times,* July 29, 1995, p. A10.

65. Robert McGarvey, "Getting Your Goals," *U.S. Air,* July 1989, p. 28.

66. Bruce A. Baldwin, "Barriers to Success," *U.S. Air,* June 1992, p. 18.

67. Fadiman, *Be All That You Are,* p. 45.

68. Pete Engardio and Peter Finch, "Kazuo Wada's Answered Prayers," *Business Week,* August 26, 1991, p. 66.

69. Mike Hernacki, *The Ultimate Secret of Getting Absolutely Everything You Want* (New York: Berkley Books, 1988), p. 35.

70. Adapted from Bloomfield and Cooper, *The Power of 5,* pp. 492–493.

Credits

Case Credits

Chapter 1: Rochelle Sharpe, "Being Family Friendly Doesn't Mean Promoting Women," *Wall Street Journal,* March 29, 1994, p. B1; Sue Shellenbarger, "Work and Family," *Wall Street Journal,* June 1, 1994, p. B1; Milton Moskowitz, "Best Companies for Working Mothers," *Working Mother,* October 1996, pp. 10–45; Sue Shellenbarger, "Two-Income Couples Are Making Changes at Work and at Home," *Wall Street Journal,* February 14, 1996, p. B1.

Chapter 2: Rick Atkinson, "Mercedes Workers Polish Their Y'Alls and Howdies," *Denver Post,* February 27, 1994, p. 3H; Jack Yamaguchi, "Eagles Are Landing in Japan," *Road & Track,* July 1994, p. 24; "White House Watch," *The New Republic,* October 25, 1993, p. 48; Justin Martin, "Mercedes: Made in Alabama," *Fortune,* July 7, 1997, p. 158.

Chapter 3: David M. Garner, "The 1997 Body Image Survey," *Psychology Today,* January/February 1997, pp. 30–48; "Altering Your Image: Strategies from the Trenches," *Psychology Today,* January/February 1997, p. 80; Mary Pipher, *Reviving Ophelia* (New York: Ballantine Books, 1994), pp. 183–184.

Chapter 4: Jennifer J. Laabs, "Beef About Employee Benefits Causes Religious Group to Boycott Disney," *Personnel Journal,* August 1996, p. 11; "Southern Baptists Take on Disney," *U.S. News & World Report,* June 24, 1996, p. 18; Kate Clinton, "The Lull Before the Lull," *Progressive,* August 1996, p. 46.

Chapter 5: Hal Lancaster, "Office Politics: It's Almost Impossible to Get Ahead Without It," *San Jose Mercury News,* April 16, 1997, p. 6G; Cheryl Shavers, "Moving the Rock Called Organizational Politics," *San Jose Mercury News,* March 30, 1997, p. 3E; Cheryl Shavers, "Corporate Politics Part of Being Effective Player," *San Jose Mercury News,* June 15, 1997, p. 2D.

Chapter 6: "Brush Up Your Business Etiquette," *Training,* July 1997, p. 10; Susan Goodman, "Interview with Judith Martin," *Modern Maturity,* March–April 1996, pp. 56–64; Stephanie Shapiro, "Civility Movement Hopes to Put White Gloves on Clenched Fists," *News & Observer,* February 23, 1997, p. 3E.

Chapter 7: Edward Felsenthal, "Supreme Court Agenda Touches Everyday Life," *Wall Street Journal,* September 29, 1997, p. B1; Elsa C. Arnett, *News & Observer,* November 22, 1997, n.p.; Linda Greenhouse, "Key Case on Racial Diversity Settled," *News & Observer,* November 22, 1997, p. 1A; "Affirmative Action Case Helps Define Boundaries," *USA Today,* November 24, 1997, p. 14A; Tony Mauro and Gary Fields, "Settlement Prolongs Affirmative Action Fight," *USA Today,* November 24, 1997, p. 4A; Steven A. Holmes, "Tough Times for Affirmative Action," *News & Observer,* November 23, 1997, p. 18A.

Chapter 8: Sue Shellenbarger, "Jo Browning Built a Child-Care Agenda into a Factory's Plan," *Wall Street Journal,* August 6, 1997, p. B1.

Career Corner Credits

Chapter 1: Louis S. Richman, "How to Get Ahead in America," *Fortune,* May 16, 1994, pp. 46–54; Ronald Henkoff, "Winning the New Career Game," *Fortune,* July 12, 1993, pp. 46–49.

Chapter 2: Jennifer Laabs, "Personnel File Data Base: Universal Access?" *Personnel Journal,* July 1994, p. 85; Shannon Peters, "Standard Policy Clears Confusion Over E-Mail," *Personnel Journal,* June 1994, p. 123.

Chapter 3: Maxwell Maltz, *Psycho-Cybernetics* (New York: Pocket Books, 1972), pp. 6–7.

Chapter 4: Hal Lancaster, "You Have Your Values; How Do You Identify Your Employers?" *Wall Street Journal,* April 8, 1997, p. B1.

Chapter 6: "How Much Can Employer Dictate Your Lifestyle?" *San Jose Mercury News,* May 2, 1993, pp. 1 PC and 2 PC; Susan Barciela, "Looks and Dress Still Count, Though the Lawyers Might Argue," *Roanoke Times & World-News,* June 19, 1993, p. D2; Susan Bixler, "Your Professional Presence," *Training Dimensions,* Vol. 9, No. 1, 1994, p. 1.

Chapter 7: "Good Customer Phone Form," *Training & Development,* December 1992, p. 9.

Chapter 8: Sue Shellenbarger and Carol Hymowitz, "As Population Ages, Older Workers Clash with Younger Bosses," *Wall Street Journal,* June 3, 1994, pp. A1 and A5.

Total Person Insight Credits

Chapter 1

p. 13: William Raspberry, "Topmost Priority: Jobs," *Washington Post,* (n.d.) 1977; **p. 9:** Marsha Sinetar, *Do What You Love . . . The Money Will Follow* (New York: Dell, 1989); **p. 16:** James Baughman quote from Frank Rose, "A New Age for Business?", *Fortune,* October 8, 1990, p. 162.

Chapter 2

p. 34: Paul R. Timm, "The Way We Word," in *Effective Communication on the Job,* ed. William K. Fallon (New York: AMACOM, 1981), p. 74; **p. 45:** Gerry Mitchell quote from "Listen, Listen, Listen," *Business Week,* September 14, 1987, p. 108.

Chapter 3

p. 97: Nathaniel Branden, *The Six Pillars of Self-Esteem* (New York: Bantam, 1994), p. 19; **p. 101:** Belleruth Naparstek, "About Face," *Common Boundary,* July/August 1996, p.64; **p. 106:** Nathaniel Branden, *The Six Pillars of Self-Esteem* (New York: Bantam, 1994), p. 105.

Chapter 4

p. 122: Peter Senge quote from Brian Dumaine, "Mr. Learning Organization," *Fortune,* October 17, 1994, p. 147; **p. 134:** Dan Rice and Craig Dreilinger, "Rights and Wrongs of Ethics Training," *Training & Development,* May 1990, p. 105.

Chapter 5

p. 149: Denis Waitley, *The Winning Generation: The Self-Esteem Training Program for Youth* (Cedar Falls, Iowa: Advanced Learning, Inc., 1987), p. 18; **p. 159:** Pamela R. Johnson and Claudia Rawlins, "Daydreams and Dialogues:

Key to Motivation," *Supervisory Management,* January 1991, p. 2.

Chapter 6

p. 282: Janet G. Elsea, *The Four-Minute Sell* (New York: Simon & Schuster, 1984), p. 34; **p. 294:** Judith Martin, "Low Income Is Not Low-Class," *Roanoke Times & World-News,* March 13, 1988, p. E 10.

Chapter 7

p. 389: Jack Pluckhan quote from Beau Bauman, *The Most Important Thing I've Learned in Life* (New York: Simon & Schuster, 1994), p. 150; **p. 392:** Vernon E. Jordan, Jr., "Look Outward, Black America," *Wall Street Journal,* October 27, 1995, p. A14; **p. 403:** Lewis Brown Griggs and Lente-Louise Louw, *Valuing Diversity: New Tools for a New Reality* (New York: McGraw-Hill, Inc., 1995), p. 9.

Chapter 8

p. 330: Gordon Lippitt quote from "Managing Conflict in Today's Organizations," *Training & Development,* July 1982, p. 3; **p. 332:** Harold H. Bloomfield and Robert K. Cooper, *The Power of 5,* Emmaus, Pa.: Rodale Press, 1995, p. 374; **p. 340:** Roger Fisher and William Ury, *Getting to Yes* (New York: Penguin Books, 1981), p. 4.

Chapter 9

p. 453: Amy Saltzman, *Downshifting: Reinventing Success on a Slower Track* (New York: HarperCollins Publishers, 1990), p. 15; **p. 456:** Hugh Prather poem from *Notes to Myself.* Copyright © 1970 by Real People Press. Used by permission of Bantam Books, a division of Bantam Doubleday Dell Publishing Group, Inc.; **p. 463:** Julie Connelly, "How to Choose Your Next Career," *Fortune,* February 6, 1995, p. 45; **p. 467:** Fred Huyghue, "Merging Spirituality with Work," *Business Ethics,* July/August 1994, p. 27; **p. 468:** Susan Smith Jones, "Choose to Be Healthy and Celebrate Life," *New Realities,* September/October 1988, p. 17.

Name Index

Note: Page references beginning with "A" stand for Notes Appendix, chapter, and note number.

Subject Index